HOW COLLEGE ATHLETICS ARE HURTING GIRLS' SPORTS

HOW COLLEGE ATHLETICS ARE HURTING GIRLS' SPORTS

The Pay-to-Play Pipeline, with a New Preface

Rick Eckstein

ROWMAN & LITTLEFIELD
Lanham • Boulder • New York • London

Published by Rowman & Littlefield
An imprint of The Rowman & Littlefield Publishing Group, Inc.
4501 Forbes Boulevard, Suite 200, Lanham, Maryland 20706
www.rowman.com

86-90 Paul Street, London EC2A 4NE, United Kingdom

British Library Cataloguing in Publication Information Available

Library of Congress Cataloging-in-Publication Data Available

Previously published under a different title:
How College Athletics Are Hurting Girls' Sports: The Pay-to-Play Pipeline

ISBN 978-1-5381-7680-1 (paper : alk. paper)
ISBN 978-1-5381-7758-7 (electronic)

∞™ The paper used in this publication meets the minimum requirements of American National Standard for Information Sciences—Permanence of Paper for Printed Library Materials, ANSI/NISO Z39.48-1992.

To the players, parents, and coaches of the Radnor Black Blitz travel soccer team, and to my fellow lunatics on the Bulldogs. Thanks for remembering (usually) that sports should be fun.

CONTENTS

PREFACE TO THE PAPERBACK EDITION

A PERSONAL NOTE

This book may be more relevant now than when it was first released in 2017. If anything, the pay-to-play pipelines connecting youth sport and higher education have become more omnipresent, even while also being more scrutinized and criticized. Recreational youth sports programs not enmeshed in the pay-to-play pipelines continue drying up. Higher education institutions increasingly tie their financial survival to larger and more costly intercollegiate athletics programs restricted to an increasingly elite population that has access to youth sports. Young athletes, regardless of their gender identities, continue to suffer physical and mental injuries in frightening numbers. Stories of coaching excesses and athlete suicide have become ubiquitous.

This is and was not just an academic issue for me but also a personal one. As you have read or will read in the book's acknowledgments, my younger daughter was (in 2017) a high school junior with a reasonable desire to play college soccer. In 2022, she graduated from a small liberal arts college where she received a great education, enjoyed a successful soccer career, survived a worldwide pandemic, became remarkably mature, and even learned how to cook. Our journey through the college application/recruitment process was relatively stress-free and she has avoided both the serious injuries and emotional burnout, which is discussed at length in chapter 5 of this book, and which I am currently researching for my next book on the structural causes of college athlete stress and anxiety.

At the risk of sounding self-serving, the research and writing of this book contributed greatly to my daughter's relatively positive experiences with youth and college sports. Knowledge, in this case, was truly golden. She had these mostly positive experiences *without* having specialized in soccer at age eight, *without* having joined an "elite" soccer club, and *without* ever having played in a so-called "showcase" tournament. We never hired a personal trainer to help with her running style, a professional film crew to produce her highlight video, or a specialized counselor to sniff out hidden scholarship money. She continued to enjoy other sports and nonathletic activities all through high school. Awareness of the insatiable and growing demand for college athletes, especially in women's sports, gave us a leg up in recruitment. Understanding youth sports as a business provided a critical lens to assess whether various companies and individuals really had our family's best interest at heart or whether they were just grifting. True, things might not have turned out as well for my daughter if she wanted to attend a larger school or one of the increasing number of small colleges where sports success has become a central (if unstated) part of the schools' mission. But she wanted to *play* soccer, not just say she was "on scholarship" at a semi-famous school. It was about the fun, not the prestige.

It was thrilling to experience firsthand the secondhand accounts presented in the book. We enjoyed watching coaches react when we proactively mentioned various "secret" components of the athlete recruitment process. After one "ID camp" (see chapters 4 and 5), an impressed coach wanted to know all about my daughter's club soccer and tournament experience. I thought the coach would spontaneously combust after hearing that such a soccer commitment would have conflicted with summer swimming and high school jazz band. Another coach at a fantastic liberal arts college with a mediocre (at best) soccer team insisted that, before being an official recruit, my daughter must participate as a "guest player" with some random team at a tournament two thousand miles from home. She told the coach to take a hike (nicely, though).

The point is that the information in this book is not just interesting but also useful. Since it first came out, and after giving dozens of public presentations on the topic, I have been contacted by hundreds of parents, and a fair number of kids, about how this information provided a roadmap for avoiding the worst of youth and college sports. Many were grateful for destroying the myth about lucrative sports scholarships. Some appreciated insights into the recruitment process and the myth of needing a club sport pedigree. By far the most gratitude came from parents eager to prevent their daughters (especially) from suffering catastrophic physical injury. Understanding sport specialization as a business model rather than as an athlete-development model gave them the courage and ammunition to just say no. I know the mother whose story opens the book wishes she had learned about the horrors of specialization and overuse a few years earlier.

PIPELINES THEN AND NOW

When this book was first released in 2017, youth sports hypercommercialization was reaching new heights, especially for girls' sports. Mirroring the already entrenched trend for boys' sports, families were pouring literally tens of thousands of dollars per year into the girls' youth sports industry, if they had the money and if there were actual opportunities in their communities. Social class, racial, ethnic, and geographical constraints on these opportunities were becoming more pronounced as the youth sports landscaped became increasingly "pay-to-play." Organized youth sports, with a few notable exceptions, had morphed into an exclusive playground for already privileged individuals and families to perpetuate their social advantages.

I argue in the book that the youth sports industry's rampant expansion during the last two decades was being driven by its systemic, symbiotic relationship with higher education and intercollegiate athletics. Colleges and universities of all shapes and sizes were putting significantly more emphasis on and resources into their nonrevenue varsity sports programs, especially women's programs (in relative terms). This served as rocket fuel for a youth sports industry eager to help fill an increasing demand for college athletes. At the heart of this commercial relationship was a fundamental misrepresentation of college athletic scholarships and sports-based admissions advantages. Colleges were very close-lipped with accurate data about the number of athletic scholarships available and their actual dollar amount. Youth sports organizations eagerly exploited this information vacuum with inflated promises of young athletes reaching "the next level" so long as they purchased the correct products and services. Parents relentlessly pushed their kids' sports consumption, not as a means to compensate for their own past sports failures but to extract social prestige from their children's sports success. This "success" was increasingly tied to playing college sports, especially with a scholarship in the largest programs. Unfortunately, the hypercommercialization of youth sports and a parallel intensification at the collegiate level has spawned a cataclysmic rise in serious injuries (physical and mental) to young athletes, especially girls and young women. It has also led to a "masculinization" of girls' and women's sports. In essence, this means that women's sports are increasingly being played and judged by the parameters of men's sports, with a corresponding surge in the number of men who are involved with the administration of women's sports. This reflects an ironic contrast with the supposed successes of the federal legislation known as "Title IX."

YOUTH SPORTS UPDATE

In the six years since this book first appeared, the symbiotic relationship between youth and college sport has only intensified despite a modest upswell in critical academic research and writing about all elements of the pay-to-play pipelines. Some economic analyses maintain that youth sports in 2022 was a $19 billion per year industry, or almost as much as NASA's current annual budget. Many serious observers predicted that the COVID-19 pandemic would temper the youth sports industry's excesses and move it away from this restrictive pay-to-play model dominating the landscape for the last two decades. In fact, though, the opposite has unfolded. With local government budgets tapped out and non-for-profits going belly-up, low cost and accessible youth sports options are disappearing. Public schools in relatively marginalized communities are also paring back their low-cost sports options.

A research project I am currently working on demonstrates how athletic interest by secondary school students is directly related to earlier community sports exposure. Assuming that sports participation has the potential for positive personal and social benefits, schools, and the communities they serve, should be working together to expand affordable, accessible, and enjoyable youth sports options. If, that is, they have the resources.

There has been a notable upswing in outstanding youth sports research and writing over the past five years. New waves of reliable data are streaming out of Utah State University's Families in Sport Lab and the National Sports and Society Survey at The Ohio State University. Well-respected organizations such as the Aspen Institute's Project Play are advocating relentlessly for youth sports reform and the expansion of noncommercialized youth sports opportunities. US surgeon general, Vivek

Murthy, and a long list of current and former professional athletes have all been weighing in on the potential benefits of youth sports and criticizing what youth sports has become. Academic and independent scholars such as Kirsten Hextrum, Chris Bjork, Rachel Allison, Linda Flanagan, and Jen McGovern are increasingly looking at youth sports not just as stages for performing and reinforcing patriarchy and heteronormativity (a common sport sociology angle), but also as a conduit of capitalist exploitation. We are finally understanding youth sport as a business rather than just a childhood pastime.

Focusing on youth sport as a business adds a new sociological layer of understanding to events normally viewed through a psychological lens. Our cultural landscape has become overwhelmed with horror stories about convicted sexual predators Larry Nasser and Jerry Sandusky, and credible accusations launched against hundreds of other adults involved with pay-to-play youth sports. As I write this preface in October 2022, a horrific sexual assault scandal is tearing through women's professional soccer in the United States. More appalling allegations within women's college soccer and girls' youth soccer (and other sports) are likely close behind. The organization SafeSports, created to police sexual misconduct in organized sport, collected data in 2020 showing significant abuse of children and young adults across fifty sports. Over 90 percent of those athletes describing abuse to SafeSports did *not* report this abuse when it was occurring. We all watched as elite athletes like Simone Biles and Naomi Osaka struggled with mental health challenges, despite enormous personal success. Reports of young college athletes committing suicide are becoming disturbingly common. Historically lower suicide rates among girls and young women are now converging with suicide rates of boys and young men.

And yet the hypercommercialized, pay-to-play youth sports industry continues to expand. Sports federations and schools tinker at the margins while doing nothing about the systems and structures enabling nightmarish individual behavior. Parents interviewed for this book insisted they would have picked up on their own kids' warning signs before anything got out of hand; that their kids would never become another innocent victim of childhood games run amok. Unfortunately, one of the key patterns in these interviews is manifest parental blindness to the physical and emotional plight of their athlete children. The harmonious siren song of college athletic scholarships, admissions advantages, and family prestige drown out the increasing harm of contemporary pay-to-play youth sports, not to mention other forms of organized sport.

HIGHER EDUCATION UPDATE

In keeping with this book's central theme, I believe that these increasing excesses of pay-to-play youth sports are being driven by recent changes in college sports and higher education. The causal relationship between corporatized higher education and commercialized youth sports, especially for women and girls, has never been stronger. Given these recent sea changes in higher education and intercollegiate sport, I could have easily added twenty to thirty pages of text to chapter 2 of this book, which focuses on college sport. In lieu of that option, however, here are some of the highlights that are contributing most to the destructive excesses of commercialized youth sports.

The last several years have brought a significant number of big and small changes to intercollegiate athletics. These changes have an impact on youth sports in diverse and, sometimes, contradictory ways, and this is especially true of girls' youth sports. For example, a lot of recent airtime, column inches, and tweeting has focused on the allegedly revolutionary "name/image/likeness" (NIL) changes in college sports. In essence, these changes remove prohibitions against college athletes monetizing their behavior like any other college student can. Monetization realms might include endorsing products, charging for autographs, and receiving royalties from those making money off an athlete's photo or named jersey. Critics of NIL changes argue it is moving college sports further away from its alleged amateur roots and pushing it closer to professionalization. Supporters of the changes contend that it is a matter of fairness and justice that college athletes who, unlike other college students, are prohibited from benefitting tangibly from their talents and skills. My own feeling is that critics, including universities, are most worried about NIL allowances being a steppingstone to "NILL," where the second "L" refers to "labor." Those running college athletics probably feel that giving a little philosophical ground on the NIL restriction (which they will *not* have to pay for) is more palatable than admitting college athletes are engaged in value-producing labor (which they *will* have to pay for).

But how will these NIL changes have an impact on youth sports and, especially, girls' youth sports? Now that the initial Chicken Little histrionics have died down, the answer seems to be "not much." Most NIL endorsement money has been concentrated in the already hypercommercialized realms of NCAA Division I football and men's basketball, where the ships of "amateurism" and "student-athlete" have sailed long ago. Youth athletes drawn to these sports are still more interested in the professional payoff, despite its rarity, than in endorsement deals during college. The silver lining for universities, as mentioned above, is that the exploited labor of athletes in these two sports can now be subsidized and softened by outside money. I'm sure there are university captains of solvency (see chapter 2) that appreciate any assistance in distracting these athletes from unionization.

In the so called "nonrevenue" sports, which includes all women's and girls' sports, the NIL changes have only marginally had an impact on the pay-to-play youth sports pipelines. While a few marquee athletes in women's sports, such as Connecticut's Paige Bueckers, have signed lucrative endorsement deals (Gatorade), that is by far the exception rather than the rule. More often, less visible athletes in nonmarquee sports are signing endorsement deals with local companies for pocket money or the equivalent of lifetime free trips to the soup and salad bar at Pat's Diner. Judging by the current marketing strategies of the girls' youth sports industry (see chapter 4), the exaggerated promises of scholarships, admissions advantages, and family prestige still take precedence when trying to sell products and services. In terms of "how college athletics are hurting girls' sports," NIL changes are more smoke than substance.

Admissions Advantages

The same cannot be said for the significant admissions advantages offered to recruited athletes at colleges large and small. Just after this book was initially published, admissions advantages started becoming a more central issue than potential scholarships in the pay-to-play youth sports pipelines. More colleges were expanding their early decision programs by increasing the number of slots available through this admissions process, or by adding a second early admission period for prospective students. As chapter 2 will explain, it is in a school's best marketing interest to lower its application acceptance rate (hence raising its alleged selectivity and prestige) by admitting more students outside of the "regular" admission process. The view of early admissions offered in this book has been accentuated by other excellent research released more recently. In *Who Gets in and Why*, journalist Jeff Selingo embedded himself in an actual admission office and offers firsthand accounts of how colleges decide to fill their incoming classes. Veteran education writer Paul Tough's many writings on higher education include candid interviews with Angel Perez, current CEO of the National Association for College Admission Counseling, and a former enrollment director at Trinity College (Connecticut). Both Selingo and Tough vividly detail how the college admission sausage gets made, where metrics involving a family's ability to pay sticker price often trump academic credentials. These inside accounts offer a blistering challenge to the conventional wisdom of college admissions as a meritocratic process, unless family income is equivalent to merit.

Varsity athletics receives only passing reference in Tough's and Selingo's discussion of admissions. But, based on research I have done in the past few years, intercollegiate sports have become an even more critical force behind the expansion of early admissions and the incessant need to admit more higher-income students, regardless of a school's rhetorical commitment to diversity, equity, and inclusion. Varsity athletics is uniquely positioned to help with these admissions goals in at least two ways. First, as explored in chapter 2, recruited athletes almost always apply through a school's early decision process. Coaches will tell prospective students that their spot on the team can only be guaranteed if they apply and are accepted early. Otherwise, if using the regular admissions portal, they will have to try out for the team as a walk-on with no promise of being selected. After putting so much time, money, and emotional angst into the pay-to-play pipelines, athletes and their families are very susceptible to this kind of subtle extortion. They are willing to forfeit the more generous financial aid offers accompanying admissions offers in the regular process when some schools are getting nervous about filling their first-year classes.

In fact, though, college rosters at schools of all shapes and sizes are continually expanding so that walk-ons are almost always welcomed whether they end up playing or not. Several athletic directors at a mix of schools have told me about the pressure from upper-level administrators to expand team rosters beyond what might be considered athletically appropriate. The evolving college admissions process, with a relatively constant number of schools fighting over a dwindling high school population, has no qualms exploiting the nervousness of youth sports families who feel their kids might miss out on the brass ring of playing college sports after all those years of schlepping through the pay-to-play pipelines. For the price of a few more team-emblazoned backpacks and some extra food vouchers during preseason, schools get to lock in more early admits and avoid the hypertensive crapshoot of regular admissions.

The second advantage of targeting recruited athletes in early admissions is that they are not only more *willing* to forgo financial aid for a guaranteed place on the team but are also more *able*. As discussed at length in chapter 1 and repeated throughout the book, families embroiled in the pay-to-play youth sports industry are not representative of the entire US population. Pipeline athletes and their families are wealthier, whiter, and more suburban than their nonpipeline counterparts. The further someone progresses in the pipeline, the more pronounced these demographic factors become. By the time young athletes (regardless of skill) show up at the college recruiting meccas dubbed "showcases," only those families with the most disposable income and fewest time constraints are generally left standing. Others have been weeded out or simply never make it through the pipelines' entry portal. The pay-to-play youth sports pipelines are far more adept identifying the best *payers* than the best *players*.

This is especially true in girls' and women's sports where rowing and ice hockey have the fastest growing intercollegiate footprints (see chapter 2). This, in turn, has created huge opportunities for the youth sports industry to meet this soaring demand. Rowing, especially, is the epitome of a play-to-play sport. It is simply not available or accessible to most people outside of a very expensive and geographically specific demographic. Public high schools that could hypothetically satisfy this demand do not offer crew teams at the varsity level where high participation costs can be subsidized, much like they are for football. According to 2021 data from the National Federation of High School Associations, only six state athletic associations recognize crew as a varsity sport. About 4,500 high school students participate on these varsity teams, equally split between those identifying as either women or men. Outside of the overtly pay-to-play rowing clubs concentrated in certain areas, any slack demand for potential college rowers is taken up by advantaged public schools who loosely support pay-to-play club rowing teams and by private schools with tuitions often approaching $50,000 per year. Coupled with the expanding admissions advantages for rowing recruits, crew has become a powerful conduit for reproducing social class, racial, and geographic inequality. This has been clearly documented in Kirsten Hextrum's recent book, *Special Admission*. Girls' youth ice hockey works pretty much the same way even though it is recognized as a high school varsity sport by a few more (sixteen) state athletic associations.

Operation Varsity Blues

It was just another typical sports and society class in March 2019 when a student deviously checked their phone and cried out, "They're arresting Aunt Becky!" Before I could reprimand the student for violating course policy on electronic devices, they offered more details on the US Justice Department's indictment of dozens of people associated with a sports-based college admissions fraud. Silly course policies became moot and what became known as "Operation Varsity Blues (OVB)," held our collective attention for the rest of the semester. Unlike other previous examples of admissions irregularities (see chapter 2), this one grabbed headlines and hooked public interest, probably because two high profile actors were involved—Felicity Huffman (an actress from TV shows *Desperate Housewives* and *American Crime*) and Lori Loughlin (the aforementioned Aunt Becky from the TV show, *Full House*). The alleged crimes were almost universally called a "scandal" or "fraud." But for anyone familiar with the systemic admissions advantages offered to certain college applicants, the so-called scandal was just a slight variation on business as usual.

OVB had everything you would want for a low-budget TV movie and, in fact, eventually became the subject of a Netflix "mockumentary" where actors recreated actual dialogue from FBI wiretaps on a series of central characters. There was slick mastermind Rick Singer, a self-styled college admissions counselor who figured out a way to game the admissions system by exploiting so-called "side doors" to college acceptance. Singer was accompanied by a who's who list of fabulously wealthy and entitled business executives who had no qualms spending oodles of money to ensure their children would attend a culturally prestigious college, even if it meant leveraging options not available to an average (or even above-average) family. And, of course, there was Aunt Becky, which gave the whole story star power beyond any alleged criminal fraud.

The "fraud" in question had two pieces, both devised by Singer. The first piece involved cheating on standardized tests by hiring very smart proxies to substitute for the aspiring college student and by also hiring test observers who would literally change students' answers to ensure a higher score. Felicity Huffman was charged with this offense, in case you are keeping score. Frankly, there's not much to dispute here. This is a pretty good example of fraud since it involved falsifying medical evaluations, identities, and test results where the lines between right and wrong were very clear. True, it begs the question of how wealthy families can *already* leverage their advantages on these tests by accessing the ubiquitous test-prep industry and private tutors. Not to mention the superior schools they attend where test preparation is often woven into the curriculum. But even with these systemic advantages, everyone still expects the person nominally taking an exam to actually be that person.

The second piece of OVB, though, is far murkier when it comes to being truly fraudulent. This part of the scheme involved Rick Singer's well-heeled clients buying access to the recruited athlete admission process even though their children were not recruited athletes and, in some cases, did not even play the sport in question. Rick Singer had correctly deduced that the admissions advantages for recruited athletes far outweighed those for the offspring of wealthy families who might, for example, make a large financial gift to the school. It is unclear if Rick Singer consulted the systematic research on admissions advantages presented in chapter 2 of this book or just figured it out on his own. Either way, with some photoshop skills and the assistance of well-compensated coaches and athletic administrators, Singer got his clients' kids into prestigious schools through the portals allegedly reserved for "real" athletes.

But Rick Singer and his entitled clients did not build this so-called side door. They did not design the advantageous admissions process for athletes recruited from the pay-to-play youth sports pipelines. Rick Singer figured out a way to bypass these pipelines and monetize a shortcut to the "athletes only" side door built by higher education's captains of solvency. I do not wish to romanticize this scheme as a Robin Hood-esque, antihero subversion of a corrupt system that is "sticking it to the man." Rick Singer's clients *are* "the man." They aren't sticking it to anyone or anything. They are entitled, privileged, powerful people who could pay Singer's price for access to this secret portal, but the portal was already in place. None of these peoples' fabulous wealth, or Singer's scheming, would have done much good without the already existing athlete admissions advantages that remain completely taken for granted within higher education and the rest of society. Do we really think that potential college athletes are entitled to this special treatment? Or have we just been brainwashed not to question it?

When giving presentations on Operation Varsity Blues, I am inevitably asked how coaches would even consider having poor players (or nonathletes) on their rosters. After all, isn't the point of sports to win games and meets? My answer to this is twofold. First, having poor athletes on a team in no way interferes with on-field success as long as you have enough good athletes. Team rosters at schools of all configurations are *already* filled with products of the pay-to-play youth sports industry who will never see one minute on the field or in the boat during a game or race, regardless of their club team pedigree. On a women's college soccer roster already teeming with thirty-five members, or a women's college rowing team exploding with ninety members, what's the harm in adding one or two more "players" when it only costs a little swag and can serve particular organizational needs?

Second, it is increasingly anachronistic to believe that college and youth sport is mostly about winning or appreciating the aesthetic marvels of the human body. As this book will discuss in detail, organized sport at every level is decreasingly about the activity itself and the personal growth of individuals participating in an activity. Organized sport is now more about profit, revenue, occupational compensation, and organizational prestige. Culturally, we accept that professional sport is a business even if that business sometimes interferes with the "purity" of the game itself, but we seem more culturally resistant to acknowledge that nonprofessional sport is increasingly a business in the sheep's clothing of fun and games. If we understand how the business of college sports fits within the corporatized world of higher education, then Operation Varsity Blues is no anomaly. It's just business as usual—only with an Aunt Becky to help us take notice.

ACKNOWLEDGMENTS

This book was greatly influenced by countless conversations in my Sports and Society classes over the past ten years, and I thank all the students who made me think more clearly about the topic and dared me to write about it. Villanova undergraduates Stephanie Uibel and Jessica Swoboda were, at times, indispensable collaborators as the project took shape and we began more serious research. Jess was also my field hockey guru since I knew less than nothing about this sport, which became a key part of the book. Cheryl Laz, Bill Werpehowski, and Ed Royce have been helping me think clearly for more than thirty years. Ed also introduced me to Sarah Stanton and the enthusiastic staff at Rowman & Littlefield. More recent intellectual guidance was provided by Sally Scholz, Jim Pennell, Mike Jensen, Corey Dolgon, Tony Ladd, Tim Maher, Chuck Koeber, Woody Doane, Mike Russell, Steve Adair, Greta Pennell, Mary Chayko, David Karen, and Kathleen Fitzgerald. Kevin Delaney, as always, entertained my wildest ideas and provided some needed diversions. Mike Messner and Doug Hartmann offered excellent although, unfortunately, unofficial suggestions on an early draft. Thanks also to Seth Whidden, Jerusha Conner, Catherine Warrick, Kelly Welch, Mike Levitan, Mark Doorley, Jenny Joyce, Brianna Remster, Christopher Kilby, and other colleagues in Villanova's Faculty Congress for gallantly resisting the corporatization of higher education that is, among other things, largely responsible for taking the fun out of youth sports.

Within the youth sports world itself, my daughters and I miraculously avoided most of the madness written about in this book, although it was always lurking close by. Almost every person I coached youth sports with has tried to keep our kids' eyes on the prize of having fun and building friendships rather than capitulating to the siren song of a potential intercollegiate payoff. They include Tracy d'Entremont, Robert Saionz, Emily Remphrey, Mike Coffey, Fred Kauffmann, Gary Rathsmill, Bob Miccolis, Bill Remphrey, Jennifer Saionz, Marty Conner, and Scott Landry. I have enjoyed more lengthy and gratifying coaching relationships with Scott d'Entremont, Gary Havertine, Mark Maz, Mark Kolber, and Jim "Skipper" Cunilio. Finally, enormous kudos and gratitude to Steve Gerber, Chris Smith, Meghan Brogan, and Kim Wakiyama for helping to keep our little youth soccer world from being overrun by commercial insanity.

I could not have written this book without the enthusiastic cooperation of players, parents, coaches, league officials, and others who shared their experiences and perspectives with me. I cannot thank them all publicly, especially the kids and parents, since I insist on protecting their confidentiality, even if they wouldn't mind the notoriety. But some individuals (not kids or parents) provided exceptionally helpful suggestions and guidance, whether or not they were quoted in the book: Glenn Crooks, Janet Rayfield, Celia Slater, Don Sabo, Joanie Milhous, Sara Bergfeld, Meghan Brogan, Michael Gaynor, Nick Gaynor, Melody McNulty, Karen Klassner, Simon Hoskins, Sam Snow, Tim Feeman, Regina Barr, Tom Farrey, Mike Barr, Chris Branscome, Josh Steinbach, Donna Helgenberg, Vince Nicastro, Tina Booth, Mike Gentile, Carol Rossignol, and the entire staff at USA Ultimate.

My immediate family actually provided more substantive support than emotional support during this project. Daughters Carolyn Eckstein and Emma Nicosia play (respectively) soccer and ultimate Frisbee, and this opened useful networks to explore these sports and receive foundational insights from "the trenches." Carolyn was poised to become a full-time, year-round youth soccer player wending her way through the pay-to-play pipeline until I became enmeshed in this project and put a parental stop to that particular option. Instead, she has developed and maintained an eclectic interest in several sports and nonathletic activities, although soccer remains a passion she hopes to enjoy for many more years. As a high school junior, she will soon test the waters of playing division III intercollegiate varsity soccer after (mostly) voluntarily eschewing that sport's pipeline so she could continue swimming, playing softball, learning karate, and playing the saxophone. It will be interesting to see if she will be able to play soccer in college via this increasingly nontraditional route. Emma, a college senior, also played multiple sports while young, but started specializing in ultimate late in high school despite my requisite fatherly protestations to do otherwise. Fortunately, we did not have to contend with a commercialized youth ultimate to college pipeline, and her experiences with the sport both in high school and college have been universally positive. My wife, Monica Nicosia, is an avid adult figure skater and has helped me understand and navigate around a sport I don't fully appreciate or enjoy but wanted to include in the book for reasons that will soon become clear. Because of her purposeful and accidental guidance, I could simultaneously mollify and impress interview subjects by tossing around words like "salchow" and "lutz," and referring to a story in the latest issue of *Skating* magazine. Now, with the book finished, I can thank her more meaningfully by cleaning up my third of the home office we share.

INTRODUCTION

> I'm the reason Susan can hardly walk anymore. My beautiful Susan. I should have said "enough." Isn't that what parents are supposed to do? Set limits? Protect their kids? But she wanted to play. She was so happy on the field. She would get hurt and insist on playing through it. Said if she doesn't keep playing she won't make the [all-star team]. I should have said "no." Practice was two hours each day, three nights a week. It was on the other side of the city, during rush hour. They said she could get a scholarship, and she wanted it so badly. But we could have paid for her college. And she only got a half scholarship. So did her friends. Nobody told us that. Now she has had all those knee operations and will limp for the rest of her life. And almost every one of her travel team friends has blown out a knee or had a series of concussions. For what? A few thousand dollars? Seeing their names and picture on the roster? Was that worth it?

This was part of an emotional interview with Susan's mother, Kim. Susan played soccer at a prestigious, well-known NCAA Division I university and also had a passionate story to tell:

> You have to understand how much I loved to play. Our travel team coach was always telling us how these former players were at big state schools or Princeton or Yale or wherever, and we could be just like them if we worked a little harder. He would get us into the best camps. He would help us get scholarships. He knew people. And we all got scholarships. But we didn't know what we were getting into. My [college] teammates all have different

> scholarships and we aren't supposed to discuss it [winks]. They use scholarships like rewards and punishments. I don't get it. It's not like we make money for the school. Nobody is at the games, even when we are playing at [big-time women's soccer school]. My parents still have to pay a lot of money, and I'm not allowed to work during the school year. There's no off-season because of conditioning. I'll bet [former travel coach] is telling his new players about us. I feel like going back [home] and telling them the truth about college sports and to just have fun playing soccer before they have their knees cut open three times. Or just have fun, period. Go to the movies with your friends. Have some friends who don't play soccer! I should show them my scars [laughing]. But probably I wouldn't have cared if somebody had showed me their scars six years ago. I was that crazy. I just had to reach that next level. There was always a next level.

Other players and parents from a variety of sports shared similar sentiments, although rarely so poignantly and rarely so intensely. Claire earned an athletic-based scholarship for soccer at a flagship state university:

> It was after my sophomore year [in college] that the wheels began to come off. I felt like my body was wearing out and [the coach] was all over me since I had a larger scholarship than most of the other players. Everything hurt, but I felt like I couldn't stop. My whole life had been built around playing college soccer. Then I started missing classes and falling behind on my assignments. I *never* missed classes unless we were on the road. I would burst into tears in the middle of my room for no reason. Finally, I just freaked out during practice. I don't even remember it. And that was it. My college soccer career was over. Fortunately, [my school] let me keep my scholarship and helped me get some counseling. At first I thought I was a loser, that I couldn't hack it. Then I learned it was a bigger problem than just me. A lot of my teammates and some of the other athletes were barely holding it together. Some of my high school teammates had similar meltdowns, and their schools usually just brushed them aside and gave their scholarships to other players. Like survival of the fittest. The pressure is unbelievable. Thirty hours a week of practice, games, meetings, films. Soccer is our entire life. The coaches tell us that the rest of college is just a distraction. But this isn't what I heard from my [youth team] coaches. Hope Solo never talks about these things during interviews. I never heard this on recruitment visits. I was sold a lot of empty promises. Maybe I can keep other girls from making these mistakes before they have a breakdown.

Susan and Claire have reached these troubling points in their lives only after a long, arduous journey through the world of serious youth and college sports, in this case soccer. Similarly, Kim's lament over her daughter's knee operations is another consequence of contemporary youth and intercollegiate sports systems that may be out of control. Despite conventional wisdom and rhetoric extolling the benefits of highly competitive girls' youth sports, this social phenomenon may pose more harm than good to its direct and indirect participants.

UNDERSTANDING GIRLS' YOUTH SPORTS

Writing a book about girls' youth and college sports was actually not on my radar until professional and personal experiences combined to pique my interest. The culmination of a multiyear project on publicly financed professional stadiums led me almost by accident into the oft-neglected field of "sports sociology" where, in developing a new undergraduate course, I noted lots of attention being paid to the *meaning* of sports but general neglect toward the *business* of sports.[1] This neglect was magnified by a useful sports sociology paradigm that identifies a historical shift in emphasis from "play" to "organized sport" among children. Play is associated with participant-centered activities with intrinsic value designed to reinforce friendships and, well, be fun. Organized sport is more rule centered with a greater adult presence and emphasis on outcomes, with fun being a secondary consideration except as it is tied to winning. But organized sport is also an increasingly commercial enterprise. It is a business. It is about buying and selling products and services, not climbing trees and building spaceships out of discarded refrigerator boxes. Organized youth sports are increasingly about consumption rather than just adding a formalized framework to certain games. Kim, Susan, and Claire's relationship with youth and college sports was primarily driven by economic calculations, not by a desire for more structured play.

As we dealt with these topics in my Sports and Society courses, a large number of students shared their own experiences with organized youth sports, a topic given little systematic attention by sociologists. A surprising number of these stories were horrific, and women's stories seemed to be worse than men's. I began to notice patterns in these anecdotes: a general reluctance to challenge conventional wisdom about the personal and social benefits of organized sports; the increasing time and expense necessary to participate in youth sports; the pressure to specialize at earlier ages; the boorish behavior of adults. But three patterns stuck out the most. First, I kept hearing the term "the next level" used when students were referring to their youth sports and, when applicable, intercollegiate sports experiences. Kids and parents wanted to find teams at the next level, coaches wanted to push players to the next level, universities wanted to hire certain coaches and join certain conferences so their programs and schools could reach the next level. The idea struck me as an almost perfect marketing mantra for rampant commercialism, so long as you never run out of next levels. Second, for those who had become varsity intercollegiate athletes, there was a shocking abundance of severe physical injuries and mental anguish, especially among the women. More and more of my female students were hobbling into class or talking about yet another teammate who tore her anterior cruciate ligament (ACL) or received a concussion. Inside and outside of the classroom, young women would frequently start crying when recounting their youth and college sports experiences. Many athletes literally couldn't wait until they graduated so they wouldn't have to touch a soccer ball, softball bat, or basketball ever again. Third, and perhaps most important, almost all of these young adults (and their families) involved in serious youth sports had been *driven* by some thoughts of a college scholarship or admissions advantage, even if those thoughts were derailed at some point before college. It seemed as though there was an actual commercial "pipeline" connecting the ideal of youth sports with the ideal of subsidized intercollegiate athletics. This "pipeline" was not just a metaphorical construct but a tangible set of social relationships that were a central part of these young women's lives. Yet for those who managed to play on a college varsity team, there was widespread disillusionment about the reality of intercollegiate athletics not corresponding with the rhetoric they had been consistently exposed to while younger. It seems that these young women and their families had been sold a bill of goods, and that the misrepresentation of intercollegiate athletics was at the heart of this deception.

Susan and Claire embody these trends. They have both successfully completed their pipeline journeys with a subsidized college education, although at great physical and emotional cost, not to mention their disillusionment with intercollegiate athletics. Without more systematic evidence, I would hesitate to say that "most" girls suffer these consequences, but I believe it is accurate to say that "far too many" girls experience them, and this book is designed to reflect this important phenomenon regardless of its frequency. There are surely countless other girls (and their families) in soccer's and other sports' pipelines, with similar visions of college scholarships dancing in their heads, with little or no idea about the personal problems they may soon face. Parents like Kim pour unbelievable amounts of time and money into youth sports as investments in their daughters' futures. Five-year-old girls (sometimes younger) are increasingly treating youth sports like a job that will eventually pay off with the ultimate promotion: being on a college varsity team. Playing in international competitions like the Olympics and World Cup may enter the equation, but nothing is more important than securing a financial (or other) subsidy to attend college. A myriad of people, organizations, and social institutions are responsible for embellishing the likelihood of receiving a subsidy and the grandeur of playing intercollegiate athletics. Higher education occupies the epicenter of this exaggeration, although it is rarely implicated for it. Until now.

On a more personal level, my two daughters and I have been mostly eager participants in organized youth sports, they as players and me as a volunteer coach and low-level league official. Oh, the things I have seen! I have been approached by parents who wondered why I wasn't being meaner to eight-year-old travel soccer players. I knew nine-year-old girls who quit a sport they loved (softball) in order to specialize in a less-liked activity (lacrosse) that would more likely pay off with an Ivy League acceptance in seven years. I watched ten-year-old girls leave community teams filled with friends and ample playing time to join more elite teams where they sat on the bench. I witnessed parents pouring thousands of dollars into camps, equipment, and personal trainers in order to get their daughters to that ever-elusive "next level" that would eventually (or so they thought) pay off with a college athletic scholarship or preferential admission to a prestigious school. I saw other families drop out of organized youth sports because they could no longer afford the expanding pay-to-play system. I saw coaches screaming at young kids for dropping a fly ball or missing a penalty kick, and heard about parents taking away their daughter's TV privileges for doing poorly in a skating exhibition. I was worried that my own kids would have to deal with this, and I tried very hard to insulate them and the other girls on my teams from the madness, but the madness was everywhere.

Beyond my own daughters, it was hard to miss the rampant commercialism infiltrating youth sports, from the increasing use (and cost) of professional coaches for younger players and the proliferation of year-round tournaments in sports that had once been seasonal. Recreational sports programs such as Little League Softball were under siege from allegedly more prestigious commercial organizations that were always promising a commodified path to the next level, rather than heralding the intrinsic fun of participation. As a college professor (for over twenty-five years) heavily involved in campus governance, I witnessed the increased emphasis on cultivating my school's "brand" and how visible and expensive intercollegiate sports were central to the ongoing "corporatization of higher education." Experiences from colleagues at other schools plus systematic data from the Knight Commission on Intercollegiate Athletics, the Drake Group, and the Coalition on Intercollegiate Athletics (COIA) underscored this corporatization as a widespread trend. The notions of corporatization, commercialization, and commodification are deeply embedded in sociology's historical roots, and it was both intellectually exciting and morally depressing to watch them at work in the milieu of girls' youth sports. Parents and other adults who place too much importance on youth sports were making conscious decisions, but they were making them under social and historical conditions not of their own choosing.[2] They have been bombarded with messages from a plethora of cultural sources extolling the marvels of organized sports generally and intercollegiate athletics specifically. But rarely, if ever, do they hear about the horror stories. Just as important, participation in youth sports was becoming class restrictive; it was increasingly "pay to play," and parents increasingly had to divert family resources in order to meet their commercialized youth sports obligations. By corollary, racial and ethnic minorities (and nonsuburbanites) had limited access to this pay-to-play system. Contrary to conventional wisdom, then, college athletic scholarships and admissions advantages are *not* a conduit of social mobility but a spoil increasingly available only to those who can afford it. Organized commercial programs in most youth sports are akin to affirmative action benefiting families already enjoying economic and cultural advantages.

CHOOSING WHICH (FEMALE) SPORTS TO STUDY

The conscious decision to study only female sports, and five specific sports, will be detailed in chapter 1. Of course, I doubt the multitudes of people who have studied and written about *male* sports would feel obliged to defend that choice! For the moment, suffice it to say that I believe female versions of youth and college sports are quite different from their male counterparts. They are not better or worse, just different. Similarly, female youth and college sports are at different historical junctures than male sports. So while a good deal of my argument is equally valid for male youth sports to college pipelines, much of it is unique to the female iteration. In terms of the sports selected, the project originally included only two: soccer and ultimate Frisbee. These are the yin and yang of female youth sports to college pipelines. Youth soccer is incredibly commercialized and commodified, reflecting its significant intercollegiate varsity presence. Ultimate, despite being played by a growing number of kids, has practically no commercial presence. I believe this is largely *caused* by ultimate's lack of an intercollegiate varsity footprint. After starting the research, and after being gently prodded by a longtime friend and colleague, I added field hockey and figure skating to the mix in order to capture the nuances excluded from the soccer and ultimate extremes. However, while exploring female figure skating, I accidentally learned about a seismic movement of young girls from figure skating to ice hockey, almost always justified by the exaggerated lure of college scholarships, which do not exist in figure skating. Thus a fifth sport was introduced, although it is presented in the book as something of a Ms. Hyde to figure skating's Dr. Jekyll (or vice versa). These five sports reflect very different youth sports to college pipelines (including the absence of any pipeline) and demonstrate the overarching importance of higher-education policies in driving the world of girls' youth sports, often for the worse. However, these five sports are not treated equally. Soccer, with the most intense commercial youth sports system, is the headliner with field hockey playing a crucial supporting role. Ultimate, figure skating, and ice hockey will make smaller but still important contributions to the story. The absence of pipelines in figure skating and ultimate is just as important as their presence in soccer and field hockey.

Other sports could have been substituted for these five. At the most commercialized end of the spectrum, soccer could have been replaced by volleyball, softball, basketball, swimming, and track. All are played throughout the United States with significant intercollegiate footprints and highly commercialized youth sports systems. Among female sports with smaller intercollegiate footprints and more modest pipelines, rowing and lacrosse could have supplanted ice hockey. All are geographically restricted but with rapidly growing intercollegiate varsity footprints driving a corresponding (although dissimilar) youth sports expansion. Field hockey, figure skating, and ultimate really have no alternatives, although gymnastics probably could have been squeezed in somehow. Field hockey is one of the few truly team sports with a static (and possibly shrinking) intercollegiate footprint, which reverberates up and down its pipeline. Figure skating has no intercollegiate varsity presence but has always been highly commercialized and extremely class-exclusive (much like gymnastics). Organized ultimate also has no intercollegiate varsity presence but, in contrast to figure skating, is generally associated with *non*exclusivity and universal accessibility. However, even the generally egalitarian nature of ultimate may be under assault from the powerful historical currents affecting all girls' youth sports.

Finally, this research is specific to the United States. Youth sport and college sports in the United States are significantly different than in other countries. Most important, college sports as we know them simply don't exist elsewhere. They have no counterpart outside of the United States. This in and of itself creates an enormously different social dynamic. Similarly, there are very few other countries where organized sport is so thoroughly intertwined with precollege education. In short, there is no other place in the world where formalized sport and formalized education exist in the same structural and ideological spaces. Intercollegiate and interscholastic (high school) sports are part of the conventional US cultural landscape. This unique relationship between sports and education in the United States is at the heart of the exceedingly commercialized and commodified youth sports pipelines.

A DEEPER UNDERSTANDING

This book is intended for a general audience beyond those few hundred people who consider themselves "sports sociologists," or undergraduate students lucky enough to be enrolled in a sports sociology course. Anyone interested in the commercialization of youth sports, the corporatization of higher education, and how these are connected, should find this book interesting and maybe even important. However, while I have tried to write in a nontechnical style, this is absolutely a work of social science. In a sense, *How College Athletics Are Hurting Girls' Sports* straddles the line between journalism and sociology, an area sometimes called "public sociology." Journalists tell good stories with lively characters, but their "evidence" leans toward the anecdotal. Sometimes these stories and characters will highlight important social injustices like the social-class and racial barriers to participating in youth sports. In contrast, sociologists try to discern patterns in social behavior through more systematic data collection (as opposed to random anecdotes) driven by certain central ideas (or theories). These ideas can be a mixture of old standards and new melodies. For instance, commercialization, commodification, and corporatization have been central to sociological thinking for over one hundred years. These classical ideas have become the building blocks of the "pay-to-play youth sports to college pipeline" idea that drives the book's empirical research. But rather than trying to "prove" how good this model is (a common sociological approach), I am using it to tell a compelling story about a very important social phenomenon that harshly impacts many individuals. Sociologist C. Wright Mills called this connecting personal troubles with social issues, and it is at the heart of what we sometimes call "public sociology" or "humanist sociology."[3]

The data gathered for this book reflect what is often called a "mixed-methods" approach. First, I draw extensively on descriptive quantitative data collected by various organizations such as the National Collegiate Athletic Association (NCAA), the National Federation of State High School Associations (NFHS), the National Center for Education Statistics (NCES), the US Department of Education, and the US Census Bureau. Some of these data are presented in their natural state and other times I have reconstructed them to help make a point. This secondary data analysis is supplemented by primary data mined and organized from different raw sources such as youth sports websites or college team rosters. Second, and far more important, I use qualitative approaches where individual actors reveal (through words and actions) their experiences with and interpretation of youth and college sports. These methods include detailed ethnographic observations of and systematic interviews with over one hundred people (mostly, but not all, female) representing athletes, parents, coaches, vendors, and administrators (broadly defined). Hundreds more athletes, coaches, and parents were systematically observed in their "natural habitats."[4]

In straddling the line between good sociology and good journalism, I used these systematic interviews to create "composite characters" that make for more compelling stories. Many of the characters quoted, then, are actually amalgamations of several individuals who spoke similarly about certain topics. The experiences of young women like Susan and Claire were mirrored by many other college athletes I interviewed and observed. Kim reflects the genre of sports parents who have come to regret some of their actions. Any person referred to by first name only is a composite, with altered names and demographic characteristics. All interviewed parents and athletes are treated this way. Those referred to by title alone are *not* composites, but I chose to disguise their identity even though most of them granted permission to use their names. So when someone is introduced as a coach of a Division I college field hockey program, then they are a real individual with that status. In a few cases, actual names (first *and* last), titles, and gender identities will be used in order to lend some necessary legitimacy or nuance to a person's perspective. This eclectic approach may get me into trouble with the guardians of sociological orthodoxy, but that's a small price to pay for telling a better story about an important topic. Naturally, this project can be replicated by anyone so inclined, and I will further explore some of these methodological issues in the book's appendix.

OUTLINE OF THE BOOK

Chapter 1 will introduce us to a few more girls and parents enmeshed in what will be referred to as the pay-to-play female youth sports to college pipeline. I will examine details about the structure and function of the pipelines (including their social-class biases), explain why female pipelines are unique (with special attention to Title IX), and differentiate between and among pipelines in different sports. Girls and their families have a misguided view about these pipelines, which leads them to greatly overestimate their potential payoff in athletic-based college scholarships and/or admissions advantages to elite universities.

Chapter 2 explores the driving force behind the female youth sports to college pipelines and the rampant misperception of their likely payoff: an increasingly corporatized system of higher education that has been diverting more scarce resources to women's intercollegiate athletics in order to directly and indirectly improve a school's "brand" visibility. While there are certainly some potential bonuses at the end of the youth sports to college pipelines, these windfalls are greatly embellished by higher-education organizations (including the NCAA) through withholding crucial information about athletic-based scholarships and granting preferential treatment to potential intercollegiate athletes, although not nearly as much as many families have been led to believe. Ironically (perhaps), the corporatization of higher education has greatly contributed to increased college costs that only feed the growing obsession of families to secure some sort of athletic-based financial support. Also ironically (perhaps), the pipelines' social-class biases ensure that only relatively wealthy girls can access this particular form of college financial aid.

Chapters 3 and 4 explore the commercialized and commodified youth sports industry, where a myriad of products and services are available to help girls reach that all-important next level of the pipeline. Chapter 3 focuses on the "supply side" of the youth sports industry that has been taking advantage of the explosive rise in girls' youth sports over the past thirty years. Chapter 4 details the creation of "consumer demand," where clever marketing strategies try to separate families from their money. At the heart of these strategies are promises that only certain products and services will guarantee a successful trip through the pipeline and into a subsidized college education. Even for those families that do not really need financial support, there is prestige involved with being able to say that your daughter is "going to {some school} to play {some sport}." This is a sociological variation on the more psychological assertion that parents are trying to reclaim unattained youth sports glory through their kids.

In conjunction with the historical trends of commercialization, commodification, and corporatization, chapter 5 examines how female sports are increasingly judged on male terms, or what might be called the "masculinization" of female sports. This masculinization operates in two ways. First, female sports are commonly compared to male sports, with the legitimacy of female sports (and female athletes) dependent upon how well they mirror the male standard. This has, among other things, contributed to a rash of serious physical injuries (like Susan's) and emotional distress (like Claire's) among girls and young women in the pipeline as they continue trying to meet male-centered expectations. Successfully addressing this problem means adopting a perspective of "irrelevant essentialism" where we acknowledge the differences between male and female sports and athletes without placing these differences into an ordinal hierarchy. The second aspect of masculinization is the increase in males coaching girls' youth teams and, more important, women's college teams. As women's sports in general have become more economically viable and culturally legitimate, men have flocked to their coaching and administrative slots. In addition to reflecting certain labor market realities, female players and their families often think that male coaches are better equipped than female coaches to help them successfully navigate the youth sports to college pipelines. The negative effects of masculinization are an ironic unintended consequence of the Title IX legislation that enormously expanded athletic opportunities for girls and women.

Chapter 6 offers suggestions about reducing the rampant commercialization and commodification of girls' youth sports, and making these childhood activities more about having fun and less about getting a leg up on adulthood. While other people have long argued that youth sports should become less serious, this may be the first systematic assertion that changes in youth sports will *not* materialize unless preceded by changes in intercollegiate athletics. These proposed changes in college athletics run the gamut from completely eliminating all intercollegiate sports to simply mandating that those involved at every stage of the youth sports to college pipeline (especially colleges) thoroughly disclose accurate information that would allow girls and their families to make well-informed decisions. There will, of course, be strong resistance to any changes in the pay-to-play youth sports to college pipelines. A lot of individuals and organizations have a vested interest in maintaining the status quo. To do nothing, though, perpetuates a significant social injustice. Those girls and young women who can't afford to even participate in the pay-to-play system will be less likely to experience the intrinsic fun and joy that organized sports can offer, not to mention their being excluded from any possible college subsidy. Those who can access the pay-to-play system will increasingly find the potential fun and joy of organized sport trampled by a rampant commercialization that, at ridiculously early ages, is turning childhood into an apprenticeship for adulthood and often leaving them physically or emotionally wounded. If nothing else, I hope this book can provide an alternative, nonromanticized perspective into the interconnected worlds of girls' youth sports and women's college athletics. With any luck, there will be fewer Susans and Claires, and more kids who can enjoy their childhoods and continue having fun playing cherished sports beyond their teens.

1

THE FEMALE YOUTH SPORTS TO COLLEGE PIPELINE

Caroline, a seventh-grader, lives in a Midwestern suburb and has always loved playing soccer:

> Some days I just want to quit. It's not fun anymore. My dad won't stop bugging me. He makes me stay around after games to work on things he thought I did wrong. He's always screaming at me during games. One of my coaches on [my previous team] the White Stallions always put me on the side of the field away from the parents so I couldn't hear him. Now I'm playing on this weird travel team instead of the Stallions. We have tournaments like every weekend. They're usually far away. Next year I have to play soccer all year, so no more softball or summer swimming. [My new team] is good but [former teammate] Grace would be our best player. I miss my old team. They were so goofy. Even the [private school] girls. My favorite part was going to lunch during tournaments. Especially the lunch court at Kroger's. Annie would always put a mountain of food on her plate. It was so gross! Next year [my dad] says I may move to a private high school where he thinks I can play center midfield because Grace plays that position [at my current public school]. He says that colleges are always looking for center midfielders. He thinks he knows everything.

Caroline's dad, Robert, has a slightly different assessment of the situation:

> I could see early on that Caroline had a lot of soccer talent, she just needed to be more disciplined. She had a lot of fun on the [White Stallions], and I

> let that go for a few years, but she really needed to play at the next level once she was older. I think the problem was the coaches. They didn't push the girls enough. One year we had a chance to do a really prestigious tournament in August, but the coaches thought it was too far and we would probably get killed and get demoralized. The other parents all went along since they probably didn't want to disturb their vacations. My thinking is you don't get better unless you play against the best teams. So, yeah, Caroline is going to play for a premier team in [a certain premier league] where there are trained professional coaches dedicated to success. I hear that college coaches flock to the tournaments that this team plays in. Caroline has got to get on their radar. Nobody is coming to watch [the White Stallions].

Caroline started playing soccer when she was six. As with many young girls, she first played in her town's recreational league that was organized and run by local volunteers, received priority access to community and school district fields, and charged a relatively small participation fee of $125 that was waived or reduced for low-income families. Games were three against three on "small-sided" fields with lots of action and lots of "touches." All the coaches were parents. There were no referees. Nobody kept score. Watching six-year-olds in a recreational league reminds us about the true meaning of play. The kids are laughing all the time, whether they are in the game or not. Some are well coordinated physically, others have trouble with basic skills. But they're mostly having fun, whether or not they are mastering soccer.

In third grade, Caroline moved from "recreational" soccer to "travel" soccer, along with Grace and other local friends who wanted a more intense playing experience and, as many of them told me, team sweatshirts with their names and numbers on the back. They named themselves the White Stallions. Some of Caroline's other friends did not move to the travel team, preferring to remain in the relatively small recreational program or giving up soccer. The White Stallions, like her previous recreational team, was affiliated with the town's not-for-profit soccer program, and only those living in the town (or who attended school in the town) were allowed on the team. Games were eight against eight on small fields. There were yearly tryouts, but the program tried to create enough travel teams to accommodate interest, so very few girls were "cut" and forced to play in the recreational program against their desires. There were about fifty girls playing in this age group at U9. By the time the girls were U12, only fifteen remained. The rest had stopped playing soccer.[1]

Caroline would play on the White Stallions, from the U9 to U12 levels. She and her friends competed against other teams in the Southeastern Michigan Girls' Soccer League based on age and self-identified ability level.[2] Most of these games were played within fifty miles of home, with the vast majority against other township-based travel teams within twenty miles. The Stallions would also participate in two or three tournaments in the fall season. These tournaments were generally not more than a two-hour drive and did not necessitate overnight stays. The team did not have structured practices outside of the fall season, although some of the girls voluntarily played in an indoor winter league. Participating on this team cost about $800 per year, with small scholarships available to low-income families. Some of that $800 went toward paying a professional soccer coach who provided technical instruction to the girls twice a week. For a few hundred more dollars from each family, that professional coach could also lead the team during actual games. Caroline's township-based soccer club will soon be *mandating* that the top-level team in each age group have a paid professional coach for both training *and* games, so this $800 yearly fee would have risen to about $1,200 at the U13 level if Caroline had stuck around. A league officer from a different soccer club explained the logic, which seems to assume a lot of parents are thinking like Robert:

> A lot of our teams are hemorrhaging girls to other programs that do not have residency requirements. When [the board] looked into this we found that the girls were almost always going to soccer programs that were more serious. They practiced more. They went to bigger tournaments. They had more training. We didn't think that ending the mandatory residency requirement would do much since the trend is against clubs like ours that are a little less intense. So we mandated that every top team has a professional, licensed game-day coach. We contracted with a company that provides these coaches plus trainers for the other kids. There was some resistance, but overall it seems to be working. Some of the second- and third-tier teams are now demanding they also have the chance to pay for a professional game coach. I guess they think their girls will have a better shot at moving to the top team. It's too early to know for sure, but we think the bleeding has stopped. The families around here all want intense experiences for their daughters, even the nine-year-olds. If we don't adjust, the soccer club will probably fold.

Caroline's new U13 team, FC Arsenal, is part of an elite club that promises players and their families a much more intense soccer experience, guaranteed to get players to "the next level." At practices, there is very little talking during drills, and water breaks are spent drinking water rather than catching up on the latest middle school scandals, which is not altogether surprising since only a few girls attend the same school. Two minutes later they are back on the field. When one girl slips and falls, they all laugh hysterically, then quickly correct themselves when the coach starts glaring. FC Arsenal is highly selective, and girls come from all over the area to try out. Many get cut. They practice locally two or three times per week. The team does not compete in a regional league but plays all its games in weekend tournaments against similarly selective teams from the entire Great Lakes region. Sometimes they might travel two hundred miles to play in a tournament against a similar elite team that practices a few towns over from Caroline's. Between fees, uniforms, mandatory summer camps, required training gear, and tournament costs, Caroline's family pays about $5,000 per year to be on this team. That is actually far less than they might pay on some other premier teams that hire strength conditioners, nutritionists, videographers, and sports psychologists to help girls (and their teams) reach that ever-elusive next level. Caroline's costs will be increasing next year since the U14 team plays in additional tournaments. That team also requires that its players commit to year-round soccer training and stop playing other sports that might interfere with this training. Currently, Caroline plays spring softball for her middle school and in the local Little League, and swims for a YMCA club team in the summer. She will have to give those up in order to participate in (and pay for) the spring and summer soccer training sessions even though, according to her friends, she's pretty accomplished at those other sports. For the time being, she can continue playing school soccer, although that might change.[3]

Elizabeth lives in the same town as Caroline but is a year older. Their soccer histories were almost identical, including moving from a town-based travel team to a more selective program, and transferring out of public school to play in a more prestigious private school setting (albeit a different school). There were some differences, though. First, the elite team Elizabeth joined at U13, called FC Manchester, did not play in a tournament-only league but in the top division of the Southeastern Michigan Girls' Soccer League. Both Elizabeth's previous team (the Hurricanes) and the White Stallions played in Division Five (out of ten total). The new team was part of a premier segment of an adjacent township's soccer program. This premier segment did not have residency restrictions so could accept girls based on talent rather than geography. In addition to playing in the local league, FC Manchester participated in about a dozen tournaments a year, including some very prestigious "showcase" tournaments that drew dozens of curious college coaches looking for future intercollegiate players.

The second difference between the two girls is that while Caroline jokes about quitting soccer, Elizabeth is actually going to do it. Completely. When we spoke, she hadn't yet told her parents and swore me to secrecy:[4]

> I'm quitting because I'm not playing. On my old team I was the starting striker and played long shifts. Most of us also played together on the [middle school] team. Both teams did OK. Not great. But we really didn't care much. My parents cared way more than I did. They were always asking if I wanted to play on a really good team. I pretended not to hear them. Eventually, they just decided for me and made me do a tryout. I was thinking of doing really bad at the tryout but probably would have gotten grounded. So I made the team. I admit it felt cool at first. But then I never played in the games. My parents told me to be patient. They said not playing on a great team was better than playing on a bad team. That seemed weird. My new school team is terrible. I mean, the team is good but the coach is horrible. He yells at us all the time. Two girls have already quit. [The coach] says they are babies. I think I'm going to run cross country next year but haven't asked my parents. They're going to flip out. They think soccer should be the most important thing in my life.

Elizabeth's mom, Rebecca, explained the parental logic at work here:

> [My husband] and I understand better than Elizabeth that certain paths lead to certain places. If she's going to get into a really good college, it won't be by playing on a mediocre travel team or mediocre public school team. A lot of our work colleagues have kids who got into good colleges by playing sports, but you have to make your kid visible. These are not all brilliant kids. One of them got into [an Ivy school] not with brains but as a lacrosse goalie. She even got a really good financial aid package. The college coaches only watch the best teams at the best tournaments and best high schools. What good is it being a great player on a bad team that nobody cares about? Elizabeth is only fourteen, so she doesn't see the bigger picture. What teenager does? They live for the moment. It's up to us to look ahead and make sure she can be successful. That means going to a prestigious college. It seems to us that sports are the best way to make that happen, and Elizabeth just happens to be a good athlete. So we're going to focus on that. She's also pretty smart, but so are a lot of kids.

THE GIRLS' YOUTH SPORTS TO COLLEGE PIPELINE

Elizabeth and Caroline (and their parents) are enmeshed in what I am calling the "girls' youth sports to college pipeline." Allegedly, young girls enter this pipeline around age five and, ten to fifteen years later, exit into a desirable college where they will be the beneficiaries of athletics-based scholarships and/or preferential admissions considerations. Some kids may even enter the pipeline at age two! Conventional wisdom holds that an abundance of advantages awaits those girls who develop their skills and talents within the pipeline. While the pipeline has many important characteristics, its very existence is predicated on what happens at the exit. Higher-education policies generally, and intercollegiate athletics specifically, drive the action. Girls and their families are deceptively lured to and pulled through these incredibly expensive pipelines by the largely exaggerated promises of a financially and/or academically subsidized college education, although many other social institutions aid and abet in this deception. The pipeline ejects many of its participants while those who make it through find a far different higher-education reality than the one promised.

While higher-education policy is the most important force shaping youth sports pipelines, other factors are also important. First, pipelines are shaped by larger social and historical forces that significantly influence the actions and beliefs of all pipeline participants. The pipeline is a "modern" phenomenon that reflects overall historical trends of commercialization, commodification, and corporatization within a complex capitalist society. Second, gender matters. There are pipelines for boys and girls, but they look and act differently and have a different social and historical context. The research in this book primarily focuses on girls' sports. Third, the pipelines do not look and act the same way for all female sports. Youth sports without intercollegiate varsity footprints do not really have pipelines, even though they may still be somewhat commercialized. Fourth, the pipelines are judgmental and often dangerous. Girls are increasingly leaving organized youth sports because of physical injury, emotional burnout, and the absence of fun. Ironically, even as the pipelines grow larger and stronger, there has been a decline in girls' overall youth sports participation. Finally, the pipeline is elitist and discriminatory; it is truly "pay to play." Significant financial resources are required to enter the pipeline and to advance through its many stages. This prevents low-income families from taking advantage of the pipeline's real, if exaggerated, benefits. Similarly, there are racial, ethnic, and geographic biases to the pipeline that reflect overall income inequality and residential segregation.

The "pay-to-play youth sports to college pipeline" is what sociologist Max Weber would call an "ideal type." Ideal types are not meant to precisely reflect reality but to provide an analytical model for guiding social scientific research. The ideal type of youth sports to college pipeline manifests in different ways the characteristics mentioned above, and this book's empirical examination of female sports in the United States is framed and steered by this ideal type. What are the historical, structural, and biographical factors that contribute to variations from the ideal model? How do geography and culture matter? How and why do different sports adhere to or stray from the ideal model? How might social factors having nothing to do with sports themselves impact different iterations of the pipeline? Why do certain sports have no pay-to-play pipelines? Why are intercollegiate athletics, regardless of the competitive level, so crucial in creating and shaping the pipelines?[5]

THE LARGER SOCIAL AND HISTORICAL CONTEXT

Commercialization, commodification, and corporatization are seminal ideas drawn from the classical sociological works of Karl Marx and Max Weber that explore the dynamics of capitalism and the growth of complex organizations.[6] These ideas have rarely been systematically applied to the social institution of sports, especially youth sports. They are not mutually exclusive concepts but do differ somewhat in emphasis. Commercialization refers to using something in order to make money from it. This money might be profit or it might be wages. For example, an apparel company wants to make money by selling state-of-the-art shin guards to young soccer players, and would like to encourage more youngsters to take up the sport and protect their shins with its product. A young British ex-soccer player (probably male) might fancy moving to the United States and earning a living by coaching teams and working camps in the ever-expanding commercial world of girls' youth soccer, a world that is far more developed in the United States than elsewhere. The new programs that Caroline and Elizabeth participate in are an especially robust part of commercialized girls' youth sports.

Commodification refers to doing something for extrinsic rather than intrinsic reasons; doing something as a means to an end, not as an end in itself. Participating in youth sports, then, is increasingly *not* about having fun, developing personal skills (physical or emotional), or building friendships. Rather, youth sports are becoming a conduit for something else: winning Olympic medals or getting a leg up on college admissions. As parents, Robert's and Rebecca's approach to youth sports reflects this trend. Within higher education itself, money is poured into intercollegiate athletics not necessarily to enhance the educational experience of community members (both players and nonplayers), but as a clever strategy to lock in prospective students, influence external rankings (also a commercialized process), and enhance a school's "brand" to outsiders. While this kind of commodification is not necessarily a bad thing, it is increasingly apparent in youth sports at ever younger ages. For example, some premier soccer programs, such as the ones Caroline and Elizabeth play in, are recruiting six-year-olds to become seriously involved in the youth sports to college pipeline, where thinking about college in twelve years takes precedent over learning to tie your own shoes.

Corporatization occurs when we apply a profit-oriented business model to human activities that aren't primarily about profit. A number of scholars and social commentators have recently written about the permeation of a corporate mentality into both K-12 and higher education (see chapter 2, notes 1–15). The corporatization of higher education, for example, reduces abstract notions of "learning" and "education" to standardized quantifiable indicators such as course evaluations, student-teacher ratios, job placements, and admissions yields. The corporatized university is obsessed with its "brand" as an end in itself and will constantly monitor the number of media branding "hits" received per dollar invested, even if that notoriety has absolutely no impact on the university's educational mission. Rankings, such as those offered by *U.S. News and World Report*, become the centerpiece of strategic planning even if they are based on irrelevant criteria and are easily manipulated. K-12 school districts reflect a corporatized approach when they focus policies on anything that can raise their median standardized test scores or the number of students taking (or scoring well on) AP exams.

In the corporatized university, revenue (and endowment size) becomes an end in itself, often necessitating increased expenditures on alumni relations and advancement in order to raise more revenue, which then gets invested in more revenue-raising schemes rather than in core academic areas. It's not unlike a for-profit corporation trying to raise the share price of its stock no matter how it impacts the company's stated mission. In sports, corporatization can take many forms. Evaluating a particular program or coach, for example, is not a question of whether the sport's participants have become better people or make contributions to the community, since that is difficult to quantify. Instead, evaluations will focus on the number of conference championships, the number of players who go on to play sports in college, the number of players who qualify for national teams, the number of travel players "placed" on premier teams, and the won-lost percentage of a team within the context of its resource base. At the youth level, teams, players, and programs are increasingly judged by their rankings on some arbitrary (and often commercialized) scale, how many elite tournaments a team plays in, or the personal pedigrees of coaches and program coordinators, including whether they speak with an exotic accent. Again,

Robert and Rebecca were very clear that these were the factors driving their soccer decisions for Caroline and Elizabeth. The girls having fun and enjoying their childhoods was not part of this commercialized, commodified, and corporatized equation.

FEMALE SPORTS ARE DIFFERENT

As briefly alluded to in the introduction, there are several reasons why this book focuses on female youth sports to college pipelines. First, when it comes to scholarly or journalistic discussions of organized sports, men and boys receive almost all of the attention. With college sports, this is not necessarily due to an overt patriarchal bias but because the research focus has been almost exclusively on "big money" sports such as football and men's basketball.[7] More systematic examinations of female sports are not unheard of, but they are rare and often enmeshed in broader concerns with issues like Title IX.[8] At the youth level, girls playing organized sports is not ignored in journalistic accounts, but gender itself is not viewed as a central issue.[9] Two notable exceptions are Michael Sokolove's *Warrior Girls*, which specifically examines the explosion of serious injuries among girls and young women playing organized sports, and Joan Ryan's (out-of-print) *Little Girls in Pretty Boxes*, which explores the sordid underbelly of girls' competitive gymnastics and figure skating.[10]

Youth sports have received scant social scientific attention, especially in the past twenty years. This is partly due to the increasingly problematic barriers erected by university institutional review boards (IRBs) that frustrate scholars wishing to pursue "human subjects research" on children under eighteen, even when this research is in no way intrusive or invasive. Within the parameters of many IRBs, a researcher would need "consent" to quietly observe a U10 girls' soccer game in a public space. There also isn't significant attention paid to female sports using macro-level concepts such as commercialization, commodification, and corporatization. Instead, there is an emphasis on how sports participation acts as a powerful agent of socially constructed ideologies, especially although not exclusively about gender. For example, Hilary Friedman examines the role of organized youth sports (male and female) in creating and reinforcing normative beliefs heralding competitiveness, with a distinction between how this unfolds differently for boys and girls. Noel Dyck's detailed ethnography of Canadian youth soccer identifies how the social meaning of sports is constructed by "negotiation" among its many participants, regardless of gender. Michael Messner's significant body of work dissects the many ways that sports generate, reflect, and perpetuate conventional beliefs about "male" and "female." Sherri Grasmuck's in-depth ethnography of youth baseball in Philadelphia identifies important components of gender socialization, but primarily for boys.[11] These academic studies do not ignore larger economic factors such as commercialization, commodification, and corporatization, but they treat them more in passing rather than as central analytical concepts. Most important, much of this research (journalistic and academic) sometimes identifies the important connections between youth sports and intercollegiate athletics, but never elevates this connection to an overarching causal relationship whereby intercollegiate athletics (and higher education) *drive* the commercialization, commodification, and corporatization of girls' youth sports.[12]

A second reason to concentrate on female sports is to allow an emphasis on the *sports* part of the term rather than the gender part. Female *sports* are different from male *sports* at both the youth and college levels. This is reflected in how we think about male and female sports, how they are organized commercially, and how they get expressed in the various youth sports to college pipelines. Starting from a foundation that might be called "irrelevant essentialism," I would that argue that males and females have certain physical differences (on average), that the organized *sports* they play are somewhat different (on average), and that this has *nothing* to do with superiority or inferiority. They are simply irrelevant differences that we have socially constructed into a hierarchy, which should be unsurprising within a patriarchal society expressing what is often called "hegemonic masculinity." We have learned to think that the female-centered variations of organized sports are less valuable than corresponding male-centered variations. And while there has been some eroding of this legitimacy gap during the past several decades, the gap still remains. So, for example, there is "lacrosse" and "women's lacrosse"; "soccer" and "women's soccer." We don't normally say there is both "soccer" and "men's soccer." Female versions of most sports are not treated as the standard or baseline of the game. Interestingly, this and other factors are leading to a masculinization of female sports, causing an increase in serious physical injuries and emotional burnout among female athletes who continually strive to be "as good as the guys." The masculinization of female sports will be more fully addressed in chapter 5.

Female organized sports are also at a different historical juncture than male organized sports. They are relatively new with still-unfolding cultural, organizational, and economic dynamics. Female organized sports began sprouting organizationally only after the passage of Title IX in the early

1970s, and only started blossoming fully after 1990. The data are clear on how Title IX opened the floodgates for female participation in organized sports. But numbers aren't everything. Female organized sports at every level are, at best, in an adolescent stage, while male organized sports are fully mature. Historical phenomena like commercialization, commodification, and corporatization have been evident in boys' youth sports and men's college sports for a long time but are only recently becoming prominent in female sports. The college-driven commercial assault on girls' youth sports is happening *now* or, at least, quite recently. There is more commercialism in male youth sports than in female sports, but it has been growing faster on the female side during the past three decades. It's as if we have developed a quasi-laboratory setting to examine the construction and expansion of youth sports to college pipelines. By no means do I intend to romanticize the "good old days" when women's/girls' sports were pure and untainted with commercial influence, just to illustrate that the social and historical forces that have already commercialized male sports are now also at work on female sports. Similarly, I will not be treating Title IX as a flawless panacea that has eroded barriers for females, but as a complex social phenomenon that has simultaneously challenged *and* reinforced traditional gender constructs.

Finally, there are few if any professional opportunities for female athletes growing up in the United States. A handful of women can make a living (often a good one) in individual-oriented sports such as tennis, golf, and figure skating, but generally there are few occupational options for female professional athletes in team-oriented sports.[13] Players in the Women's National Basketball Association (WNBA) earn about $35,000 as rookies and have salary caps of approximately $110,000. There are opportunities to play professional basketball outside the United States, but there are far fewer of these opportunities for women than for men, and most teams based in other countries limit the number of American players on their rosters. Women's professional soccer has failed to gain much traction in North America. The average salary in the nascent National Women's Soccer League is about $30,000, but that is skewed upward by some large salaries for marquee US National Team players such as Alex Morgan. In addition, there are some professional opportunities for women in European leagues.[14] In 2016 members of the ultra-successful women's national soccer team filed a lawsuit against the US Soccer Federation, claiming it supported them at far more paltry levels than the far less successful men's national team.

For most females in the United States, then, obtaining a college scholarship or preferential college admissions has become the primary endgame for entering and participating in the youth sports pipeline, outside of any possible intrinsic value derived from playing sports. The corresponding boys' pipelines exit into occupational opportunities in addition to higher education, even though those professional opportunities are extremely rare. Nevertheless, male college athletics may themselves be a commodified (if exaggerated) means to an occupational end as partly dictated by the arbitrary credential requirements established by many professional sports leagues. But there are probably very few girls or young women who see college sports as a brief training program on the road to being a professional athlete.[15] With the cost of higher education skyrocketing along with the perceived importance of obtaining the "right" college degree, college admissions advantages and/or athletics-based scholarships have become a very attractive goal. Lila is a thoughtful and energetic ten-year-old girl:

> I'm so excited that I made the [Hotshots] travel team. The girls are really good, and I'm going to get way better. My coach says that to be the best and play in the Olympics we have to play soccer all year. So I'm going to stop playing [travel team] basketball and [recreational league] lacrosse. I want to play in the Olympics like Abby Wambach!

Lila told me that she likes basketball better than soccer, but people say she is too short for the sport. At ten years old! I asked her father, Christopher, about the possible pitfalls of Lila's sports specialization at such an early age. He seemed to be more concerned with Lila's college options than with her idolization of Abby Wambach's Olympic glory:

> It's not that I can't afford Lila's college. But I need to make sure she gets into a good school. I see my friends' kids getting into Ivy League schools even though they aren't valedictorian types but because they play lacrosse or row. None of them got into Princeton because they play the cello or took fifteen AP physics courses. All the kids applying there play the cello and take AP courses. But it seems like being a recruited athlete is more important. So she's going to focus on soccer. Yes, she likes basketball better, but she'll forget about it. What if she doesn't grow? And you need more players for a soccer team than a basketball team, so your odds of getting in are better. This [Hotshots] program is pretty solid. They say a lot of their girls go on to play [in college]. I don't think I buy this stuff about overuse injuries. Look at these women playing in the Olympics. They've probably played just soccer since they were three. And even Lila's hero, Abby Wambach, played at North Carolina first.[16]

The female youth sports pipelines have been built around these higher-education dreams. Trends within higher education, fueled by a changing legal landscape, have led to an enormous expansion of women's intercollegiate sports opportunities. Women's college sports are becoming as serious as men's college sports. And while the availability and substance of these intercollegiate subsidies are greatly exaggerated, they are still significant, and the possibility of obtaining them has had a tremendous impact on the continuing commercialization, commodification, and corporatization of girls' youth sports.

THE TITLE IX LUBRICANT

What we commonly refer to as "Title IX" may be one of the single most effective laws ever implemented in the United States, yet not without its ironic unintended consequences. Contrary to popular lore, Title IX of the Educational Amendments of 1972 was never really about sports. Its purpose was to update Title VII of the Civil Rights Act of 1964, which banned many forms of discrimination in employment but mentioned nothing about discrimination in education. Most supporters at the time seemed to be thinking about dismantling barriers to attend prestigious undergraduate colleges or medical/law/professional schools. Sports were really not on anyone's mind, at least not within educational organizations. After all, women already competed in many Olympic sports and could prepare for this participation without institutionalized school programs. During the congressional hearings about Title IX, athletics were barely mentioned except when some people wondered, almost jokingly, if it would mandate coed football teams.[17] Since Title IX's explicit language talked about discrimination in "any educational program or activity receiving federal financial assistance," it was unclear whether organized sports in school settings (excluding physical education classes) were covered under the law, since these programs did not directly receive federal financial assistance.

In the years immediately following Title IX's passage, implementation of the law was drifting toward including *all* programs and activities within educational settings that received *any* financial assistance. This financial assistance even included indirect payments such as federally backed loans that helped students pay for college. Thus, both interscholastic (high school) and intercollegiate sports *programs*, not necessarily individual teams, would need to provide equal extracurricular opportunities for male and females. Into the late 1970s, there was still confusion about how compliance with the law should look in the trenches and significant resistance to the spirit (if not the letter) of the law. In reality, it took almost twenty years for Title IX compliance to really kick in. It is possible that opportunities for female athletes, especially in non-Olympic sports, would have increased even without Title IX. The commercial opportunities were simply too vast even within the context of a patriarchal culture. But without Title IX, these opportunities (both commercial and noncommercial) would have unfolded much more deliberately. Title IX's impact can be seen in sports like women's soccer where the United States is far ahead of most countries in identifying and developing female talent to compete in contests such as the Olympics and World Cup. Title IX was a lubricant for the growth of organized female sports and the construction of commercially oriented pay-to-play youth sports pipelines. Ironically, perhaps, Title IX's contribution to expanding opportunities for women has simultaneously encouraged both social-class bias and the masculinization of female sports.

WOMEN'S INTERCOLLEGIATE ATHLETICS LEAD THE WAY

Despite Title IX's passage and implementation in the early 1970s, school-based athletic opportunities for girls and women increased very slowly. Figures 1.1 and 1.2 illustrate that there was significant absolute growth in the 1970s and 1980s, but the growth was mirrored on the male side of

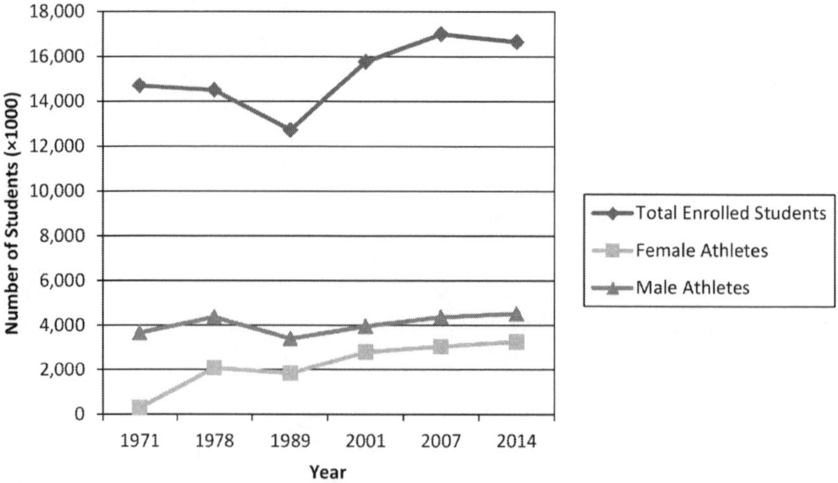

Figure 1.1. High School Sports Participation by Gender, 1971–2014
Source: National Federation of State High School Associations (NFHS)

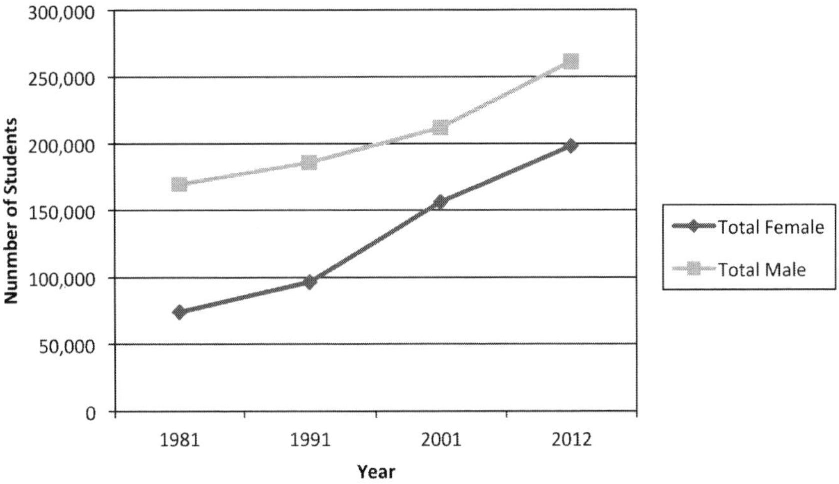

Figure 1.2. Intercollegiate Athletics Participation by Gender, 1981–2012
Source: National Collegiate Athletic Association (NCAA)

the ledger. Both male and female high school interscholastic participation dipped in the 1980s, primarily due to declining high school enrollments. However, opportunities for girls declined more slowly than those for boys, so something resembling parity started to emerge indirectly.

Intercollegiate athletics opportunities during the 1980s increased symmetrically for women and men. This coincided with the National Collegiate Athletic Association (NCAA) replacing the Association for Intercollegiate Athletics for Women (AIAW) as overseer of female intercollegiate sports. The NCAA had never been eager to embrace or promote female intercollegiate sports and had been a vociferous opponent to Title IX. The AIAW was established in 1971 to deal with this vacuum in the still-minuscule world of female intercollegiate sports. It was only after Title IX was clearly not going away and after opportunities for women college athletes started slowly to increase that the NCAA changed its approach and mounted a "hostile takeover" of the AIAW.[18]

The 1990s was the golden age of equalizing opportunities in both high school and college sports.[19] At the college level, new women's teams were created and new slots were added to existing teams. Overall, there has been a 168 percent increase in women's intercollegiate opportunities between 1981 and 2015, compared to a 54 percent increase in men's opportunities during that period. Most of the increase for women's sports was between 1990 and 2000. Even with the enormous expansion of women's opportunities, however, men still account for 56 percent of intercollegiate athletes despite comprising only 43 percent of current undergraduate students.[20] The residual gap between male and female intercollegiate athletics opportunities is primarily a result of football. Despite some popular rhetoric indicting women and Title IX for the precipitous decline in sports such as wrestling and men's gymnastics, it was the explosive, and some might say unnecessary, growth of football squad sizes over the past three decades that forced schools to reduce other male opportunities and still be in compliance with Title IX. Between 1981 and 2014, the average size of football teams has grown 18 percent in Division I, 38 percent in Division II, and a staggering 49 percent in Division III.[21] As we will see in chapter 2, this might be less about sports themselves than about securing enrollments that can help a school's "brand."

The absolute and relative growth of women's intercollegiate athletics opportunities has been the single most important catalyst for the expansion of commercialized girls' youth sports to college pipelines. Even though high school sports are only a tangential piece of these pipelines, the data suggest that large increases and decreases in the number of women's college teams in particular sports get reflected several years later in the number of high school teams for those sports. For example, the number of women's college soccer teams increased 340 percent between 1981 and 1991, with the bulk of the increase closer to 1980. The number of high school teams showed a similar trend between 1984 and 1994, with the largest increases between 1988 and 1992. In field hockey, the number of college teams started flattening and declining between 1998 and 2008, foreshadowing a similar pattern in high schools between 2002 and 2012.[22] This general trend was also identified by a now-retired teacher who coached girls' high school soccer from 1985 to 2004:

> Some of the local college coaches were already sniffing around [in the late 1980s] just as we were getting our team off the ground. In those days, they came right to the high schools, but so many of the schools barely had teams or had players that weren't very good. Remember, there was no recreational soccer like there is now, where young girls can get their feet wet. High school girls were learning the game on the fly. A lot of teachers in the area started pressing for more girls' soccer teams. Some of them were [physical education] teachers but many, like me, weren't. There seemed to be girls' softball, basketball, and field hockey teams all around but very little soccer. But the college programs kept coming around. It was like they couldn't get players fast enough to fill their rosters. Some of my early players were recruited to play college soccer, but they weren't very good.

DIFFERENT SPORTS, DIFFERENT PIPELINES

Soccer, field hockey, figure skating, ice hockey, and ultimate Frisbee represent very different iterations of the "ideal-type" youth sports to college pipeline. Figures 1.3 and 1.4 show changes in the number of college and high school participants in these and a few other select sports. Soccer is

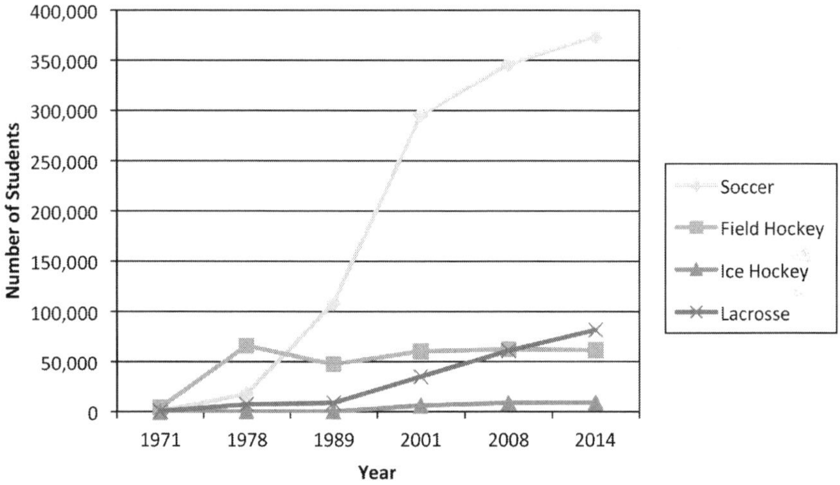

Figure 1.3. US High School Girls' Participation by Sport, 1971–2014
Source: NFHS

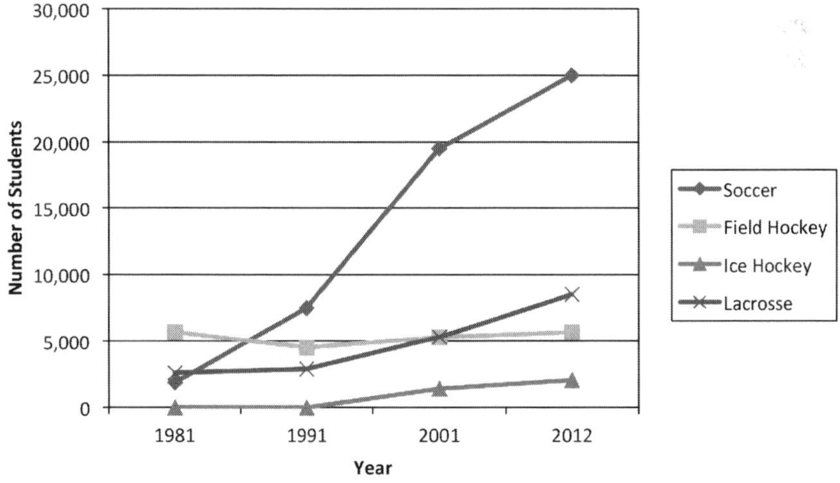

Figure 1.4. Women's Intercollegiate Athletics Participation by Sport, 1981–2012
Source: NCAA

one of five women's sports that have a very large intercollegiate footprint, not to mention a large high school interscholastic presence. The other female sports with large intercollegiate footprints are basketball, softball, volleyball, and track. These sports come closest to the "ideal type" of a female youth sports to college pipeline. Soccer is interesting, also, because its growth spurt started much later than the other four popular sports and continues to grow.

Organized female youth soccer in the United States is staggeringly complex (see figure 1.5). This will be discussed at some length in chapter 3, but a brief overview will help illustrate why soccer comes close to the ideal-type youth sports to college pipeline. There are a number of competing organizations that coordinate girls' youth soccer teams and leagues in the United States. While all of these organizations are affiliated in some way with US Soccer and the US Soccer Federation, only US Youth Soccer (USYS), started in 1974, is closely aligned with the federation, and oversees both "recreational" and "elite" programs. The others, such as US Club Soccer (USCS), US Specialty Sports Association (USSSA), and the American Youth Soccer Organization (AYSO) compete with USYS for soccer-playing customers, although technically kids can play for teams in both organizations. USCS began in 2001 specifically for identifying and developing elite players; it makes no claims to service kids who might just be looking to have fun playing soccer.

USSSA's elite soccer program has been around since 1997 but has not gained much commercial traction within soccer's youth sports to college pipeline. It was probably no coincidence that USCS's emergence followed soon behind the explosion of women's intercollegiate soccer, and initial Olympic and World Cup success. Similarly, in 2009, USCS created a female-only elite club system, the Elite Clubs National League (ECNL), to commercially benefit from USYS's alleged inattention to elite female player

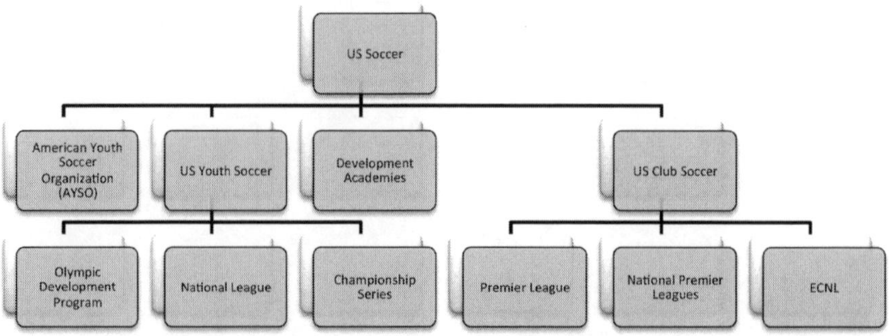

Figure 1.5. Girls' Youth Soccer in the United States

development. The new premier team that Elizabeth was moving to played in the ECNL. She would soon be participating in a myriad of "showcase" tournaments in front of curious college soccer coaches. These tournaments have become perhaps the most important piece of the girls' youth sports pipelines, and will be discussed fully in the next two chapters. All "elite" programs revolve around these tournaments, as do the recruiting strategies of college coaches. AYSO is very much an outlier within the contemporary world of youth soccer. Created in 1965, AYSO is completely dedicated to organized recreational soccer. It is about kids having fun playing, not using youth sports as a commodified conduit for intercollegiate success.

Field hockey's intercollegiate footprint is much smaller than soccer's, and it is barely growing at all. Thus, it has a much more modest youth sports to college pipeline. Interestingly, field hockey was at one time one of the most popular intercollegiate and interscholastic sports. In the early 1970s there were far more high schools and colleges with varsity field hockey teams than with varsity soccer teams. But the number of intercollegiate field hockey programs is almost exactly the same now as it was in 1981. Due to this static intercollegiate footprint, field hockey's pay-to-play youth sports pipeline is much smaller than soccer's, although they do share many of the same commercial qualities. The organizational structure of field hockey in the United States is as simple as soccer's is complex. USA Field Hockey coordinates almost everything related to the sport. All teams and activities fall under its umbrella. There are no parallel groups such as US Club Soccer and AYSO that maintain a loose affiliation with USA Field Hockey but act independently from it. There is no myriad leagues and only a few tournaments run independently of USA Field Hockey (although with its blessing). In fact, the largest independent college showcase tournament, sponsored by Disney/ESPN, may be closing shop due to a concurrent tournament recently established by the National Field Hockey Coaches Association (NFHCA).[23] There simply isn't enough consumer demand to support two simultaneous elite tournaments. Girls' youth soccer does not face this constraint.[24]

Field hockey's unique characteristics may account for this trend. For one thing, in the United States it is mostly played by females, which may foster cultural perceptions that it isn't a real sport and thus gets overlooked when schools expand their sports teams, or when players and families are looking to get involved with a well-known activity.[25] Interestingly, Olympic field hockey was a strictly male sport until 1980, when women's teams also started competing. Women's and girls' field hockey in the United States is also geographically concentrated in the northeastern and middle

Atlantic states, with only a smattering of teams beyond those areas.[26] Perhaps the most important distinction between the sports is that field hockey has almost no recreational option for kids. Youth field hockey revolves completely around a restrictive pay-to-play club system that is primarily designed to funnel girls and young women into college slots, with some concern for stocking the national team that plays in the Olympics and other international contests. USA Field Hockey is hoping to counter this trend with its FUNdamental Field Hockey program, which provides free equipment, instruction manuals, and even a carrying bag to groups (or schools) who want to introduce the sport to young kids between ages seven and eleven. As we will see in chapter 3, leaders of USA Field Hockey were hoping that this recreational focus and an expanded tournament system would emerge independently of the national federation. But this has not happened, and the trend suggests it probably won't. Without a significant or expanding intercollegiate footprint, there isn't a viable commercial market for a pipeline independent of USA Field Hockey.

Although not explored much in this book, women's lacrosse provides a direct counterpoint to field hockey. Both sports are played in virtually the same limited geographic region, but lacrosse has been expanding rapidly since 1991, while field hockey is barely treading water (see figures 1.3 and 1.4). There are now 40 percent more intercollegiate lacrosse programs than field hockey programs. With this expanding intercollegiate footprint, the pay-to-play youth to college pipeline in lacrosse has exploded, with new commercial hot spots emerging in Colorado and California.[27] Again, there is probably a patriarchal element at work here that intersects with economic factors such as commercialization. While women's lacrosse is significantly different from men's lacrosse, it is still lacrosse and it is still played by a large number of males. Thus, as one USA Field Hockey official disapprovingly explained, it does not carry field hockey's stigma of being a "girlie" sport associated with elite New England boarding schools.

THE IMPORTANCE OF PUCKS

Female figure skating has no intercollegiate varsity footprint; thus, it has no commercialized youth sports to college pipeline. It also has no varsity-level presence within high school interscholastic sports. To be sure, competitive female figure skating is "pay-to-play." It has always been a sport with formidable economic barriers to participation, creating no illusions (like soccer) that it is a sport of the masses and accessible to all regardless of social class.

But this pay-to-play system is not a pipeline constructed around intercollegiate opportunities. Thus, female figure skating's commercialization is far more subdued than soccer's, even though it has been a very popular Olympic sport since 1908 and is currently among the most highly watched winter events. Like field hockey, all competitive female figure skating falls under the umbrella of a national federation, in this case US Figure Skating. The federation sponsors all official competitive events that might eventually lead toward national or international championships (including the Olympics). US Figure Skating is not on the verge of financial collapse, but its membership is down 9 percent since 2006, with a notable decline among kids older than twelve. Without the catalyst of an intercollegiate footprint (aided by Title IX requirements), female youth figure skating may continue contracting. A former youth skating prodigy, now retired from the sport after a long career, remarked,

> Figure skating was never seen as a gateway to college for young women. The girls who got into figure skating were generally very wealthy. It's the same girls who would take up tennis or golf. It's a country club sport without the country club. Yes, some of the kids and their parents are thinking about the Olympics, but not nearly as many as you might think. For most of them, it is like showing off that they are wealthy. It's an exclusive sport at the higher levels, although there are a lot of non-rich kids who try it out just for fun. They start leaving when they're about ten, around the time they might outgrow group lessons and need personal coaching to keep improving. I was a little unusual since my family was middle class and I stuck with the sport, but I never really got involved in the high-level competitions, even though I was doing very well in local events. I just loved skating. Serious skaters and rink officials didn't mind my doing that thirty years ago, but I don't think they would be as accepting today when so much of the sport revolves around keeping coaches occupied and bringing recognition to the skating club by winning medals at regional or national events. But now everybody is really worried about hockey.

Figure skating's declining appeal is not independent of youth sports to college pipelines. Title IX–driven changes within intercollegiate athletics have led to the rapid growth of women's college ice hockey programs (mostly to balance football). This is luring girls to abandon double toe loops, put on the pads, and start hitting the puck. As a result, a highly commercialized youth sports to college pipeline is starting to take hold in girls' ice hockey, largely modeled on a similar male version. The Olympic lure of women's figure skating (augmented by exorbitant costs) cannot by itself create an extensive commercialized youth sports figure skating industry. Female ice hockey, though, has both an Olympic lure and a burgeoning intercollegiate footprint, making it ripe for a highly conspicuous pay-to-play youth sports pipeline. According to data at the USA Hockey website, only about 50,000 girls are currently registered on youth teams (as of 2015) compared with 260,000 boys. But the number of registered girls is increasing at a faster rate.

THE CONTRAST OF ULTIMATE

If soccer is the zenith of a commercialized, pay-to-play youth sports to college pipeline, ultimate is the nadir. Like figure skating, ultimate has no varsity intercollegiate or interscholastic presence. Unlike figure skating, though, it is a team sport with a multitude of girls and young women participating in organized high school and college settings. At the high school level, the National Federation of State High School Associations (NFSH) does not recognize ultimate as an "official" sport, nor do any of the fifty state federations that sponsor official championships. Locally, high schools generally do not recognize (or fully fund) ultimate as an official varsity sport except in certain hot spots such as Seattle, Washington, and Amherst, Massachusetts. Ultimate does not even have an Olympic component like figure skating, although the US Olympic Committee (USOC) and the International Olympic Committee (IOC) have recently recognized mixed-gender ultimate as an "official" sport, thus setting the stage for *possible* Olympic inclusion down the road. Despite these organizational constraints, an estimated 4.5 million people currently play ultimate in the United States (over 50 percent male), far more than are involved with figure skating, ice hockey, field hockey, or lacrosse. But the way they participate in the sport is much different.[28]

There seems to be something of a consensus about ultimate's origins as a sport.[29] The modern game emerged in the late 1960s somewhere in the northeastern United States. First played mostly ad hoc in high schools, it spread to colleges, where it became increasingly popular, with one thread retaining a "pickup" orientation and another thread morphing into something more "organized," with set teams, leagues, schedules, and tournaments. The basic rules, though, were mostly the same regardless of how seriously the players took the games. In 1979, the Ultimate Players Association (UPA) emerged in the United States, providing something akin to oversight, even though the idea of a central bureaucracy seemed philosophically at odds with ultimate's countercultural origins. In 2010, the UPA morphed into USA Ultimate, which remains the sport's governing body. USA Ultimate is headquartered in Colorado Springs along with many other Olympic sports federations. Tommy has been playing ultimate for over thirty years. He attended college at a (then) ultimate hot spot and has played on dozens of competitive men's and mixed-gender teams. Additionally, he has coached a few youth teams and was a local league administrator in the Bay Area, one of the game's current hot spots:

> We were always arguing about whether the game should remain informal and participant-directed or develop a bureaucratic structure like other sports. I think most people agreed that the sport would grow and become more popular if it had a coordinated framework, but even here many people didn't know if that was necessarily a good thing. I remember one of my friends storming out of a team party screaming "bigger isn't always better." So you had one group that thought we should bring the game to the masses but making damn sure it didn't lose its off-center charms, and another group that was sure such a move would destroy the game we loved and make it just like all the other team sports we had played and abandoned because people were taking things too seriously.

The "off-center charms" mentioned here are commonly referred to by ultimate players as the "spirit of the game." This is not just a quaint colloquialism that grew from postgame indulgence in psychedelic drugs, but is one of ultimate's enduring central tenets. The spirit of the game (SOTG) is prominently displayed in the first section of the Official Rules of Ultimate (eleventh edition):[30]

> The integrity of Ultimate depends on each player's responsibility to uphold the Spirit of the Game, and this responsibility should remain paramount. . . . Ultimate relies upon a spirit of sportsmanship that places the responsibility for fair play on the player. Highly competitive play is encouraged, but never at the expense of mutual respect among competitors, adherence to the agreed upon rules, or the basic joy of play. Protection of these vital elements serves to eliminate unsportsmanlike conduct from the Ultimate field. Such actions as taunting opposing players, dangerous aggression, belligerent intimidation, intentional infractions, or other "win-at-all-costs" behavior are contrary to the Spirit of the Game and must be avoided by all players.

You will not find this sort of philosophical foundation in other team sports. For those unfamiliar with ultimate, it is something of a combination of traditional team-oriented field sports, perhaps with a little basketball thrown in. The most interesting part of ultimate is that players can advance the disc toward a goal *only* through teamwork. Running with the disc (for more than a few steps) is not allowed. Passing between and among teammates is foundational to the game. You cannot, as in some sports, have an unstoppable dominant individual who single-handedly controls a game's outcome. You *must* pass the disc repeatedly in order to achieve your objective. In a sense, the game itself is built on the idea of community participation and community success, not individual glory.

Another unique element of playing ultimate is that transgressions are identified by the participants themselves rather than by some independent referee or official. In this regard, ultimate somewhat resembles competitive golf and tennis (below the championship level), except that those activities are individual-oriented rather than team-oriented. Self-policing has always been central to the spirit of the game, although recently the approach has come increasingly under fire. Even without a varsity intercollegiate athletic footprint, ultimate has become increasingly intense over the past ten to fifteen years, with a corresponding increase of players who think winning is more important than some anachronistic platitude about spirit. As a result, many high-stakes ultimate contests use "observers" to mediate between opposing players and teams who may not be able to reach consensus about an alleged rule violation. Tommy remarked,

> Introducing observers was the beginning of the slippery slope. Once we admitted to ourselves that some people were focused on the winning rather than the playing, we lost the moral high ground about our sport somehow being different. The fight over using observers was a more modern version of the earlier battles over the game's overall philosophy. I think that the necessity for observers was driven more by the men's game, where players started migrating over from more traditional sports like lacrosse, where they had learned to win at all costs and thought the spirit of the game was just crazy talk. Eventually, that started to impact the women's and mixed-gender games. I watched my daughter play in a college championship tournament this year, and observers were used in the semifinal and finals. They hadn't become obtrusive yet, but it looked like a different game with a lot more contact than usual. It was almost like introducing observers caused people to initiate more contact rather than being a response to more contact. That slippery slope.

The symbolic importance of using observers was not lost on some of USA Ultimate's leaders:

> Man, we have really struggled with this one. It doesn't help at all that the men's professional teams are using referees and couldn't care less about the spirit of the game. But we also realize that the world of competitive sports has a certain boilerplate. Like when we were first pitching the game to the

> [US Olympic Committee], they couldn't understand this whole self-officiating thing. At the [International Olympic Committee] level, there was even more confusion. How can you have a game without referees and judges? I think the only reason they stayed interested was that we were pushing the mixed-gender format and they thought that might be a marketable niche.

Many people might be surprised that there are men's professional ultimate leagues. Actually, there are currently two leagues, the American Ultimate Disc League (twenty-four teams) and the newer Major League Ultimate (eight teams). It is something of a stretch to call these "professional" leagues, since very few players earn regular salaries. Instead they sometimes hold ownership shares in the team and receive a portion of gate receipts. Nobody makes a living playing ultimate. But regardless of this quasi-professional status, the existence and increasing (if still muted) popularity of these leagues is impacting nonprofessional ultimate, including the women's and mixed-gender games. Many people within the larger ultimate community, including leaders of USA Ultimate, find this influence increasingly problematic.

THE IRONY OF PIPELINES AND PARTICIPATION

Youth sports participation is simultaneously heading in several possibly troublesome directions. First, kids are decreasingly involved in action-centered "free play" and more involved with outcome-oriented sport.[31] This is not necessarily bad except that there is usually more sitting around by those engaged in organized sports rather than free play. Second, within the world of organized sports, youth participation rates are declining, although not across the board. Between 2009 and 2014, there was about a 10 percent drop in the number of kids playing organized sports regularly, whether those sports were "recreational" or "serious."[32] Most of this attrition is taking place between the eighth and twelfth grades, or after kids reach the age of thirteen. But while sports such as soccer (–8 percent), field hockey (–16 percent), and basketball (–6 percent) have had drops in participation, there has been growth in lacrosse (+29 percent), ice hockey (+44 percent), and so-called emerging sports like ultimate (+21 percent). Within soccer, however, the participation data is slightly misleading because while fewer kids may be playing soccer overall, they are increasingly playing in elite pay-to-play settings.

For example, player registration within US Youth Soccer has leveled off since 2000 despite an almost 3 percent growth in the total number of

US kids under eighteen. However, US Soccer has announced it will be starting a new elite Girls' Development Academy in 2017 to parallel an existing development academy for boys (see figure 1.5). This is likely an organizational response to US Club Soccer starting ECNL in 2009, and will also directly compete with US Youth Soccer's already established Olympic Development Program (ODP), since those participating in the new Academy (who will practice four times a week) will be prohibited from playing elsewhere. The overall issue of exclusivity is controversial in and of itself. Programs within US Youth Soccer (including ODP) cannot prevent players from participating in US Club Soccer programs (including ECNL) and vice versa. However, these programs can and often do forbid players from participating in school programs. There is disagreement about whether this is a good or bad thing but, regardless, it encourages a shift away from relatively low-cost school settings and toward relatively high-cost commercial settings within the youth soccer to college pipeline. This trend is also expressed by the declining availability of recreational-oriented programs like AYSO. While no hard data on AYSO participation trends were available, veteran youth soccer officials are absolutely convinced that recreational soccer is becoming an anachronism. One commented,

> My friends across the country all tell me the same thing that is happening here. We have fewer players and teams that want to play for the fun of it and more that are highly competitive and serious. We don't have any AYSO programs in this area, but I know they are getting killed elsewhere, especially in the wealthier suburbs. Parents don't think the emphasis on fun is going to help their daughters develop into Alex Morgan or Carli Lloyd. Here's how it might play out: in one of our regional leagues, there was a huge debate about whether to let the kids play 3v3 and 8v8 games for one extra year.[33] If you have ever watched ten-year-olds playing 11v11 on a full field you would know why most knowledgeable soccer people support at least an extra year of small-sided games. But the parents think it will stunt their girls' ability to participate at the next level. When the league went ahead and implemented the delay, a lot of parents moved their kids to [premier] programs that [still used] the full field at the earlier ages. They wanted to make sure their eleven-year-old daughters had a leg up for college scholarships. What they don't realize is that touching the ball is way more important to player development than running aimlessly around a full-size field until you collapse from exhaustion. But the elite teams pitch it as though they will be at a disadvantage if they don't move to the full field earlier.

Field hockey's youth participation decline is less nuanced since so little of the sport is played recreationally. Despite valiant efforts by USA Field

Hockey to expose more kids to the sport and initiate recreational programs, almost all participation continues to take place in the expensive pay-to-play pipeline. With field hockey's intercollegiate footprint in stagnation, especially at the DI level, there is less reason for girls and their families to spend time on that sport. In contrast, the expanding college footprint of women's lacrosse keeps generating youth opportunities, reaching even into formerly undeveloped areas like the West Coast. With this recent explosion of interest in lacrosse, consumer demand has been strong enough for growth in both elite club and recreational domains. Female figure skating and ice hockey provide still more permutations on participation trends. While purely recreational skating has been increasing somewhat, the number of competitive skaters has declined 9 percent between 2006 and 2014.[34] In contrast, girls' youth ice hockey has been growing at both the recreational and elite club level, with some indication of greater expansion within the fast-growing pay-to-play pipeline. However, some leaders of US Hockey have implemented and expanded a recreationally focused program to stave off what they see as a disturbing attrition rate in youth hockey. But this program seems to focus mostly on boys, where the supply of high school–age players is greater than the intercollegiate demand. On the girls' side, where intercollegiate demand is eclipsing the current domestic supply, there is an unabated emphasis on getting kids into the pay-to-play pipeline.[35] As usual, ultimate is hard to definitively figure out. There has certainly been a well-documented increase in the number of female ultimate players at every level, and there has been a noticeable expansion of teams, leagues, and tournaments, but it's not clear if these are "elite" teams and tournaments or some quasi-recreational format where people can simply enjoy the sport without any commodified intentions.

BARRIERS TO YOUTH SPORTS PARTICIPATION

Even though Title IX does not directly impact female sports outside of an educational context, there is no escaping its indirect effect on the expanding girls' youth sports to college pipelines. In fact, these pay-to-play, noneducational, commercial opportunities have largely replaced high school interscholastic athletics as a conduit to the "next level." Girls and young women are still playing high school sports, but it is no longer the primary pathway to obtain preferential college admissions or scholarship aid. Instead, the pipeline from youth sports to intercollegiate athletics is an increasingly commercialized and prohibitively expensive pay-to-play system that bypasses high school interscholastic sports and severely limits participation by modest- and low-income families. This phenomenon also has a racial and ethnic component due to an overrepresentation of blacks and many cultural groups within poorer income brackets. In contrast to the conventional American narrative, then, a sport-based pathway to upward social mobility via intercollegiate athletics is increasingly available only to families who are already relatively well-off. Women's intercollegiate athletics subsidies have become a de facto affirmative action program for wealthy, primarily white, suburban families.[36]

There is a frighteningly strong relationship between social class and every stage of youth sports participation. Family income is strongly correlated with when kids start and stop playing sports. In the aggregate, children from families with incomes over $100,000 per year start playing organized sports at 6.3 years old, while kids from families earning less than $35,000 per year start at 8.1 years old. Families with annual incomes above $75,000 report that 51 percent of their kids younger than six participated in sports or athletic activities over the past year, compared with 33 percent from families with incomes under $30,000. Among older children, the participation rates are 84 percent and 59 percent, respectively, in high- and low-income families. Thus, high-income children are 1.5 times more likely to participate in organized sports than low-income children, a trend that seems to be growing. These class-based influences are more pronounced among girls than among boys.

Social class also explains who is playing specific organized youth sports at any given moment. Despite its global reputation as an inexpensive and accessible sport, 35 percent of organized youth soccer players in the United States come from families with annual incomes above $100,000 (who account for 25 percent of the total population) compared with 13 percent from families with annual incomes below $25,000 (who account for 24 percent of the population). In the United States, anyway, youth soccer is clearly not a sport of the masses. Also, 43 percent of organized youth swimmers and 56 percent of youth lacrosse players come from high-income families. High-income families are even slightly overrepresented among organized youth basketball players. While hard data are not readily available for field hockey, ice hockey, or figure skating, it is highly likely that these expensive sports would show the same social-class bias. Even ultimate, which has no pay-to-play youth sports to college pipeline, has become a high-priced activity, at least in its *organized* form, by emphasizing regional tournaments rather than local leagues for serious players. These tournaments often require travel, per diem expenses, and possibly missing work or school.

Attrition from sports is also highly class-sensitive, although this sensitivity is more heavily influenced by gender than overall participation rates. For example, between 2008 and 2012, there was a 31 percent drop in boys' soccer participation and a 52 percent drop in girls' soccer participation after the age of thirteen. For boys, however, social class did not seem to influence that trend, while for girls there was a linear (if modest) class impact. Poorer girls drop out of soccer at a higher rate than middle-income girls, who drop out at a higher rate than wealthy girls. The same general (and modest) trend is true for field hockey. In lacrosse and ice hockey, it is harder to be certain about the class impact on attrition since so few low-income girls are involved in the sports to begin with. In terms of race, African American girls are much more likely to stop playing organized soccer after eighth grade than either white girls or Latina girls. While this is mostly related to family income and place of residence, there are also some cultural factors that creep into the equation. A community activist who has tried to start a girls' youth soccer league in an East Coast urban setting commented,

> Soccer just doesn't resonate with a lot of the African American families in [this city]. These girls don't see any or many dark faces on the World Cup team, if they even know it is going on. All of the black women athletes in the Olympics on TV are playing basketball or running track, so they think that's all they can do, too. Aren't any black swimmers, that's for sure. There aren't many [Latina] women visibly playing soccer either, but I'm not sure that would matter anyway. Some of the first-generation Latino families seem to dissuade their daughters from playing any organized sport. It's just not the way girls and women are supposed to act. The high schools around here don't have soccer programs because they are operating under the same cultural myths. So the girls and their families start thinking that it's almost their destiny to play basketball or run track if they are going to do some traditional sport. I get a lot of young African American girls interested in [the soccer] program, but they don't stick around long. I think their friends make fun of them for playing a stupid game. With the [Latina] girls, they play until middle school and then their families want them to learn how to cook instead. I know it's sexist, but it's hard to fight certain traditional sexist values. It's kind of like an American *Bend It Like Beckham*, just without the happy ending.

Ten-year-old Olivia is one of those girls:

> I really liked soccer, but only a few girls wanted to play, and the field near our house is filled with broken glass and trash. There are goals, but they don't have nets. The boys don't really like soccer either, so we can't even make teams of boys and girls together. A girl in my church has a cousin who lives a few miles

> from here, and she plays on a real team with uniforms. I would love to do that, but my parents probably wouldn't let me. They think it's OK for my brother to play basketball but don't think I should do sports. But I like to play. Maybe I can go live with my friend's cousin.

The lack of diversity on the US Women's World Cup team is extremely important. On the 2015 championship squad, there was only one African American woman, Sydney Leroux, who is actually biracial, grew up in Canada, and moved (by herself) to Arizona during high school for a more intense soccer experience than she could receive in British Columbia. Leroux's family was not wealthy, but they certainly were not poor. Examining the hometowns of the team's other members shows that they grew up in areas with family incomes well above the national median.[37] The 2016 Women's National Team does include Crystal Dunn, an African American woman from Long Island, New York, who was raised in a town with a median family income of $95,000.[38] The same demographic reality is apparent on the US National Field Hockey Team, where almost all the players hail from relatively wealthy suburbs in the northeastern and mid-Atlantic states. All of them are white. Some of the younger women's and girls' soccer national teams seem a bit more ethnically diverse, but this does not necessarily mean the teams are more economically diverse. Field hockey's younger national teams appear to be all white.

The same social-class and racial bias holds true when looking at NCAA Division I intercollegiate soccer and field hockey players. An exploratory analysis of ten Division I women's soccer programs and ten Division I field hockey programs shows that scholarship or recruited athletes have higher family incomes than the overall student bodies at those schools.[39] In one highly ranked program at an extremely prestigious school, the recruited players had a median family income roughly 40 percent higher than the overall student body. Among the twenty programs examined, recruited or scholarship athletes had family incomes approximately 21 percent higher than those of students as a whole.[40] Field hockey players on the whole seem to have moderately higher family incomes than soccer players, at least in this limited sample. However, that could simply be reflecting the higher cost of living in field hockey's more limited geographical playing area. Among the top ten NCAA DI field hockey programs, there are three African American players. Two attended $25,000-per-year private high schools and the other attended public school in a town with a median family income of $106,000. In the top ten soccer programs, there are sixteen African American women among the approximately 250 recruited players (there are also four Canadians of African or Caribbean descent). The median family income of these players' hometowns is around $90,000. The mean family income of this group would have been even higher due to a few of them hailing from very wealthy areas.

Although rowing (aka crew) was not examined in detail for this book, it provides perhaps the single best example of a phenomenally expensive and socially exclusive pay-to-play youth sports to college pipeline. Rowing's intercollegiate footprint for women is exploding. There are seven times more women rowing on varsity teams in 2015 than were rowing in 1990. The number of male college rowers has pretty much held constant during that period. The average size of a women's college rowing team has grown from twenty-seven in 1990 to fifty-one in 2015. Most of this growth has taken place at the DI level, where the average team has more than sixty participants and awards a relatively large number of financial scholarships. The intercollegiate expansion of crew has unfolded mostly as a way for schools to maintain compliance with Title IX as football teams keep expanding (see note 21). But this expansion has an equally important impact on youth sports. Only seven states recognize rowing as an official interscholastic sport eligible for substantial school subsidies, with a total of 4,200 girls participating on those teams.[41] Assuming an even split among class years, this means that just over 1,000 public school seniors are looking to fill the almost 1,900 slots for first-year college rowers (female only). Expensive private schools do have rowing programs that fill in some of this gap, but not all of it. Women's rowing, along with ice hockey, is a rare case when intercollegiate demand for youth athletes actually exceeds the domestic supply.

In response to the lack of official public high school rowing teams, pay-to-play "club" rowing teams have expanded rapidly in schools with families that can afford them. Such club teams may receive tacit varsity status from the high school, whereby the team can identify itself as part of the school and participants may receive varsity letters. Club rowing teams are generally run by a parent board that coordinates equipment purchases, boat placement, scheduling, and transportation. With little or no school subsidy, club rowing is phenomenally expensive for participants. A new eight-person rowing shell can cost anywhere from $15,000 to $35,000, not including oars at $600 apiece. Most teams would need several eight-person shells and some smaller ones. Adding in a coach or coaches, it is not uncommon for a family to pay between $5,000 and $10,000 per year for their daughter to participate on a high school crew team. And, given crew's growing intercollegiate footprint (for women), this participation is much more likely to pay off with preferential admissions to prestigious schools and/or athletic scholarship money than is participation in soccer or field hockey. Indeed, college rowing coaches have been known to scour the campus student center in search of powerfully built women who can fill their boats.[42] Coming out of high school with rowing experience gives young women a far above-average chance of being college athletes. But these chances are clearly restricted to wealthier families and communities that can bear the costs. There aren't many (or any) high school club crew teams in poor urban neighborhoods. Again, intercollegiate athletic subsidies for women's rowing, either financially or in admissions advantages, is little more than an affirmative-action program for wealthy suburban families.

The same basic dynamic is apparent in women's ice hockey, where a fivefold increase in the number of female intercollegiate players since 1990 has created something of a domestic player shortage.[43] Only sixteen states recognize high school girls' ice hockey as an "official" sport eligible for school subsidies. Among these sixteen states, twelve have only one or two dozen programs each, with opportunities for around 1,000 girls total.[44] With the growing demand for female intercollegiate hockey players, expensive pay-to-play youth clubs and leagues are sprouting quickly to fill the varsity high school gap, even as male-centered youth ice hockey programs may be leveling off. As with crew, private high schools not under the jurisdiction of state interscholastic sports federations will satisfy some of this player shortage, but not all of it. Wealthy families in wealthy communities are much more likely to take advantage of an ice hockey–oriented college subsidy for their daughters.

The primary takeaway from this preliminary analysis is that the youth sports to college pipelines are selective and restrictive when it comes to social class and, by corollary, race and ethnicity. The enduring myth of sports as a conduit of social mobility simply does not play out in reality. Girls and their families must have significant financial resources to access and traverse the pay-to-play youth sports pipelines that could eventually empty into a college admissions advantage or athletic scholarship. Even though there is a very small likelihood of receiving significant athletic scholarships, and only a slightly larger chance to receive preferential admissions, girls and their families continue pouring tens of thousands of dollars into these sports-based dreams. True, sports such as ice hockey and crew have a better chance of paying off and, ironically, they are the most class biased, where those families with the deepest pockets can literally buy their way onto intercollegiate teams, often at prestigious schools. But even soccer, the so-called sport of the masses, operates a highly restrictive youth sports to college pipeline. While many families who get sucked into these pipelines should possibly know better about the long odds they are facing, they have also been greatly misled by the hyperbole of individuals and organizations that benefit commercially (and sometimes noncommercially) from any deception, whether intentional or not. These families are making decisions, but they are making them in conditions not of their own choosing.

THE SOCIAL EXAGGERATION OF SPORTS

For the past ten years, I have asked students at my school and elsewhere to estimate what percentage of US residents define themselves as sports fans (without defining any specific sport). Overall, they presume that about 75 percent call themselves sports fans. Some have suggested 90 percent, and a very few believe it is lower than 60 percent. Most of these people are quite surprised to learn that, in fact, only 56 percent of US citizens define themselves as sports fans, with a significant gap between males (66 percent) and females (46 percent).[45] They are also surprised to hear that those with higher family incomes are more likely to consider themselves sports fans than those with lower family income. These young people are certainly not alone in exaggerating the social importance of sports. This exaggeration of sports is a very important piece of the pay-to-play youth sports to college pipeline, especially in terms of a young woman's likelihood of successfully navigating a pipeline and emerging with some college admissions advantage and/or athletic scholarship. The three most important conduits of this exaggeration are higher education, the youth sports industry, and family ignorance (which is somewhat dependent on the other two factors). Each of these will be addressed separately in chapters 2 through 4. But there are other social channels that exaggerate both the overall cultural importance of sports, and the probable payoff from entering a pay-to-play youth sports to college pipeline.

High Schools

The United States is the only country in the world where organized sports are embedded within formal education.[46] Despite the declining importance of high school interscholastic sports in all but a few youth sports to college pipelines, they maintain an important symbolic role in the overall exaggeration of sports' cultural significance. Organized sports almost always occupy the apex of a high school's extracurricular status hierarchy. In mixed-gender and all-male schools, football or some other male sport will generally hold this position. And while there is no systematic empirical evidence to support the assertion, I suspect that sports teams (and those playing on them) are increasingly likely to top the status hierarchies of all-female schools, although perhaps not to the same degree. A veteran math teacher and multisport coach at an expensive all-girls' high school commented,

> It's really quite surprising to see how much more emphasis we are putting on sports now than we did ten to fifteen years ago. The school has definitely changed its orientation. I have seen the shift from emphasizing educational extracurricular activities like the chemistry club and robotics club to emphasizing sports. The number of teams is expanding, practices are getting longer, and our literature now stresses who is getting an athletic scholarship to what prestigious school, rather than who is studying engineering at Cal Tech. We actually go out and recruit athletes instead of just good students with deep family pockets. None of the college coaches actually come here looking for players, except maybe for crew. It's all done in the travel leagues. But the [Ivy League schools] do seem to be impressed with our athletes, or maybe it's just with their ability to pay tuition without a lot of financial aid.

Within mixed-gender public schools, nonathletic extracurricular activities are not shunned, but they do not receive the same attention as sports. There are no pep rallies for the Model UN before it heads off for a major competition in New York. There are no abbreviated class periods and all-school sendoffs for the marching band before it performs before fifty thousand people in the Magic Kingdom. And students do not receive a half-day off when the band returns from Orlando with a "superior" rating, but may when the mediocre school football team beats an equally mediocre team from the adjacent town. High school sports teams often require their own specialized administrator who can schedule games, juggle fields, purchase uniforms, replace equipment, and provide rudimentary oversight for the dozens of teams and coaches in an interscholastic program. Even with their diminished role in the youth sports to college pipelines, high school sports reinforce the overall ideology that sports are serious business and that participating in them can have big payoffs beyond intrinsic rewards like having fun and getting exercise.

This is well illustrated by the exaggerated attention high schools give to a student's "commitment" to play intercollegiate sports. Every year, high schools will hold the equivalent of press conferences and saturate their websites with announcements and pictures of seniors signing their "letters of intent" to play in a college program. The National Letter of Intent (NLI) program is coordinated by the NCAA as a completely voluntary option for future intercollegiate athletes and their host colleges. By signing such a letter during senior year of high school, the student is agreeing to stop looking at other schools and the college is agreeing to provide one guaranteed year on the team with some athletically based financial aid. NLIs only apply to Division I (DI) and Division II (DII) schools, and *only* when some amount of athletics-based aid is offered. By definition, Ivy League and Division III (DIII) schools cannot participate in the program since they do not offer athletics-based financial aid, at least not officially.

However, high schools will create the impression that their students are signing these prestigious letters of intent when, in fact, they might be signing blank pieces of paper during carefully staged events. Even if an intercollegiate program guarantees a spot on the team (and in the school) and a high school senior agrees to play in the program (and attend the school), the agreement is not binding to either party *unless* there is some actual athletics-based financial aid and both parties agree to participate in the NLI process. In any event, the commitment is only for one year. After that, both schools and athletes are relieved of their obligations. This seemingly harmless charade breeds misconception in two ways. First, it exaggerates the notion of "commitment" since both athlete and college can change their mind without penalty if no sports scholarship money is on the table.[47] This is especially true at DIII schools, which are literally forbidden from establishing anything resembling a binding agreement to play on a sports team, even if preferential admission has been offered.[48] Second, it exaggerates the alleged payoff from successfully navigating the youth sports to college pipeline. Parents see these events and think that everyone on stage is receiving a "full ride" that will cover a lofty college price tag for four years.[49] In reality, these high school seniors may or may not be receiving any athletics-based financial aid, and any financial assistance they may be receiving could disappear after a year.

Local Media and Government

In addition to dutifully reporting on the National Letter of Intent shows, local media spend a good deal of air time and column inches reporting on the travails of local high school sports. These could include large regional papers like the *Philadelphia Inquirer* and small local papers like the *Mayberry Weekly Gazette*. These papers print high school schedules and scores and run regular stories on successful teams or players. Most important, these stories almost always announce (when applicable) what intercollegiate program a high school player has "committed to," is "heading toward," or is "being recruited by." These announcements make no distinction between actual binding commitments (such as with the NLIs) or nonbinding oral commitments to anybody that falls outside of the very narrow NLI and NCAA parameters. For example, mention will be made of a junior field hockey player or sophomore soccer player who has committed to play at some college, but that is misleading, since even eligible DI and DII colleges are not permitted to "sign" a player until their senior year. They can recruit these youngsters, and can make pinkie-swear promises that they will receive a tangible offer in one to three years, but neither party is bound by such a "commitment." A high school athlete being "recruited by" a college may merely have made phone contact with a coach or unofficially visited a school to informally meet some players. And, of course, the DIII schools can never make such an official binding promise to any future athlete. But you would never know it from the newspaper stories, and there is never any follow-up about apparent commitments somehow evaporating, as often happens due to an injury or a coaching change on the college team. Again, observers are left with an exaggerated perspective on the likelihood that investment in a youth sports pipeline will handsomely pay off with some college admissions advantage or athletic scholarship.

Local governments can also contribute to the social exaggeration of sports by subsidizing athletics activities and privileging them over other cultural events. Township-based soccer clubs, such as the ones Caroline and Elizabeth played in, usually receive preferential access to public fields and available space at public schools. If some local residents want to have a softball party at one of the public parks or play pickup basketball in the middle school gym, they will likely have to work around the local youth leagues' schedules. Sometimes these not-for-profit sports organizations will partner with the local school district and local government on capital projects such as scoreboards or constructing artificial turf fields that will be available to school teams (3 p.m. to 6 p.m.), club teams (6 p.m. to 9 p.m.; weekends), and the general public (when not being used by the high school or club teams). It is likely, although not imminent, that the public resources directed toward youth sports exceed the resources directed toward the public library or the public arts center. It is a chicken-egg argument about whether such prioritization *causes* youth sports to be exaggerated or merely *reflects* a youth sports system that is already culturally magnified. Regardless, it reinforces the cultural exaggeration of sports in general, and youth sports in particular. Watching your six-year-old daughter play in a publicly subsidized youth soccer league on a publicly subsidized field may be the start of her (and her parents') journey through the youth sports to college pipeline. This journey may include a side trip through middle school and high school sports, and include some write-ups in the town's weekly paper when her travel soccer team wins a local U11 tournament or her high school field hockey team qualifies for the state tournament. But nothing is more important to this journey than the great allure of preferential admissions to an elite college or an athletics-based financial aid package to defray higher education's skyrocketing cost. That is the holy grail of the pay-to-play girls' youth sports pipeline.

2

HIGHER EDUCATION AND THE YOUTH SPORTS TO COLLEGE PIPELINE

While many social institutions contribute to the cultural exaggeration of organized sports' personal and social benefits to girls and young women, none play a more important role than higher education. American colleges and universities, catalyzed by the legal requirements of Title IX, have created a system that appears to reward the athletic prowess of prospective female students even more than their academic prowess. Part of this appearance is real and part of it is exaggerated. As illustrated in this chapter, the simultaneously accurate and exaggerated importance of intercollegiate athletics is *driving* the unusual dynamics of organized female youth sports participation, where fewer individuals are participating in the ever-more exclusive and expensive pay-to-play pipelines. In a sense, the flow through these pipelines is dependent more on the *pull* of intercollegiate athletics rather than the push of youth sports. Any attempts to address the problematic elements of youth sports, then, *must* focus on higher education's essential role in the pipelines. Creative and well-intentioned strategies to increase youth sports participation, eradicate class- and race-based barriers to youth sports participation, and provide a reality check to the exaggerated social and personal benefits of organized sports, will have little lasting impact unless they forcefully address higher education's inordinate influence over the youth sports landscape.

THE CORPORATIZATION OF HIGHER EDUCATION

> [Many insist on the] businesslike organization and control of the university . . . on an efficient system [in which] these corporations of learning shall set their affairs in order after the pattern of a well-conducted business concern. The university [is] a business dealing in [sellable] knowledge, placed under the governing hand of a captain of erudition [to maximize] output. [But] the pursuit of knowledge does not lend [itself] to quantitative statement and cannot be made to appear on a balance sheet. The imposition of any appreciable . . . standardization and accounting must unavoidably weaken . . . the work of instruction.

This critique of not-for-profit universities operating like for-profit businesses did not come from a twenty-first-century assessment of colleges such as the University of Phoenix. Instead, it is from sociologist Thorstein Veblen's 1917 book *The Higher Learning in America*, which examined mainstream, not-for-profit universities of that period. Veblen's book, originally subtitled "A Study in Total Depravity," excoriated higher education for reducing learning and the pursuit of knowledge to just another business enterprise like selling shoes. Satirizing the "captains of industry" idea taking hold in the early twentieth century, Veblen likened university leaders to "captains of erudition" and "captains of solvency" more interested in bragging about hefty revenue streams than the scholarly creativity of faculty and students. Veblen's analysis clearly reflects the ideas of commercialization, commodification, and corporatization discussed earlier, although it's unclear whether Veblen had been directly influenced by these classical writings or had developed his ideas more independently. Forty years later, C. Wright Mills warned us about the "industrialization of academic life" where revenue-centered bureaucracies were threatening higher education's important role as a vanguard of human reason and freedom.[1]

A hundred years after Veblen's critique, the "neoliberal" corporatization of higher education continues unabated, where organizational strategies genuflect before conventional tenets of the so-called free market.[2] Higher education is becoming a "giant industry," with seismic shifts in the university's balance of power. Key decisions on resource allocation are now made by financial advisors (rather than faculty) who are beholden to neoliberal market principles such as the consumer experience and unbridled fundraising where "it is hard to tell where corporate jargon ends and academic jargon begins."[3] University presidents, Veblen's "captains of erudition and solvency," are increasingly referred to as CEOs and are drawn from the world of corporate finance rather than from academia. Their main function is to maximize the volume of revenue streams while making sure that news about the institution's solvency is publicly disseminated. University CEOs hire legions of noninstructional staff who create layers of bureaucracy, spending inordinate amounts of time engaging in everything except the direct work of teaching and learning. In order to maximize bottom lines, the captains of solvency might try to replace expensive (and relatively independent) full-time, tenured faculty with more contingent part-time instructors or, better yet, subcontracted "product designers" who might develop an online course for about one-twentieth the price of a faculty salary, and with no need of an office. These unused square feet can then be expropriated by the bloated managerial class of administrators and associate vice presidents who can convene more meetings to "sift sawdust."[4]

Literally dozens of scholarly books and journalistic reports have addressed this issue over the past two decades (see notes 1–9). The rational, neoliberal university seeks to simplify the complex task of scholarship, teaching, and learning into calculable formulas and algorithms compatible with the most recent spreadsheet software. Academic freedom and creativity are rhetorically presented as hollow idioms that will not offend potential benefactors or tarnish the school's public persona by generating controversial research. Faculty "productivity" is reduced to easily quantifiable metrics such as the number of articles published, the "impact ratings" of journals where articles might appear, and the amount of external grant money procured. Faculty "efficiency" is equated with "consumer satisfaction" on standardized teaching evaluations, the number of academic majors in a departmental unit, and the number of classroom seats filled per hour of instruction. All of these quantifiable indicators will be entered into yet another software program that tracks and categorizes every calorie expended by the faculty and allows midlevel "deanlets" and "deanlings" to keep tabs on the serfs in their fiefdom.[5] Undergraduate students in the neoliberal university are encouraged to think of college as a "corporate service station" where they select from increasingly shiny product lines in order to earn "badges of ability" that announce to future employers that they excel in following orders and filling out paperwork.[6] Quaint notions about "critical thinking" and "moral development" are tossed around by university administrators amidst winks and grins, while faculty are encouraged to form "synergies" with private companies who will help establish joint "incubators" for ideas that might help these companies increase their profits and generate press coverage for the school.[7]

Higher Education as a Brand

Higher education's ongoing corporatization, and the impact this has on intercollegiate athletics, is probably most evident in its growing concern with "branding," or how universities package and present themselves to outsiders. Once again, Thorstein Veblen was on to this phenomenon a hundred years ago when he wrote how the captains of solvency focus their energies on "principles of spectacular publicity" not unlike a lottery that serves mainly to "impress potential donors" with the prestige value of the university and how important it is for wealthy and powerful people to be associated with such prestige. Such "prestige value" need not be tied to the actual "line of goods" produced by the university, but to the "intangible utility attached to these goods [that affects] the customer's sensibilities."[8] Branding occupies the heart of administrators' obsession with rankings, such as those appearing in *U.S. News and World Report*, and shifts their managerial concerns from internal educational accountability to managing the impressions of outsiders, with every school trying to outdo others and get to that proverbial "next level."[9]

The modern corporate university will assemble large internal public relations departments, perhaps euphemized as "Offices of Communications," to ensure that the company brand is standardized and tightly controlled, possibly down to the color and font used on any official letterhead, business cards, or sweatshirts. The university's name and any associated logos or symbols become product lines in and of themselves that might help one or another revenue stream. Part of the PR department's job is also to encourage, and then tabulate, the number of times the university is mentioned in various media outlets, since these "media hits" are quantifiable evidence that the brand is being spread, regardless of whether or not this notoriety has any tangible impact beyond its mere existence. This is the same logic used by corporations when they purchase naming rights to sports stadiums. While there is no empirical evidence that this investment generates increased revenues, companies see it as a strategy to increase brand recognition as an end in itself.[10] In this case, branding even trumps net revenues.

Intercollegiate Athletics and Branding

The modern neoliberal university's branding strategies are increasingly focused on intercollegiate athletics, although, again, this is certainly not a new phenomenon. In the early twentieth century, Veblen noted the increasingly large use of funds directed "toward ostentatious items of plant and grounds, including for athletic contests." These displays are visible evidence of commercialization and corporatization to "serve the cultural aspirations of the leisure class to acquire credentials" and to "encourage the attendance of that decorative contingent who take more kindly to sports . . . and social amenities than to scholarly pursuits. [These consumers] add to the numbers enrolled and also gives a highly appreciated loud tone ('college spirit') to the student body and [benefits] the corporation by drawing public attention. [Financing] these academic accessories—or side shows—[is] felt to be money well spent."[11]

More recently, former Harvard University president Derek Bok specifically identifies intercollegiate sports spending as a "chimera of profitability" within the corporatized university that obsesses over maintaining its hallowed image to outsiders and reaching some ever-changing next level. Spending on athletics "dwarfs the amount made available for community service, orchestras, and theater."[12] He also warns that intercollegiate sports spending has become ground zero for the competition among universities for market share, and that it leads to an unnecessary emphasis on the "beer and circuses" of college life rather than a school's academic prowess.[13] The modern corporate university is not overly concerned with the substance of its educational mission, since that is difficult to quantify and would require deference to academic professionals rather than relying on financial managers who draw from business-oriented models that emphasize marketing, visibility, and public image promotion:

> In this instance, the circulation of [sports] money and power on university campuses mimics its circulation in the corporate world, saturating public spaces and the forms of sociality they encourage with the imperatives of the market. Money from big sports programs also has an enormous influence on shaping agendas within the university that play to their advantage, from the neoliberalized, corporatized commitments of an increasingly ideologically incestuous central administration to the allocation of university funds to support the athletic complex and the transfer of scholarship money to athletes rather than academically qualified, but financially disadvantaged students.[14]

THE CORPORATE UNIVERSITY AND INTERCOLLEGIATE ATHLETICS

Expanding youth sports pipelines are a semirational (if exaggerated) response to higher education's skyrocketing costs over the last thirty-five years. Since the late 1970s, the cost of higher education has increased three times faster than the overall cost of living. Many factors have contributed to these increases, although increased salaries for faculty are *not* a significant one. Instead, relatively more money is being spent on student services such as career planning, grounds and facilities (including fitness centers), and student recruitment. However, the largest increases have been in noninstructional administration and intercollegiate athletics. According to multiple sources, there has been a 60 percent increase in the number of full-time administrators between 1993 and 2009, with an almost equivalent decline in the percentage of college instructors who are tenured or on the tenure track.[15]

The Athletic Trap

The increased absolute and relative spending on intercollegiate athletics is quite remarkable. Universities of all shapes and sizes are directing larger portions of their budgets toward intercollegiate sports. While football and men's basketball have been the main beneficiaries of this spending spree, most sports have shared in the largesse regardless of whether they do or do not generate net revenues.[16]

The data in figures 2.1, 2.2, and 2.3 show that institutional spending on intercollegiate athletics is increasing much faster than spending on academics and instruction. Some have likened this spending spree to an endless

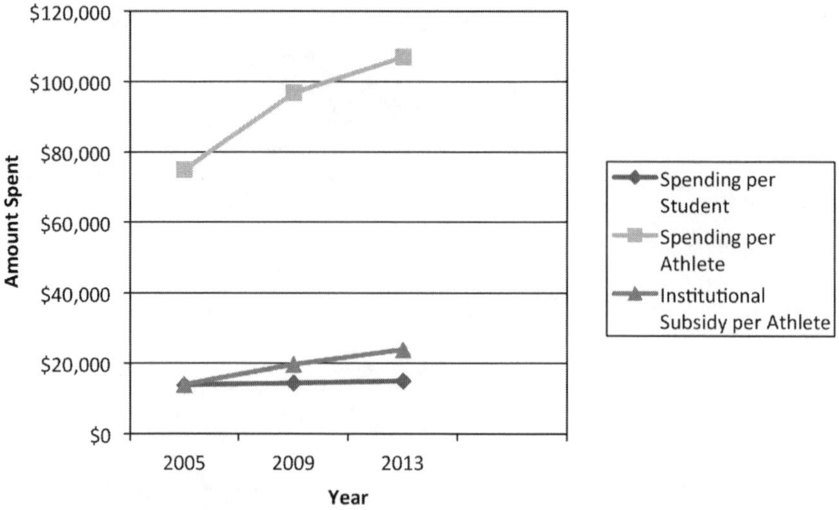

Figure 2.1. Average Spending per Athlete/Student at FBS Schools, 2005–2013 (constant dollars)

Source: Knight Commission on Intercollegiate Athletics

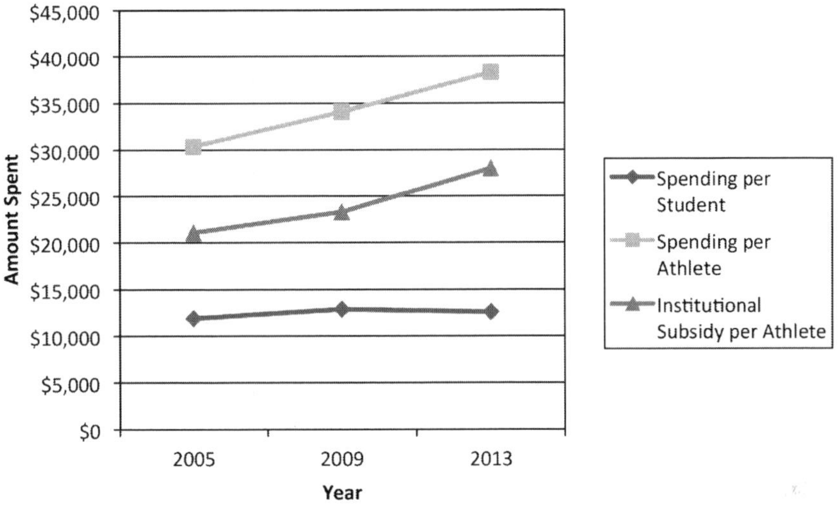

Figure 2.2. Average Spending per Athlete/Student at FCS Schools, 2005–2013 (constant dollars)

Source: Knight Commission on Intercollegiate Athletics

athletics "arms race" where schools must continually compete with each other for the most successful and visible sports programs in order to maximize revenue streams that will pay for these increasingly visible and successful sports programs, which will supposedly enhance the school's brand and propel it to the "next level."

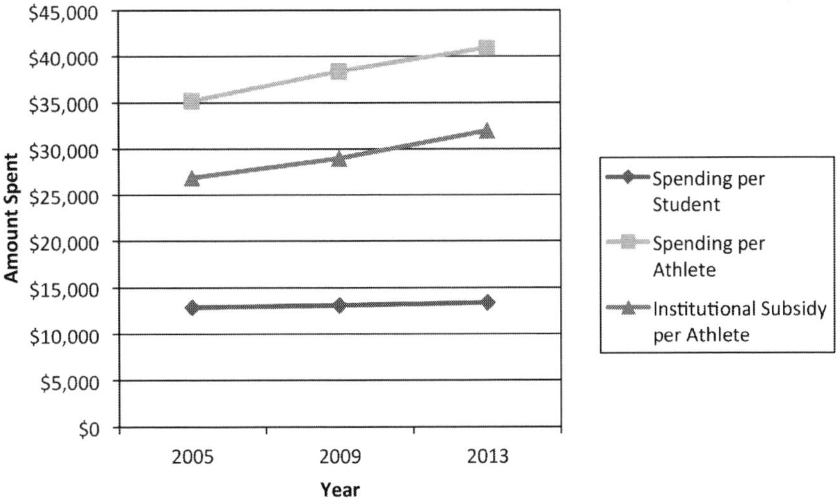

Figure 2.3. Average Spending per Athlete/Student at Non-Football DI Schools, 2005–2013 (constant dollars)

Source: Knight Commission on Intercollegiate Athletics

These data are only from Division I of the NCAA structure, although similar trends (with smaller amounts) are also evident in Division II and Division III. The NCAA clearly acknowledges the explosive spending on intercollegiate sports at all divisional levels and reminds us that only twenty-four schools (as of 2014) actually generate net athletics revenue, all at the elite Football Bowl Subdivision (FBS) level (figure 2.1).[17] Schools at the less elite Football Championship Subdivision (FCS) level, and those without football programs, are more financially strained by the increasing resources directed toward intercollegiate athletics (figures 2.2 and 2.3). This is consistent with the neoliberal emphasis on branding and the near obsession of some FCS schools to join the "big kids" in the FBS, even if it means financial sacrifice.[18] In these cases, the obsession with branding even extends to nonrevenue sports that are unlikely to receive much media attention.

Howard Nixon II calls these neoliberal trends an "athletic trap" that ensnares universities in the incessant commercial requirements of visible and successful intercollegiate sports programs.[19] Supporters of large athletics programs insist that they will deliver all sorts of tangible and intangible rewards for the institution, including enhanced revenues from TV contracts and postseason appearances, better connections to local employers who might hire a school's graduates, more alumni loyalty and contributions, and increased "brand" visibility to prospective students and benefactors. Once this trap becomes entrenched, presidents and other decision makers are unable to extricate their schools from intercollegiate athletics' insatiable financial appetite. Because so few intercollegiate athletics programs generate net revenues, almost all schools find themselves diverting increasing general budget resources to athletics, or identifying significant external resources to finance the athletics arms race. In 2014, the five highest-resource NCAA conferences had an average athletic budget deficit of $2.3 million. This deficit was much higher ($17.6 million) at all other FBS schools not in these "Power Five" conferences.[20] This turns into a vicious cycle, since standard external fund-raising models typically rely on visible intercollegiate sports programs, which seem to have an insatiable appetite for expensive coaches, fields, and player recruitment strategies, even in nonrevenue sports. Consistent with the neoliberal university, presidents have become more concerned with the needs of external constituents (alumni donors, event sponsors, media) than with the internal constituencies focused on scholarship and learning. This absolute and relative growth of intercollegiate athletics has provided a prolific growth medium for the rampant commercialization of girls' youth sports.

The NCAA as Promoter and Regulator

The NCAA's historical origins are intertwined with intercollegiate athletics' growth as a university revenue stream and their growth as a branding tool that will allegedly attract more students (consumers), board members (benefactors), and female varsity athletes (to satisfy Title IX and balance football).[21] Officially born around 1910, the NCAA was at first a response to President Teddy Roosevelt's concern with the growing fatalities in college football. Its creation was riding an already-established trend where "promotion" of intercollegiate athletics was hard to distinguish from its "regulation." At different historical moments, the NCAA would offer slightly more stringent *internal* regulations of college sports in order to stave off possible increases in *external* oversight, usually from state or federal agencies that focused on labor rights, workplace safety, and the validity of tax-exempt organizational status. Perhaps the NCAA's most ingenious executive innovation came in the mid-1950s when its president Walter Byers coined the term "student-athlete" while fending off a workers' compensation claim by the widow of a Fort Lewis A&M (Colorado) football player who died from a head injury during a game. The NCAA claimed then, and in many subsequent workers' compensation cases, that student-athletes were, first and foremost, *students* who were participating in a school-sponsored extracurricular activity that just happened to pose more physical risk than, say, singing in the glee club. But they were not *workers*, and the revenue often associated with these sports teams (usually football) was defined as incidental to the students engaged in this activity.[22]

"Student-athlete" has become the marquee semantic symbol for the NCAA's successful defense of the allegedly noncommercial orientation of college sports. You will hardly ever hear anyone officially associated with college sports (either nationally or locally) *not* use the term "student-athlete" when referencing varsity players. The successful internalization of this idea into our everyday lexicon helps sustain assertions that neither a school's varsity athletics program nor the NCAA is engaged in anything more than amateur sports that are truly educative and only incidentally generate revenue for the schools and the association. Such "impression management" is also reflected in the labyrinth of NCAA rules and regulations that reinforce the purportedly noncommercial foundation of intercollegiate athletics. These might include restrictions on recruitment, limits on the number of scholarships offered in different sports, the prohibition of offering athletic scholarships in Division III schools, and a limit on how many hours/days per week a "student-athlete" can participate in games and practices. In some regards, the NCAA's simultaneous regulation and promotion of intercollegiate athletics parallels (without a government moniker) the Atomic Energy Commission's (AEC) simultaneous regulation and promotion of civilian nuclear power from 1946 to 1974.[23] The AEC would often, with great fanfare, penalize a nuclear utility for violating some minor rule to demonstrate that the regulatory system worked and to defend civilian atomic power against criticisms. Similarly, the NCAA often, with great fanfare, penalizes schools or athletes for minor rule violations or moral turpitude to show that it is engaged in meaningful oversight of noncommercial intercollegiate athletics. In both cases these *strategic* penalties help reinforce the legitimacy of the oversight bodies and help fend off more stringent *systemic* regulation.

The conflation of promotion and regulation may also be evident in the NCAA's requirement that Division I schools maintain a minimum of seventeen varsity teams, regardless of whether they actually offer any sort of athletics-based financial support to members of those teams. This allows the NCAA to reinforce the narrative that college sports are not really a money-making business, and that only a minute percentage of college athletes will eventually earn a living in their sport. These points are prominently presented on the NCAA's website and in TV ads. This narrative is also supported by the organization's refreshingly honest disclosure about the tiny percentage of high school athletes who will play any intercollegiate sport, and the even more infinitesimal percentage who will receive a scholarship for doing so. While this could simply be a case of truthful advertising, it may also be part of an overall strategy to continually obfuscate intercollegiate athletics' commercial elements. Combined with the statutory imperatives of Title IX, the NCAA's minimum team requirement necessitates that schools continually maintain and increase their financial commitments to women's varsity sports, especially as they continually increase the size of their football programs.[24] While the benefits of these increases are generally exaggerated, they still have had an enormous impact on the growth of pay-to-play girls' youth sports pipelines.

The NCAA and Revenue Streams

The NCAA constantly finds itself tiptoeing the line between acceptable and unacceptable levels of commercial activity. It's certainly possible that the NCAA (and member institutions) truly believes that intercollegiate athletics revolve around cherished ideals such as amateurism and the "student-athlete." But there is also no denying that the NCAA and its member schools benefit financially from using the noncommercial moniker of intercollegiate athletics to market college sports as somehow different from the money-centric world of professional sports. The primary tangible benefit from intercollegiate athletics' noncommercial status is that any revenue generated by varsity sports is tax-free. If intercollegiate athletics are just another piece of the school's educational mission, and the NCAA is merely a not-for-profit organization that helps colleges and universities meet these goals, then it should enjoy a tax exemption.

Approximately 80 percent of the NCAA's revenue comes specifically from TV rights connected with the annual Division I Men's Basketball Tournament (see figure 2.4). This percentage has remained fairly steady for the last two decades, suggesting that the NCAA grows and expands in sync with this revenue stream. More lucrative big-time football revenue (mostly from TV broadcasting agreements) accrues to the conferences in which schools compete, not to the NCAA.[25] Traditional postseason football bowl games are financially independent from the NCAA structure. Revenues from bowl games are controlled by their hosts, who do provide "payouts" to participating teams, although rarely enough to cover a team's expenses to participate in the game.[26] The recently introduced Football Bowl Subdivision (FBS) playoffs are also not officially sponsored by the NCAA, so, once again, all revenues from these games go to individual conferences.[27]

The less elite Football Championship Subdivision (FCS), formerly referred to as Division IAA, does hold an NCAA-sponsored national tournament,

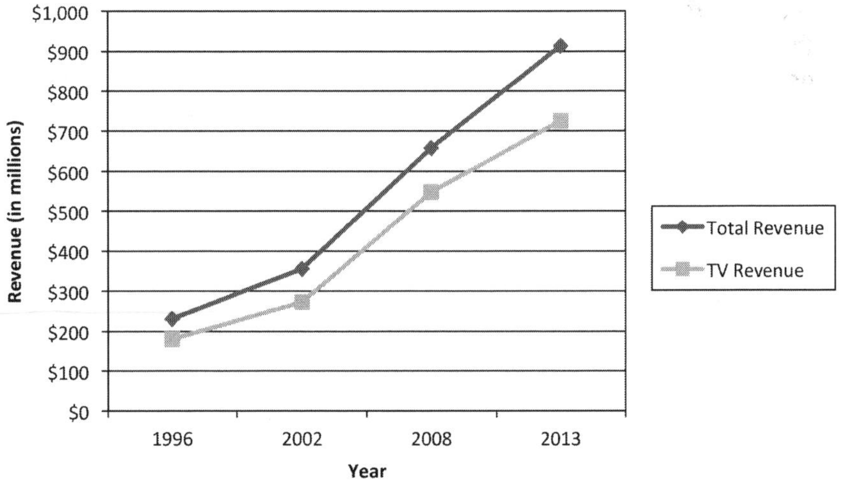

Figure 2.4. NCAA Television and Total Revenues, 1996–2013 (current dollars)
Source: NCAA; Alesia (2014)

but it generates a relatively small amount of revenue, much of which is used to pay expenses for the participating teams. Without 501(c)(3) not-for-profit status, the NCAA would be responsible for millions in federal and state taxes based solely on revenues from the men's basketball tournament. Likewise, if this not-for-profit umbrella did not extend to conferences and schools, they might also be responsible for paying taxes on what appears to be commercial activity. The NCAA also has other tax advantages. In 1999, the state of Indiana successfully lured the organization's headquarters from Kansas City to Indianapolis. The city agreed to construct a brand-new building, currently valued at about $42 million, in return for an annual rent of one dollar. Indiana taxpayers were responsible for about half of the total $50 million relocation incentive package. As a not-for-profit organization, the NCAA does not pay Indiana property tax on its headquarters, and the organization and its affiliates are exempt from paying Indiana sales tax anytime Indianapolis hosts the men's basketball Final Four.[28]

The centrality of this purportedly noncommercial model, and the important role played by female sports and male nonrevenue sports in building this model, contributes greatly to the overall exaggeration and privileging of sports discussed in the last chapter, and the size and scope of any youth sports to college pipelines. After all, we do not assign a special title to college students who participate in nonathletic extracurricular activities. The editors of the college paper are not called "student-journalists," and actors in school drama productions are not called "student-thespians" even if those individuals help generate marginal net revenue for the paper or theater club, and will likely not earn a living in those fields. Do members of the varsity golf team really experience more personal growth than members of the forensics team? Does a heavily subsidized crew team that competes in faraway regattas contribute more to the university community than a nonsubsidized glee club whose members burst into classrooms for singing valentines? Not only are these interesting questions in and of themselves, but answering them helps make sense of the complex connection among abstract ideologies of higher education, women's intercollegiate athletics policies, and the everyday reality of girls' youth sports pipelines.

INTERCOLLEGIATE ATHLETICS AND THE UNIVERSITY'S FRONT PORCH

Universities' near obsession with financing intercollegiate athletics is consistent with a neoliberal approach to higher education, where revenue streams and public perception are far more important than esoteric notions of critical thinking and informed citizens. Notable athletic achievements supposedly contribute to building the "front porch of the university" whereby prospective students might take notice and check out the inside; kind of an organizational curb appeal.[29] This is consistent with an overall approach to developing a school's "brand" rather than its academic substance, and is often targeted at nonlocal customers who live far away from the "product." Tangentially, there have been assertions that athletic success directly benefits the university financially through increased state subsidies for public universities and increased alumni donations.[30]

As previously discussed, Title IX has helped spawn far more recent growth in the number of women's varsity sports programs (and players) than men's programs. In a sense, women's sports have offered relatively more building material for front porch expansion in the last two decades, although building materials for men's sports still cost more and are featured more prominently. These policies are operating not just at Division I and II scholarship schools, but also at Ivy League and Division III schools that offer no official athletic scholarships. The contemporary captains of solvency seem completely convinced that their schools will not survive and flourish without strong varsity sports programs. Only a very few university leaders have been willing to buck this trend.[31] Simultaneously accurate *and* inaccurate signals are being received by youth female athletes (and their families), and are providing a fertile growth medium for pay-to-play youth sports pipelines. The intercollegiate athletics–led surge in university branding has created a complex system that, while not completely inaccurate, exaggerates the importance of varsity athletics within the fabric of higher education, paralleling the overall social exaggeration of organized sports' importance.

The Flutie Factor[32]

The overemphasis on using intercollegiate sports to build a university's front porch is often referred to as the "Flutie Factor," named for Boston College quarterback Doug Flutie, who completed a last-second desperation pass in 1984 to help Boston College defeat defending national champion Miami in a nationally televised game. After the 1984 season, observers pointed to subsequent 30 percent increases in Boston College's applications, giving rise to the Flutie Factor to explain how successful and visible sports programs benefit an entire university. The Flutie Factor was apparently at work a few months later when underdog Villanova University beat heavily favored

Georgetown 66–64 for the 1985 NCAA men's basketball championship. The dominant narrative then and now claimed that this victory put Villanova "on the map," instantly transforming it from a regional commuter school into a national university. Georgetown itself was supposedly a Flutie Factor beneficiary after a series of NCAA Final Four appearances in the mid-1980s accompanied a 45 percent increase in undergraduate applications.

But systematic research on the Flutie Factor suggests that it may be more myth than reality, although there is no denying the power of that myth. Research on the Flutie Factor's existence and efficacy is, at best, contradictory.[33] Regardless of the conclusions reached, most of this research looks to see whether intercollegiate athletic success translates into subsequent increases in the quantity and quality (measured by SAT scores) of undergraduate applications, the amount of alumni donations, and/or "brand recognition." More recent research seems to be increasingly suspicious of the Flutie Factor. An important part of this suspicion revolves around the substantive importance of college applications. After all, someone who *applies* to a college will not necessarily be *accepted* to that school or *attend* the school. It is quite possible that those who apply because of a suddenly appealing athletic front porch are actually *less* likely to be accepted or to actually enroll. It's also possible that intercollegiate athletic success is completely irrelevant to enrollment decisions. That counterintuitive hypothesis is borne out by 2012 Gallup poll data showing only 37 percent of US residents over the age of eighteen consider themselves college basketball fans, with even fewer (32 percent) among 18- to 34-year-olds. Over 60 percent say they are not at all fans of college basketball. Despite conventional higher-education wisdom about "March Madness" taking over people's lives, only 15 percent of respondents in a 2014 HBO/Marist College poll said they filled out a "bracket" to project the winner of the NCAA Men's Basketball Tournament. Even one of the pioneering studies of the Flutie Factor acknowledged that sports' impact on applications was almost impossible to disentangle from other factors such as increased financial aid and more residential opportunities.[34] On the other hand, increasing the number of applications in and of itself is quite consistent with a neoliberal orientation since it will decrease the school's acceptance rate, increase its perceived "selectivity," and strengthen overall brand appeal without making any substantive changes to the "product" itself.

Moving away from applicants and zeroing in on enrollees clearly challenges the universal wisdom of using visible and successful varsity sports as the foundational material of a school's front porch. Examining aggregate national data from the Educational Longitudinal Study (sponsored by the National Center for Education Statistics) and original survey data from three different universities, Peterson-Horner and Eckstein argue that highly visible intercollegiate athletics are a relatively unimportant factor weighing the *attendance* decisions of prospective college students, irrespective of where these students may have *applied*.[35] This confirms earlier conclusions from the Arts and Sciences Group, a higher-education market research firm, in a 2000 national survey of five hundred–plus high school seniors who planned to enroll in a four-year college the following fall. Among other things, the survey found the level and quality of intercollegiate sports were relatively unimportant to these students' college attendance decisions; general awareness of intercollegiate sports was superficial; those whose college decisions were influenced by intercollegiate sports (as nonparticipants) tended to be male and have *lower* academic credentials.[36]

Interestingly, while universities have been publicly and politically lambasted for their rising price tags, intercollegiate athletics remain a largely unindicted contributor to the trend. For example, in late 2015 Rider University (New Jersey) became one of the latest universities to announce significant budget cutbacks, including the elimination of thirteen academic majors and fourteen tenured faculty positions. Even the sociology major was reduced to just a minor! Decision makers at Rider blamed declining enrollments and the rising cost of instruction for the school's financial woes. However, the $13 million intercollegiate athletics program (6 percent of the total university budget) seems to have been spared the knife. While data are unavailable for Rider itself, schools in the Metro Atlantic Athletic Conference that includes Rider have literally *doubled* their net spending on varsity athletics between 2003 and 2014.[37] These schools, including Rider, have not doubled their instructional spending during this same period. Ironically, perhaps, at the time of these budget cuts, Rider's home page greeted visitors with a picture of the men's soccer team that would soon be playing defending national champion (although currently unranked) Virginia in the NCAA playoffs. Rider lost 2–0.

Elsewhere in New Jersey, a December 2015 front page story in the *New York Times* assesses Rutgers University's ongoing and expensive attempt to improve its branding reach by joining the Big Ten athletic conference with its multibillion-dollar revenue streams and media markets between Lincoln, Nebraska, and New York City.[38] This strategy is a huge leap of faith for Rutgers' captains of solvency since it will not collect a full share of conference revenue until its sixth year of membership, but must immediately crank up expenses for coaches, facilities, and scholarships. Although it may be more coincidence than cause, the changing intercollegiate landscape at Rutgers has coincided with the firing of two athletic directors and two prominent head coaches (football, men's basketball) in the last four years.

Scholarships and Footprints

While universities are increasing their spending on varsity athletics faster than on academics, that doesn't necessarily mean there is a substantially larger financial payout for those individuals who successfully enter and navigate the girls' youth sports to college pipeline. Intercollegiate athletics allocations can be spent on many things besides scholarships, such as facilities, salaries, and in-kind services like academic advising, nutritional counseling, and sports psychologists. Scholarships themselves are often misunderstood. Many people assume that all Division I athletes receive monetary scholarships, and that these scholarships are "full rides" that cover close to 100 percent of tuition, room, board, and book costs. In fact, though, fewer than 15 percent of DI athletes are on "full" scholarships, mostly in sports (basketball, football) where they are mandated by the NCAA. Only one-third of varsity athletes receive *any* athletics-based financial assistance (table 2.1). The NCAA and individual schools use the term "scholarship equivalency" to represent athletics-based financial assistance that will cover the total cost of tuition, room, board, books, and possibly a supplement for the "full cost of attendance."[39] Depending on the sport, programs can award these equivalencies as full scholarships or divide them up into smaller pieces, thus increasing the number of varsity athletes who might receive some sports-based financial assistance. Across all but a few sports, most DI varsity athletes receive only "partial" scholarships. In Division II, there are fewer scholarship equivalencies available and they are almost all partial scholarships, even in marquee sports such as football and basketball.

Table 2.1. Changes in Women Athletes and Scholarship Equivalencies, 2004–2012

	2004	*2012*
Scholarship equivalencies	21,205	26,813
Total varsity athletes	70,042	80,460
Total scholarship $	$517.3 million*	$885.4 million*
Percent athletes "on scholarship"	30%	33%

*Current dollars.

Source: NCAA

The prevalence of partial scholarships is clearer in figure 2.5. The NCAA sets a maximum number of scholarship equivalencies for various

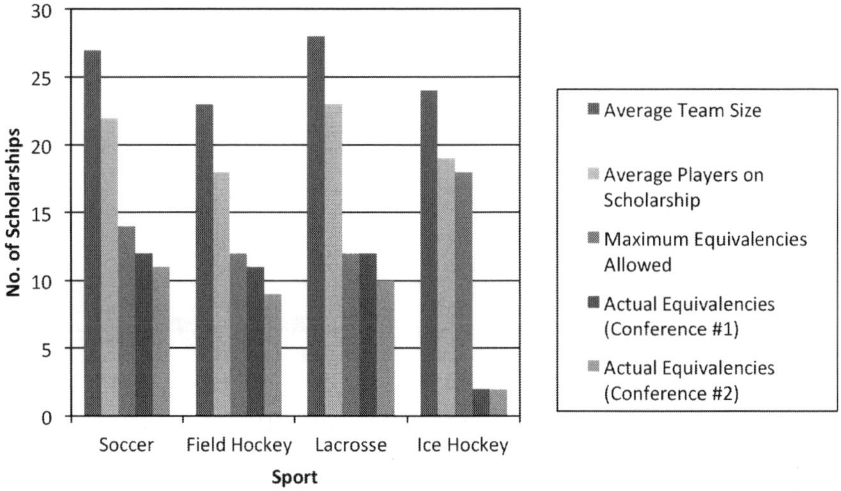

Figure 2.5. Average DI Women's Scholarship Equivalencies by Sport and Conference, 2014

Source: NCAA

sports. Individual schools, sometimes in conversation with other conference teams, have complete discretion about how many equivalencies will actually be offered in any given year. These numbers are not generally available to the inquiring public, although the NCAA provided me with data from two DI conferences.[40]

Within this matrix, there are several distinct scholarship designations, including "head count" sports where full scholarships must be offered, but only if the school is at the NCAA maximum. If the school is offering fewer than the maximum in a head count sport, it can treat them as "equivalency" scholarships and divide them up at will. For most sports, regardless of official designation, the vast majority of full scholarship equivalencies are divided among a large number of players at the discretion of coaches and athletic directors. So a soccer team that has ten scholarship equivalencies (four fewer than the NCAA maximum) will divide them up among twenty-two of the twenty-seven players typically on a Division I squad. These young women can receive anything from a "book scholarship" of a few hundred dollars a year to a full ride including the recently added "cost of attendance" supplement mentioned earlier. Most receive nothing at all. The actual *mean* dollar amount received by "scholarship" athletes in most sports is actually quite modest (figure 2.6), and has not kept up with rising college costs (figure 2.7). So yes, there is an increasing aggregate amount of money being spent on women's intercollegiate athletics, but it rarely

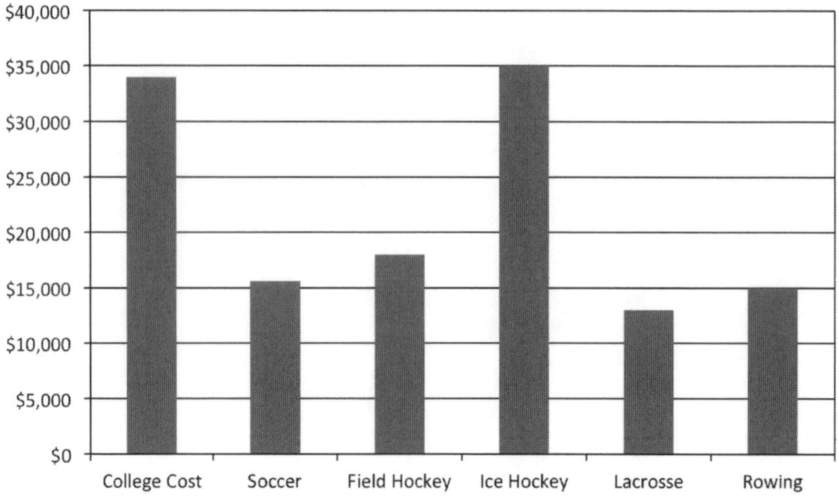

Figure 2.6. Average College Cost and Women's DI Scholarship Amounts by Sport, 2013

Source: NCAA; National Center for Education Statistics; College Board

subsidizes a large percentage of college costs, especially in sports such as soccer and field hockey. Girls and their families may have pumped over $100,000 into the youth soccer to college pipeline and only received back, at most, about $60,000 on that investment. Most receive far less than that,

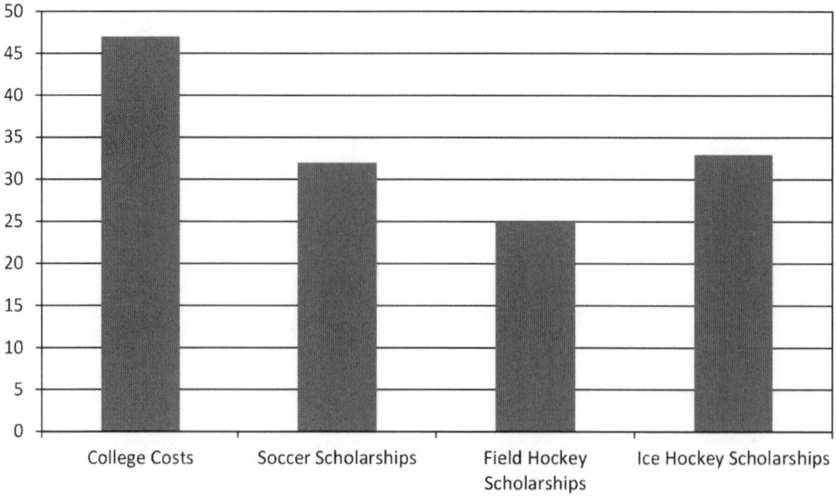

Figure 2.7. Percent Increase in Average College Cost and Scholarship Amounts by Sport, 2005–2014

Source: NCAA; National Center for Education Statistics

if anything. Among the three varsity sports primarily discussed in this book, only women's ice hockey provides a reasonable return on any monetary investment in youth sports. Of course, there may be nonmonetary returns on investment, but these are difficult to define and measure beyond platitudes like "it made them better people."

Of course, without a complete list of what scholarship percentage each individual athlete receives, it is impossible to calculate the *median* scholarship amount, which would better capture athletic scholarship reality. The mean would be higher than the median for several reasons, since even a few full (or almost full) scholarships, especially at very expensive private schools, will skew the average upward. This skewing occurs even at lower-cost public schools since varsity athletes are far more likely to come from out of state than the typical student and, thus, be charged higher out-of-state rates.[41] On the whole, these data provide a Division I focus to the varying "footprints" of the different women's sports explored in chapter 1. Soccer's growth among scholarship sports has been truly remarkable, rising from an "emerging sport" in 1981 to become one of the "big five" in 2012. Conversely, field hockey is a shadow of its former self and was eclipsed in the early 2000s by lacrosse, which shares its limited geographical niche. Ice hockey may offer the most interesting story not just because of the explosion of teams and players, but because of the huge scholarship levels. Almost 80 percent of Division I female ice hockey players are "on scholarship" and at monetary levels that are roughly twice that of soccer. These robust scholarships are *not* mandated by the NCAA, which allows ice hockey squads to divide up to eighteen equivalencies in any manner they wish. The higher scholarship levels probably reflect the sport's player composition. Approximately one-fifth of female intercollegiate ice hockey players are non-US citizens, a significantly higher percentage than in any other sport.[42] Collegiate programs may also use generous scholarship offers to stimulate a more domestic (and slightly cheaper) player pool. This seems to be working, as evidenced by the enormous shift of young female figure skaters into ice hockey. In addition to being interesting in and of itself, this supports the general idea that intercollegiate athletics are very much driving the youth sports landscape. Still, while DI universities are devoting an increasing amount of their budgets to nonrevenue varsity sports, the amount of sport-based scholarship money typically awarded to young women is quite modest, despite a conventional wisdom suggesting that pots of gold await almost anyone who successfully navigates the pay-to-play youth sports pipelines. Colleges and the NCAA could certainly do more to alleviate this inconsistency between rhetoric and reality. Perhaps they would rather perpetuate a certain amount of misperception.

Sports without Footprints or Pipelines

Figure skating and ultimate Frisbee provide an important counterpoint to the expanding corporatization of higher education, the resulting growth of intercollegiate athletics, and the impact these changes have on the commercialized girls' youth sports to college pipelines. Colleges and universities do not use figure skating or ultimate to promote their brand, attract donations, and lock in prospective attendees. A few schools have started synchronized skating teams (at the club level), and many offer ice time to figure skaters and subsidize unofficial competitions with neighboring colleges, but they offer no athletic scholarships or admissions advantages unlike with soccer, field hockey, and ice hockey. US Figure Skating offers a "collegiate" program with its own national championship, but this is independent of the NCAA and its series of national championships. In 2015, a few dozen schools fielded figure skating teams in three geographical regions within the US Figure Skating structure. The lack of a meaningful intercollegiate footprint for figure skating, combined with ice hockey's expanding footprint, has been a noticeable catalyst for girls leaving figure skating and taking up ice hockey, or for taking up ice hockey in the first place.

Ultimate poses a slightly more complicated contrast to the relationship between intercollegiate athletics and commercialized girls' youth sports. A lot of college students play organized ultimate. It's possible that more college students are actually *playing* ultimate at any given moment than are playing other organized sports. While most of this playing is at the intramural or club levels within each school, there is also a highly structured intercollegiate system managed by USA Ultimate. This intercollegiate system, like in the NCAA, has both a Division I and a Division III. Schools with more than 7,500 students must play in Division I. Smaller schools can play in either or both divisions, but with no more than one team at each level. So, for example, perennial powerhouse Carleton College (enrollment two thousand) has two separate women's teams, one in each division. The much larger University of Oregon, also a strong women's program, must play in Division I. Each year, USA Ultimate coordinates regional and national championships in both divisions. It maintains eligibility requirements for college team players that are actually far more stringent in some respects than parallel NCAA eligibility guidelines. All collegiate players must pay $25 for a USA Ultimate membership.

Where ultimate differs most from official NCAA sports is that it does not receive varsity-level resources. Instead, ultimate teams are treated like any other extracurricular club. Some receive significant funding from their schools and share access to fields; others may be completely on their own to identify resources and practice space. Ultimate teams must buy their own uniforms, arrange their own transportation to events, and pay for their own coaches. A few schools with very visible programs (within the ultimate community) do have commercial sponsorships by ultimate-specific companies such as Five Ultimate and VC Ultimate, but these might amount to a few hundred dollars' worth of apparel as opposed to the millions offered to NCAA programs by the likes of Nike and Under Armour. Organized recruitment of high school players by college teams is unheard of, although there is use of informal networks that have no links to the college itself. Most importantly, of course, outstanding ultimate players are not eligible for athletic scholarships or preferential admissions, even if they might take their programs to the next level and win a national championship. Thus, college ultimate players, like their high school counterparts discussed in chapter 1, must largely subsidize their own activity, ironically exacerbating social class–based obstacles to participating in this relatively egalitarian game.

Ultimate's almost nonexistent varsity intercollegiate footprint, especially the absence of scholarships and preferential admissions, has significantly constrained but not prevented the expansion of a pay-to-play youth system. But this pay-to-play system is *not* a pipeline, and college applicants will get very little mileage out of playing up their ultimate chops. A Division I ultimate player reflected,

> I was all about soccer in high school, but ultimate was so big [in the Eugene area] that I thought I might give it a try. I really liked it. It was so much more laid back, but I got to use the same skills as for soccer, just without kicking anything. I wanted to do both in college, but at one campus visit it was clear that the soccer coach did not look favorably on ultimate. Maybe that was just [this coach], but I stopped mentioning it when I visited other schools. Why stir the pot? It's not like playing ultimate would help me get admitted. Now I do both in college. But I can't always go to the [ultimate] tournaments because of the cost.

Likewise, universities have not embraced successful ultimate programs to help build their sports-based front porches. For example, the University of Oregon's women's ultimate team ("Fugue") has won three of the last six Division I national championships. But you will find no mention of that anywhere on the school's website even though it could hypothetically help develop the school's brand and attract students or donations. A former DI ultimate player who continues to play at a high competitive level explained,

> I wanted to go to a small school. My family is really into the whole liberal arts college thing. But I also wanted to compete for a national championship in DI ultimate. There are only a handful of schools that can do that. I got accepted to a bunch of outstanding schools but they only had DIII ultimate teams, even though some of them were really successful. But [not having a DI program] was a deal breaker for me. I have been playing ultimate for most of my life and I like to play with and against the best players.

It's possible that there are a significant number of potential female "student-athletes" who are attracted to a school's front porch by a visible and successful ultimate program. However, until ultimate develops a standard intercollegiate footprint, its youth programs will not turn into commercially viable pipelines.

Scholarships in Sheep's Clothing

Despite the absence of official athletic scholarships in the DI Ivy League, and the outright prohibition on athletic scholarships at DIII schools, these programs still employ creative financial strategies to entice varsity athletes. One heavily recruited former Ivy League player remarked,

> It was pretty obvious that I was getting money for playing [my sport]. A couple of nonathletes from my high school also go here and they didn't receive nearly as much aid, even though my family is probably a little richer and their SAT scores were way higher than mine. But I played [an important position on my team]. When I stopped playing after sophomore year, a chunk of my financial aid mysteriously disappeared even though my ability to pay had not changed and my grades were solid. The financial aid office told me that everybody's aid package was recalculated based on some new formula. It's funny how none of my twenty-two other teammates were recalculated.

The same sort of "unofficial" athletics-based monetary assistance plays a role in drawing elite athletes to smaller liberal arts colleges that proudly profess how students at their schools play sports for the love of it, not for the financial payoff. A former soccer coach at a highly respected liberal arts college recalled,

> I remember my second year when we were in the hunt for this really great defender who was certainly good enough to play DI but who wanted to go to a small school and be more than a full-time soccer player. Her grades were decent, although well below average for our school and most others in our conference. The DI schools were drowning her with offers, but she just

> ignored them. I told my AD that she was going to be on the preference list of every coach in the conference and that we will need more than just guaranteed admissions to land her, since she could probably single-handedly change a program. The financial aid and admissions office put together a hodgepodge of grants and scholarships that knocked about 50 percent off our sticker price. My colleagues at the other conference schools were putting together the same kinds of packages. One school promised her a work-study job that amounted to getting the field ready for practice. Ultimately, she didn't even go to a school in our conference! But it wasn't for lack of trying on our part. Interestingly, she only played for one year and had very little impact. I think she was burned out.

Of the approximately three dozen youth sports families interviewed for this book, only one knew about the small percentage of Division I intercollegiate athletes who received full athletic scholarships. Even ice hockey families had a slightly distorted view of that sport's intercollegiate footprint, but it was far closer to reality than the soccer and field hockey families' assessment. Interestingly, though, the players and families who were more interested in Ivy League or DIII schools *did* have a better (although still somewhat inaccurate) grip on the reality of "creative financial aid" at those allegedly nonscholarship schools. And almost all of the families regardless of divisional level *did* understand that being a recruited varsity athlete would offer some admissions advantage over people with possibly better academic credentials. In this regard, up-front spending on the pay-to-play youth sports pipeline may be less a strategy for securing financial rewards than for guaranteeing admissions into allegedly elite academic institutions.

Admissions Advantages

Sports-based admissions advantages may be more important than financial scholarships in shaping higher-education policies, a more corporatized intercollegiate athletics system, and commercialized girls' youth sports pipelines. These advantages are concurrent with financial scholarships at DI and DII schools, and (officially) in lieu of scholarships at Ivy league and DIII schools. There are two different ways these admissions advantages play out. First, recruited athletes (with or without scholarship money) are very often admitted over academically equivalent (or even superior) students who do not play varsity sports. Second, the admissions process for recruited athletes is usually streamlined. Rosters still must be filled, preferably with quality players who will take their teams and their schools to the next level of organizational visibility and success. This means granting early acceptance in return for an athletic commitment, whether that commitment is binding or tacitly understood.[43]

The Mellon Foundation's College and Beyond study provides the most comprehensive empirical exploration of the academic credential gap between recruited varsity athletes and the overall student body.[44] The admissions advantage offered to academically weaker varsity athletes has no parallel in other extracurricular domains. The College and Beyond study and other research has shown that recruited athletes are up to four times more likely to be admitted to certain prestigious schools than either legacies or members of traditionally underrepresented demographic groups, with the largest advantage accruing to those with the weakest academic credentials.[45] Except at a very few specialty schools, nonacademic admissions advantages are rarely if ever dangled before, say, an outstanding saxophonist with mediocre grades who can take the school's jazz ensemble to "the next level," or to an exceptional yet underachieving poet who can put the school's literary magazine "on the map."

Data from the Mellon study found that, regardless of sport, gender, or level of play, recruited varsity athletes' aggregate academic credentials (generally measured by standardized test scores) are almost universally lower than those of the entire student population.[46] For men, credential gaps vary widely among schools and conferences but are generally largest in revenue-generating sports such as football and basketball. However, ice hockey players at certain schools and in certain conferences actually have a larger credential gap, particularly in the Ivy League. Among female recruited athletes, the credential differences between athletes and nonathletes are less extreme but still significant, with ice hockey and basketball generally offering the largest advantage. There is also less variation among women's sports than among men's sports. This gap holds for Division I schools that offer sports scholarships as well as for Ivy League and Division III schools that do not offer official athletics-based scholarships. Historically, the academic gaps have always been larger for men (even when excluding revenue sports), but the gap has been shrinking. However, the gap has been growing, albeit slightly, between women athletes and nonathletes. In this respect, women's intercollegiate athletics are becoming more like the male versions.

The message being sent by colleges is clear, if not necessarily loud: girls who have modest academic credentials can get into academically prestigious schools if they are outstanding athletes in certain sports. Given a choice between pouring thousands into academic support (including SAT prep) or into the youth sports to college pipeline, some families are choosing the latter. Of course, paying for both is ultimately preferable, if you can afford it! However, this strategy overlooks the fact that *most* girls in the youth sports pipeline will still *not* get into schools because of their athletic prowess. They end up going to schools that they would have been admitted to anyway without having spent $100,000-plus on the youth sports pipeline. In any case, neither of these strategies to gain an admissions advantage is available to low-income families. A soccer coach at an academically respectable DIII college explained,

> We take six or seven new players each year. For those players, we probably get over a hundred inquiries. Some are just informational, but others are sending videos, press clippings, and invitations to showcase tournaments where they will be playing. One even sent the trading card from her soccer club's picture day. Of these initial hundred, maybe half are both academically qualified to attend [our school] and contribute to the soccer team. Now in addition to those fifty people, I have identified another dozen or so on my own by visiting tournaments and talking with other coaches. Oh, and I almost always take one walk-on each year. It's usually a kid who played for her high school but not for a club. In my experience they usually have lower family incomes and so couldn't play on the club circuit. They are often more enthusiastic and less likely to be hurt or burned out. So, really, we are talking about seventy prospects for five or six spots.

In terms of streamlined admissions, the College and Beyond study collected data before schools expanded their overall "early action" and "early decision" strategies.[47] Recruited athletes, though, have always benefited from some variation of guaranteed early admissions. This is an advantage both to the athlete and the school. The athlete is guaranteed an admissions slot at a school that, perhaps, she would have little chance of attending based strictly on academic credentials. She and her family can also shut down their side of the recruitment operation and take a few deep breaths. The school has sewn up a commitment for the incoming class that will no longer be left to the roulette wheel of normal admissions. More important, as mentioned earlier, by drawing a smaller percentage of incoming students from the general applicant pool, the school can inflate the "selectivity" statistics often used to accessorize its front porch. This branding coup may, in turn, attract more (if not necessarily better) applicants in the future, which further boosts its selectivity statistics and provides another coat of fresh paint for the front porch without any substantive changes in the quality of teaching and learning within the school. Once again, the school's brand is treated as an end in itself to be carefully manipulated by the captains of solvency and their public relations wizards. If these admissions advantages help the women's soccer, field hockey, or ice hockey teams reach that always-elusive next level, all the better since that might also translate into more brand exposure, even though that exposure might result in a net financial loss.

The so-called National Letter of Intent briefly discussed in chapter 1 (see also note 43) has become a way to codify this mutually beneficial resolution to the recruitment process. However, as with the "early action" trend in general, this formalized relationship between school and athlete may be more beneficial to the school, not to mention further intensifying any advantages already enjoyed by relatively richer families who might be able to forgo financial aid in exchange for a guaranteed early admissions slot. A DIII athletic director reflected,

> The letters of intent are a racket. The girls and their families are so obsessed with being "on scholarship" that they give up their freedom instead of being patient for a better offer. I can't count the number of stories I've heard about families approaching a DI or DII coach or AD about getting out of a sports commitment. It's usually when the kid's early offer from the DI school turns out to be far worse than a travel teammate's later offer from an academically superior DIII school. The DIII kid is getting more academic aid than the DI kid's quarter scholarship; she'll be starting right away rather than sitting for two years; she can still play softball in the spring if she wants; and she can still change her mind and go somewhere else right up until classes begin.

As already mentioned, DIII schools can now issue nonbinding, ceremonial letters of intent that allow these varsity athletes to share the "signing day" spotlight with their DI and DII counterparts. In addition to any other benefits or detriments of this ceremonial procedure, it does give the college's brand a little more exposure at high school press conferences while sending signals to girls and families that "playing soccer at XYZ College" is also pretty cool, and that it's probably wise to keep pouring time and money into the youth sports to college pipeline.

Admissions Advantages in Action

The "admissions list" and "admissions slots" referenced by the coaches in the last section are not just metaphoric. Varsity coaches provide the admissions office with a list of valuable recruits who they hope will be given preferential treatment. The actual process works a little differently at each level. At DI schools (including the Ivy League), the coaches' lists include *all* desired recruits whether or not they are receiving a scholarship. As long as these recruits meet NCAA minimum academic requirements, and any more stringent local academic requirements (which can be quite fluid), they will be guaranteed admission independently of the overall applicant pool.[48] In general, as discussed earlier, the "floor" of these local academic requirements is notably lower than for the general applicant pool. For example, imagine a school where 90 percent of the incoming class has SAT (math/verbal) scores between 1250 and 1390, or ACT scores between 28 and 31. Any applicants with an 1150/25 (or lower) are significantly more likely to be admitted if they are a varsity athlete rather than a legacy, a member of a traditionally underrepresented demographic group, or a great jazz saxophonist. At DI schools, only the most egregious cases are supposedly denied admissions, although there are certainly ample anecdotal accounts of intercollegiate athletes being functionally illiterate, or spending one to two years after high school in special "academies" where they can beef up their academic credentials while continuing to play sports. But this is far less likely in women's sports and nonrevenue men's sports, primarily because of the social class–based sifting and sorting provided in advance by the youth sports to college pipelines. Young women coming through the soccer and field hockey pipelines have almost all attended relatively wealthy public or private high schools. They may or may not be brilliant, but they are unlikely to be illiterate.

Admissions lists for DIII teams work a little differently. There is no standardized number of preferential admissions slots for teams, schools, or conferences. Each individual college or conference decides how much preference will be given to recruited athletes at any given moment in time. Some coaches of traditionally successful teams at heavily sports-centered schools might be given enough preferential slots to cover the entire incoming class. That is, *all* recruited athletes will be guaranteed admissions so long as they meet certain minimum academic expectations, which are often much lower than for applicants as a whole. At the other extreme, some coaches at some schools will be given *no* preferential slots for recruited athletes, who will be considered for admissions in the same process as every other applicant in either the regular or early action pools, although it's possible that admissions officers will still weigh athletic talent more than other talents. Most schools fall somewhere in the middle, with coaches receiving some guaranteed slots, but not enough for an entire incoming class.

It seems the data released from the College and Beyond study were somewhat embarrassing for many DIII schools and conferences that historically insisted that potential varsity athletes were academically equal to and treated similarly to every other applicant.[49] Perhaps in response to this or perhaps independently of this, schools in the New England Small College Athletic

Conference (NESCAC) designed a standardized system of preferential admissions slots for their varsity teams.[50] In general, each NESCAC school is allotted two slots (often called "athletic factors") per varsity sport, and fourteen slots for football if applicable. On average, each school (with a football team) gets approximately sixty-six slots annually. Coaches and athletic directors decide each year how many slots will go to each team. The permutations are almost endless, but rarely does every single team always get two (or fourteen) slots every year. According to NCAA rules, DIII schools may not formally "guarantee" admissions to any recruited athlete. However, the perception among some coaches is that if you are on a NESCAC coaches' list and have no smoking guns in your application you will absolutely be accepted, even if there is no verbal or written confirmation. Generally, academically prestigious DIII schools are extremely secretive about the slot system and the entire athlete admissions process, much like DI schools treat scholarship equivalency numbers like a state secret. This lack of transparency surely contributes to manipulation by commercial elements within the youth sports to college pipelines, and to the widespread misunderstanding by families of the college admissions process.

Coaches in NESCAC and other DIII conferences, not to mention the Ivy League, will try to use their slots for recruits who are academically weaker than the overall student body and who would be unlikely to gain admittance without preferential treatment. Allegedly, coaches then fill out their rosters with players who have been admitted in the school's regular process (either early action or standard) and who just happen to be decent in the sport in question. Rather than leaving this completely to chance, though, coaches are able to get "early reads" on potential players who are not being afforded one of the team's preferential slots. Early reads are done by admissions officers in the summer before an athlete's senior year in high school, well before the regular admissions process begins. Coaches will provide to admissions counselors a potential player's basic academic information to get a "30,000-foot" appraisal of how likely the person is to be admitted from the regular applicant pool. Coaches can then pass on those vague possibilities to potential players, giving them information helpful in their overall college search. In theory, then, potential varsity athletes outside of the official preferential slots are treated similarly to nonathletes. A longtime DIII field hockey coach (non-NESCAC), now retired, finds that assertion to be more rhetoric than reality:

> I have to chuckle when I hear some of these Ivy League and elite DIII schools claim that they don't get players beyond the two or three on their coaches'

> list. That's what early reads are for. It's like that Monty Python skit when they do "nudge, nudge, wink, wink." We claim that we are giving guidance to prospective students, but we're really alerting admissions that these kids are important to the team's success and have credentials that are in striking distance of the average student. Admissions officers follow the lead of whoever sets the university's tone. Usually the president. If the president thinks sports are more important than the debate team, then admissions will give preference to a solid midfielder over a solid debater. Coaches do have to be careful, though, and not waste the admissions people's time. You can't bring them knuckleheads for an early read. You have to save your capital for good players who are on the academic borderline. The preferential slots are for kids way below that line.

Still, there is an interesting downside to this increased importance on using sports to build the front porch of smaller liberal arts schools. Many of the DIII coaches I spoke with acknowledged that having more guaranteed slots and early reads helps greatly with team success, but it is also associated with a "corporatized" oversight more common in big-time DI athletics:

> Turns out the college had hired some new budget czar. He was some MBA who, rumor has it, wanted to get a college job in order to get tuition remission for his kids. The president said all colleges are hiring these Wall Street types to keep their finances in order. Well, the coaches started getting direct questions about our recruitment costs and how much our recruited players paid in tuition compared with walk-ons and nonathletes. We never got questions about this stuff before. Then the AD said she was also getting pressure from [the budget chief] to justify the expenses of our "unit." Maybe the budget guy wanted to see if I contradicted the AD. We had no idea how to respond. Should I talk about wins and losses? Game attendance, which is usually in the single digits if you don't count parents? How the team's GPA matches up with students in general? I don't think he really knew, but for the moment all-conference selections seem to be important. I guess he's interested in getting headlines in the *Springfield Gazette* when so-and-so makes all-conference. But we don't have a lot of superstars; that's not our style. I have no idea how this is going to play out.

RECRUITING ATHLETES TO THE FRONT PORCH

Building a school's front porch with intercollegiate athletics is one thing; getting prospective customers (and financial benefactors) to visit the porch is something else. As we will see in the next two chapters, the youth sports industry is more than willing to commodify, exaggerate, and market the availability and magnitude of athletic scholarships and admissions advantages, and young female athletes and their families are more than willing consumers of this commodity. But this embellishment begins with the increasingly corporatized world of higher education that has hitched its organizational health (and associated branding efforts) to visible and successful intercollegiate athletics programs, irrespective of the high cost involved with this strategy. The actual physical recruitment of prospective varsity players is critical to building a school's front porch around successful and visible intercollegiate athletics.

There are significant differences between recruitment at the DI/II and DIII levels. Perhaps more than any other area of college sports, the NCAA's labyrinth of rules and regulations are concerned with the recruitment of DI athletes, although these rules vary greatly from sport to sport. It is not really my purpose here to explore the nuances of intercollegiate athletics recruitment, only how these practices significantly impact the girls' youth sports to college pipelines. There have been many scholarly and journalistic forays into the world of recruitment, primarily in regard to DI football and men's basketball, where the financial and branding impact is much higher.[51] Interestingly, though, as higher education increases its overall neoliberal emphasis on intercollegiate sports, the same organizational pressures are impacting coaches in nonrevenue sports, including women's sports.

Showcase Tournaments

Chapter 3 will carefully examine the elite showcase tournament system as a critical piece of the youth sports to college pipelines and the primary interface between them and the world of intercollegiate athletics. No other single phenomenon has had more impact on the commercialization and commodification of youth sports such as soccer and field hockey. The historical origins of multigame tournaments that actually "showcase" high school athletes in front of college coaches remain fuzzy at best. Clearly, both college recruiters and the youth sports industry have developed a mutual vested interest in these tournaments. One longtime women's DI soccer coach, now retired for many years, believes the evolution of showcases was an outgrowth of Title IX's uneven initial application and enforcement:

> When the women's game was starting to take off in the early 1990s, we would receive the same number of equivalencies as the men's teams, but the rest of our budget was much smaller. We had far less money for equipment,

> travel, coaches, and recruitment. The school thought that we would be in compliance as long as scholarships were even. I think people still feel that way. Girls' youth soccer also hadn't exploded yet, so there was only a smattering of the tournaments that have since multiplied a thousandfold. One of my coach friends in a different conference was taking a short postseason vacation in [a southern state] and found out about this tournament. She said I should also come along with a few of our mutual friends. It wasn't a long-term recruiting strategy; we were just trying to have some fun in the sun. But it eventually struck us that this *could* be a long-term strategy. I'm not sure we were pioneers of this process, but we did get involved pretty early. Most of the tournaments included both boys and girls, but in the early days I remember most of the college coaches were from women's programs. We all knew each other!

Coaches at smaller DIII programs may have been an even bigger catalyst for the eventual explosion of showcase tournaments and their central rather than incidental role in the youth sports to college pipeline. A DIII athletic director and former field hockey coach explained,

> DIII coaches often recruit far more heavily than DI coaches because they don't have scholarships. We don't have dead periods [and] quiet periods.[52] We have every weekend and every week of the year when we have to track down kids who are proactive only about contacting DI programs where they assume they will get a free ride. [DIII coaches] have to be seen. We have to provide more personalized service to garner interest. Going to [showcase tournaments] is more efficient, but we're still on the road the same number of days. I guess it's better to say that it's really inefficient for us to travel an hour and a half each way to watch one player on a particular club team, when you usually know within about ten minutes if that girl is skilled enough for college field hockey. Of course, you have to stay for the whole game and then talk to the girl and her family. Now I can take that same ten minutes and use it at a showcase where I can see fifteen kids at once. That's a lot better use of my limited time and limited resources. Of course, the travel coaches exploit this trend by telling prospective customers that "they will be seen" by college coaches at these "elite" tournaments if they commit to [their travel] team. Not all of them are college-level players, but the travel coaches don't tell them that.

Currently, almost all recruiting for DI women's soccer and field hockey programs takes place at showcase tournaments. A smaller but still overwhelming percentage of DIII recruitment also takes place in that setting. So if you are a young female athlete aspiring for whatever reason to play varsity college sports, it's almost imperative that you enter the expensive, commercialized youth sports pipelines that very much revolve around these showcase tournaments.

The National Field Hockey Coaches Association (NFHCA) has recently shown how important college coaches and college recruitment are to the entire showcase system. The NFHCA, with commercial partner Corrigan Sports, has established its own showcase tournament in conjunction with the association's annual convention. This tournament will be at roughly the same time of year as the private Disney/ESPN tournament that has long been one of the largest and most prestigious showcases for youth club teams. The rumor within field hockey's grapevine is that Disney will no longer hold this event after 2016. With field hockey's somewhat modest youth sports to college pipeline, there really isn't enough consumer demand for two practically simultaneous national tournaments showcasing the same players. If the college coaches who attend an NHFCA conference prefer the NFHCA tournament, then that is that. You can't have a showcase tournament without people assessing the show. In contrast, the National Soccer Coaches Association of America (NSCAA) sponsored eight showcases in 2016, but the youth soccer world is so large that this did not significantly cut into dozens of other "private" showcases, including Disney's. The 1,030 intercollegiate soccer programs need far more showcases than the 271 field hockey programs.

Recruiting Babies

The pressure to win (for whatever reason) has led college coaches to recruit far younger players, always looking to get an edge over rival programs. While the NCAA officially prohibits "official" contacts with kids until they are in ninth grade, and has other statutory restrictions on how coaches and prospective college athletes can interact, it is not very difficult for relationships to start developing before a girl or boy is in high school. Extrawide loopholes exist where high school or club coaches can act as intermediaries between the player and the college coach. Also, girls and their families can have practically unlimited contact with college coaches as long as they do the initiating. The recruitment of very young kids generated more animated responses from college coaches than any other topic discussed in this project. To a person, the coaches I spoke with loathed the practice of recruiting kids before high school and trying to garner either an informal or semiformal commitment to attend a certain university before the girl makes an actual (or symbolic) commitment during her senior year of high school. Yet despite these moral protestations, almost all of these coaches admitted they might do it if their backs were truly against the wall and their professional careers were on the line. The coach of a women's soccer team at a small DI state university said,

> The pressure to win is outrageous, even though there's no money involved and I only make about a quarter of the football coach's salary. But since we receive the maximum allowable NCAA scholarships, on top of a relatively decent recruiting budget, we have to continually justify why we should remain a "fully funded" program. Sometimes I can't believe the things I do. I might tell a player it's OK to miss a class in order to work into a trainer's schedule so [an injury] will heal before the big game with [a rival school]. I might leave a great senior in an easy game in order to improve our scoring differential rather than let undeveloped freshmen get some important experience so they can be better in the future. Who knows, those [additional points] might improve our power rankings. But the biggest impact is on recruitment. We can't take a breath. [The coaching staff] probably spends more time on future players than on current players. One of [our coaches] is always missing practices and games because we are on the road looking for the next Mia Hamm hiding in some poorly publicized tournament in the far corner of Idaho where no one else will find her. And the showcase tournaments have kids as young as U9. Should we be looking at them? What if [another conference school] identifies and courts a ten-year-old who turns out to be Carli Lloyd? In this conference, it only takes one or two stars to get a team to the next level.

There have been many fairly well-publicized accounts in recent years of middle school girls being courted by college programs.[53] There is rarely ever any systematic follow-up as to whether these early commitments actually pan out five years later. Even University of North Carolina coach Anson Dorrance, one of the pioneers of recruiting middle schoolers, is simultaneously enamored with and appalled by this practice.[54] As we will see in the next two chapters, college recruitment of girls at ever-younger ages has had an enormous impact on the pay-to-play girls' youth sports to college pipelines, especially those with significant or expanding college footprints. The pressure to recruit babies even works on DIII coaches who have no scholarship money, and only a few preferential admissions slots:

> At most of the showcases, club teams distribute their glossy brochures with the head shots and stats for their players. The parents will even go around to the stands and make sure we have them, usually reminding us of their daughter's number. It used to be only the kids U14 and above that were highlighted. Lately, the brochures have contained information on girls as young as U10! Nobody wants to actually watch a nine-year-old, but once somebody does it,

> we all follow along like lemmings. It's disgusting, but the logic is if we don't do it and a competitor does, then we can be in trouble. There are so many kids, mostly at DI schools, who commit early and then end up sitting on the bench in college. They were great in eighth grade but never improved much while everyone else did. Meanwhile, the coach has used up at least a half scholarship for essentially a practice player. Since coaches can't control themselves despite all the hand-wringing, the NCAA needs to step up.

Many of us have probably seen a nine -year-old (with an early growth spurt) completely dominate a game or tournament. It could be, though, that this same girl eventually becomes an average player in high school after her friends have caught up physically. At the other extreme, there are probably girls who are not good enough (or wealthy enough) to enter the pay-to-play youth sports pipeline in third grade and find it difficult or impossible to break through later when they may have developed into excellent players.

INTERCOLLEGIATE ATHLETICS: THE YOUTH SPORTS PIPELINE'S POT OF GOLD

Post–Title IX higher-education policy has had an incredibly important institutional impact on the systemic exaggeration of female sports and, as we will see next, the expansion of various girls' youth sports pipelines. The neoliberal corporatization of higher education (along with its commercialization and commodification) has spawned a corporatized world of women's intercollegiate athletics that shares many of the long-corporatized patterns of male intercollegiate athletics. This goes beyond the highly commercial and profitable domains of men's basketball and football. All intercollegiate sports, regardless of NCAA divisional status, are now acting as if they are highly successful commercial ventures that must do everything possible to win games, gain notoriety, and recruit those blue-chip young women who can take a program and school to the "next level." The university's captains of erudition and solvency treat nonrevenue varsity sports the same way they treat revenue-generating sports, and increasingly see intercollegiate athletics as a centerpiece of the school's "brand" rather than as a complementary extracurricular activity. This in turn sends clear but misleading messages to potential varsity athletes and their families: sports matters. Perhaps even more than academics.

The data presented in the first two chapters clearly show that the numbers of intercollegiate programs and intercollegiate athletes are growing, especially on the women's side of the field house. This growth is not necessarily even, and each intercollegiate sport has a very different footprint with a correspondingly diverse impact on each girls' youth sports to college pipeline. Soccer has shown the most long-term expansion over the past thirty years, although ice hockey (not to mention lacrosse and rowing) currently seems to be experiencing an intense growth spurt. Field hockey, with a once-significant intercollegiate footprint, has pretty much stopped expanding and may even be contracting. Figure skating has no college presence. Intercollegiate ultimate is played at a very high competitive level but is not recognized under the NCAA's banner and thus does not offer scholarships or opportunities for preferential admissions. The focus on institutional branding and visibility has become so strong, universities are willing to spend millions of scarce dollars on programs that have little to do with the school's educational mission, and ultimately may serve only the handful of athletes who are on the varsity teams. In conjunction with the commercialized youth sports industry, universities' corporate-driven, Title IX–lubricated emphasis on expensive varsity sports has become an affirmative-action program to subsidize the college educations of relatively rich, relatively white, and relatively suburban young women. However, this affirmative-action program offers far fewer benefits to far fewer young women than is commonly believed. And it is helping to drive up college costs for everyone, although few people seem willing to acknowledge that publicly.

My contention is that this is no accident, although it also isn't an organized conspiracy to purposefully mislead millions of young girls and their families. There are individuals and organizations both inside and outside of intercollegiate athletics that stand to benefit from an exaggerated cultural portrayal of sports-based scholarships and admissions advantages. This exaggeration has many sources. But none are more important than higher education, which increasingly equates its institutional fortitude with the success and visibility of its varsity sports teams. For families facing ever-increasing college price tags, and with more cultural emphasis on having daughters (not just sons) attend the "correct" school, the message is clear, if not necessarily accurate. Sports matter. A lot. Given the tenets of capitalist commercialization central to US society, it's no wonder that pay-to-play youth sports to college pipelines have exploded to both stoke and satisfy these exaggerated cravings that are rooted in the ongoing corporatization of higher education.

3

THE COMMERCIALIZED YOUTH SPORTS TO COLLEGE PIPELINE

Among the sports explored in this book, the youth sports to college pipeline is most commercially developed in soccer, primarily due to its substantial intercollegiate athletic footprint. At the annual convention of the thirty thousand–member National Soccer Coaches Association of America (NSCAA), this commercial element of the pipeline occupies a space the size of two aircraft hangars, attracting both coaches and others involved with organized youth soccer. Hundreds of companies are looking to sell every conceivable commodity or service to help young soccer players (along with families, coaches, and clubs) get to that "next level." Apparel companies pledge that their new fabric will wick away more moisture and make players faster. A dozen technology companies promise that their videographic equipment and tracking software will allow clubs to send more of their players to Division I programs. One company offers a wide array of software to help various stakeholders in the college recruitment process, claiming that the days of using paper and pen are over. Domestic and international camps pledge that the pathway to college scholarships must go through Germany. Or Italy. Or Australia. Plenty of "pipeline consultants" will, for a nominal fee, help guide high school athletes and their families to the appropriate intercollegiate program. There are even specialized companies that advise how clubs (or other interested parties) can set up their own multiday soccer tournaments. Local tourist bureaus are also on hand to let you know how accommodating their counties could be to hosting such events. However, this commercial element was not limited to the vendor exhibit. Even many of the panels and workshops offered at the conference focused on topics such as making youth soccer leagues more financially successful.

The commercial characteristics of youth field hockey, figure skating, and ultimate Frisbee are much more modest, although certainly not undetectable. With fewer (field hockey) or no (figure skating, ultimate) college admissions advantages and scholarships, there is less fertile ground for businesses built around the youth sports to college pipeline. The National Field Hockey Coaches Association (NFHCA) has about 1,800 members, many of whom gather once a year for an annual convention. Unlike the gargantuan commercial exhibition at NSCAA, the NFHCA's meeting sports a dozen specialty vendors in a medium-size conference room. Likewise, the Professional Skaters Association (PSA), with about six thousand members worldwide (99 percent in the United States), offers a modest exhibit at its annual conference, featuring a few specialty vendors largely unknown outside the figure skating community.[1] Ultimate does not have a dedicated coaching organization or annual coaches' conference.

YOU ARE WHAT YOU BUY

One obvious commercial manifestation of the youth sports to college pipelines is the enormous amount of apparel and equipment that athletes can purchase to allegedly give them a competitive edge. Certainly at the NSCAA conference, apparel and equipment manufacturers comprised the greatest number of vendors and always with the splashiest presentations. Footwear was the most common product on display, since feet are the soccer player's most important equipment. These vendors included some of the biggest corporate names in sporting goods. Longtime conference attendees told me that the exhibition's focus over the past decade has shifted somewhat from apparel to practice equipment and "systems" for developing soccer skills, even though apparel vendors still had the glitziest displays. These products can focus on individual consumers but are more likely to target clubs and leagues that might purchase items for two dozen different teams. A practice goal (available in various sizes) purported to cleverly collect balls, allowing you to spend less practice time chasing down errant rebounds. One brand of training cone alleged that its wide variety of colors makes them much easier to see and helps younger players stay interested. A "training system" (sold as a DVD) claimed that five of its customers have nationally ranked teams. It did not say where these teams were ranked, and how many of its clients were not ranked. Kwik Goal is the five-hundred-pound gorilla in this field, with everything from a nonround "erratic" goalkeeper training ball ($80) to a custom bench shelter with twelve luxury padded seats ($38,400 per pair). A custom shelter was prominently displayed at Kwik Goal's huge exhibition, strategically located by the vendor hall's main entrance. It was quite comfortable, and I could imagine several of my former players preferring to stay on that bench rather than being put into a game on a cold, rainy October morning.

Gone are the days when "serious" soccer players threw on the cleats they also used for softball and whatever pair of shin guards they found lying around the house. A standard pair of cleats will cost around $30, but it is not unusual for girls (and their families) to spend over $100 on footwear that will probably be outgrown in a year. Many of the girls on one elite U9 soccer team told me that they have three or four different types of footwear. Some are for grass (with a backup in case the primary pair gets wet), and others for various types of turf. High-tech shin guards, as we will see in chapter 4, might also cost upward of $70 a pair. Throw in concussion-reducing headbands, special moisture-wicking base layers, and antiblister socks and a young girl may be wearing $200 worth of apparel on the soccer field. This does not include any home training equipment she might have to maintain her soccer edge between games and in the off-season.

Expensive, specialized equipment plays a slightly less discretionary role in the commercial milieu of field hockey, figure skating, and ice hockey. Many of these items, unlike in soccer, are not a luxury or attempt at conspicuous consumption. Because field hockey in the United States has a more modest youth sports to college pipeline, large sporting-goods corporations such as Nike are not really commercially involved in it. Instead, smaller specialty companies, almost all based outside of the United States, are responsible for the bulk of field hockey equipment sales, and make most of their money internationally. These companies include TK (Germany), Gryphon (Britain), Ritual (Australia), Obo (New Zealand), Slazenger (Britain), Dita (India), Grays (Britain), and Voodoo (Australia). STX is the only US-based equipment company, but its main organizational focus is lacrosse.[2] Playing competitive field hockey is expensive. Wooden field hockey sticks are still available for under $50 but, as one college player told me, the only ones she has ever seen are in public school physical education classes. Composites are all the rage now, and high-quality sticks run between $200 and $400. There are also specialty sticks for indoor play ($75–$150), and players need multiple sticks, since they do break or wear down. Protective gloves ($30 *each* hand), goggles ($50), and shin guards ($25) add to the total equipment cost before even considering footwear, which may require multiproduct specialization for different playing surfaces (Astroturf, all-purpose turf, natural grass). Goalkeeping gear can cost $300 for an entry-level package including shin guards, specialty footwear "kickers," upper-body armor, girdle, and hand protectors. Helmets are often not included in these packages (add $150). You also need a bag to carry all this stuff (add $135). Top-shelf goalkeeping equipment can run well over $1,000, including the bag. In and of itself, outfitting a field hockey player may be prohibitively expensive for some families, thus excluding them from even entering that particular youth sports to college pipeline. The contracting pipeline only exacerbates the social class bias of participation.

Figure skating equipment costs center on two specialty items, skates and apparel. Serious competitive figure skaters cannot buy their skates off the shelf at Dick's Sporting Goods. They must be custom made and can cost several thousand dollars, although you can get a reliable pair for about $750. Girls may need a new pair every year or two as their feet grow, but even highly competitive skaters who are not growing could need new boots every year and new blades several times a year. High-end blades themselves can run over $1,000 per pair. Competition dresses are also not purchased at a TJ Maxx clearance sale, although you can get some very serviceable ones for under $50. According to one skating coach, a typical competition dress for a young teen will cost between $150 and $600. The cost roughly doubles for those competing on a national stage. Even with these high equipment costs, this is only one piece of figure skating's hefty price tag. None of this, of course, is particularly surprising. Figure skating has always been an expensive sport restricted to those with plenty of discretionary funds. These economic barriers exist independently of the youth sports to college pipeline.

Ice hockey equipment is also very expensive for many girls and their families. Hockey skates are not nearly as expensive as figure skates, but a good pair can still cost several hundred dollars. Composite sticks with a variety of blade designs can run up to $300. Pads and helmets can also cost several hundred dollars, with goalies spending significantly more. And let's not forget the bag. Girls (and boys) still play hockey on frozen ponds with wooden sticks, Aunt Sophia's hand-me-down skates, and goalies stuffing their clothes with pillows and chair cushions. But this type of hockey is not part of the youth sports to college pipeline. For that, only the best equipment will help you get to the top, or so goes the conventional wisdom. And while females do not need quite as much protective padding as males, they still need some, plus all of the other accoutrements.[3] Ice hockey equipment is also dominated by non-US companies such as Bauer and Graf. However, US companies such as Easton Hockey and Reebok/Adidas are starting to sell more products. In fact, in 2004 Reebok/Adidas bought the popular Canadian company CCM and uses that label on all of its equipment except for sticks.[4] As ice hockey's youth sports to college pipeline continues to expand, especially for girls and women, there will probably be more interest from megacorporations such as Nike and Wilson.

Playing ultimate does not require a lot of specialized equipment or apparel beyond a requisite pair of cleats, and footwear companies do not market specialty cleats for ultimate as they might for soccer, field hockey, softball, or lacrosse. According to a longtime youth ultimate coach,

> A lot of our [recreational league] teams just buy a bunch of matching shirts at Target, then iron on their own numbers and nicknames. Sometimes they will just use whatever is laying around the house as long as it's almost the same color. It is decidedly low-tech. Of course, the higher-level teams try to have splashier uniforms, but often it's just the shirts. The shorts or sweatpants can be a variety of colors and the socks rarely match. In fact, for some teams, wearing nonmatching socks is done purposefully.

There is an "official" ultimate disc made by Discraft, but teams often use whatever is available as long as it is the correct weight. USA Ultimate formally endorses three small companies (Five Ultimate, VC Ultimate, and Savage) that offer allegedly ultimate-specific apparel for interested teams. Only these three companies can produce apparel bearing the USA Ultimate logo. According to several college ultimate players, this apparel isn't much different from what you might buy at a department store, and the inability to wear the USA Ultimate logo is not a deal breaker for many players and teams. The federation does not yet mandate that teams wear the logo when participating in USA Ultimate events, but that day may come if the sport can increase its commercial presence, although that is unlikely without the catalyst of a varsity intercollegiate footprint sparking a youth sports to college pipeline.

TEAMS AND LEAGUES

> I was kind of astounded that Sophie could not play intramural soccer in our town league. In her age group there were no intramural options, only travel teams. My neighbors said the travel teams are not all good and that there are no cuts, but I did not want to make that large a time or financial commitment. Even the lowest-level travel team might drive over an hour for a fifty-minute

> game. Then there are the uniform costs. Everyone needs matching shirts, shorts, socks, and sweatshirts. Some of the teams require backpacks with your name and number. In [our previous home's recreational league], everyone got a T-shirt, and they could wear whatever else they wanted.[5] Shin guards were required, but you could use anything laying around. Sophie and her friends seemed to be having fun even without matching bags. Apparently, the families around here wanted more travel team options. I don't think my neighbors are necessarily thinking directly about scholarships or world cups, but they probably don't want to close any future doors. What if their daughter is a late bloomer and could be the next Mia Hamm?

Sophie is ten years old. She really likes to play soccer with her friends even though she isn't very good. She explained,

> My favorite part of soccer I guess is playing [defense]. I like to keep the other team from scoring. It makes me laugh. And then I don't have to be in the big bunch of girls trying to kick the ball. I got a big bruise doing that once. I don't think I want to play in high school. My team got to be ball girls once [for the high school team], and all the players looked so mad and yelled at us if we didn't give them the ball right away. They were scary.

Sophie puts a face on the dropout statistics discussed in chapter 1. She (and her family) will likely become casualties of the growing trend in youth sports where fewer kids participate in more elite (and expensive) settings. There is no AYSO option in Sophie's new community like there was in her old neighborhood. While Sophie's family is certainly not poor, they were still sensitive to the financial exigencies of travel soccer, even at a low competitive level. Certainly these financial concerns would be more constraining for poorer families.

As mentioned in chapter 1, there are incomplete data on the decline in girls' recreational soccer teams and the ascendancy of travel soccer teams. But the coaches and league officials I spoke with are absolutely certain that this trend is real and growing. A youth soccer administrator with over twenty years' experience reflected,

> Of course when I first started there wasn't even a girls' recreational league. We had to build that from scratch. The boys already had [recreational] leagues plus travel teams. Once we got the recreational leagues going, the parents wanted to know why there weren't travel team options for the girls. This was the early '90s when the Women's World Cup started and the US won, so there was some fanfare for a while. Then the US women won the first Olympics in

> [1996]. Plus there was a huge increase in college soccer. The families wanted more travel teams for their daughters so they could get into the hunt for medals and scholarships. They didn't seem to care about cost.

Whether or not these families cared about cost, this trend toward travel soccer reflects another segment of the youth sports to college pipeline that is largely inaccessible to poorer families. With fewer college coaches recruiting in high schools, and with the simultaneous unwritten expectation that serious soccer players will be on serious travel teams, girls from poorer families are structurally prevented from progressing through the pipeline regardless of their talent or motivation. Girls and young women cannot just show up at showcase tournaments, pick sides, and then play soccer in front of curious college coaches. Travel *teams* play in these tournaments. Travel *teams* are ranked by for-profit companies that insist they have the best assessment algorithms. But, as Caroline and Elizabeth showed us in chapter 1, not all travel teams are created equally. Another veteran youth (and high school) soccer coach explained,

> The number of so-called elite or premier teams for girls has exploded in the last ten years. There used to be just a handful of them in this area. Now there are hundreds of them in both regular leagues and the specialty leagues from U8 to U17. It used to be that these were independent teams not tied to a local soccer club. They had arrangements with local colleges to rent their fields, so that's one reason they cost a lot. But now even the town clubs are creating elite segments alongside their "normal" travel teams. They play on the same community fields and high school fields as the regular travel teams and the [nontravel] teams. So their costs are lower. But they still charge more than the "normal" travel teams. All the premier teams try to poach players from each other, and they are always looking for hidden talent in the regular travel leagues. I have only lost two girls from my [primary] travel team over six years, but some of my friends lose that many every year. It's funny, but it's not always the best players who go to the premier teams, just those with the biggest dreams. Or maybe it's the deepest pockets. There's so many teams, they just need girls to fill the rosters.

If this perspective is accurate, then the expanding travel team system may be more concerned with identifying high-income families than outstanding soccer players; more adept at manufacturing demand for elite travel soccer teams than satisfying a preexisting cultural interest.

While girls' youth soccer has been steadily shifting its emphasis toward travel/club teams, youth field hockey has always subscribed to this "privileged" model. Outside of a school setting, girls' field hockey is played almost exclusively in expensive pay-to-play clubs rather than inexpensive recreational leagues. In southeastern Pennsylvania, a national hot spot for field hockey, there are about a half dozen clubs offering teams in the U12, U14, U16, and U19 age groups. Across the Delaware River in southern New Jersey there are at least that many as well. Some of the larger, more established clubs may offer multiple teams in each age group and/or teams for boys and adults. There are even a few U10 teams. Fees vary depending on age level, skill level, and the perceived prestige of any particular club, but they are quite comparable to the price of pay-to-play youth soccer, except that there are far fewer national tournaments adding to families' potential final cost. Many teams will play each other in loosely defined winter and spring leagues, usually in indoor facilities. Fall club team practice schedules will generally revolve around school teams. The high-level club teams primarily train for competition in the elite showcase tournaments. Unlike in soccer, elite field hockey clubs do not require players to eschew their school teams, although it is largely acknowledged that prospective college players *must* play in a club program. A DI coach explains,

> Most of the high school teams don't have cuts. They probably couldn't have a team if there were cuts. That's fine, but it doesn't help assess the really good players who might be on a high school team. Let's say "Mary" is a good forward. On her high school team, she might not really excel because nobody can pass it to her in a scoring position; or the defenders will triple team her since there aren't any other scoring threats. But on a club team surrounded by decent players, her skills are more noticeable. I guess it's like separating the wheat from the chaff. We rely on the clubs to take care of that screening. I imagine that some potentially good players get sifted out incorrectly, but that's the system we use.

Talent is not the only factor that might determine whether a girl is considered wheat or chaff. Family finances also play a central role in deciding whether or not a girl can play organized field hockey, which team or club she may play for, and how she can best position herself in the college recruitment section of the pipeline. For example, a fully committed field hockey player could face the following *annual* costs in addition to the lofty cost of equipment mentioned earlier: club dues, \$220; indoor season, \$900; spring academy \$220; National Indoor Tournament fees, \$210–\$390 (age dependent); Junior Premier Indoor League fees, \$195; Disney Showcase fee, \$150 (plus travel to Florida);[6] Regional Club Championship fee, \$125;

National Club Championship fee, $150; summer camp, $300; National Festival, $100–$200 (plus travel). According to a former club team coach,

> We didn't see a lot of girls drop out because of money. This is a pretty wealthy area overall. But it did seem to impact which club or team they might be able to play for. I knew several girls from a summer clinic in [the nearby city] who were very good but simply couldn't afford to join the club team I was coaching with at the time. At that time, our club did not give anything like scholarships. [The girls] did manage to hook up with another club that was far less serious and had no teams at Festival. But [the girls] only played for a year because getting to the practice field was really hard.

These girls might have been prime candidates for a recreational field hockey program. Such programs, however, are practically nonexistent. There is no established field hockey equivalent to soccer's AYSO or the less-commercialized threads of US Youth Soccer, although USA Field Hockey is trying to do this with its FUNdamental Field Hockey program. The absence of a recreational option actually accentuates the social class bias of field hockey's pipeline. Girls can play field hockey outside of school just for fun, but it will cost them. For example, the Philadelphia Field Hockey Association does offer an organized league for people not playing on a high school or college team, but you must be over eighteen years old and pay a significant fee. There are some people within the field hockey community who would like to expand youth recreational programs but are also cognizant of the constraints. A former college field hockey player and current youth coach explained,

> We are trying to get girls and boys interested in field hockey at a much younger age. The old-school belief was that kids didn't really have the necessary skills to play until they were around thirteen. That might be true, but you could still get kids interested earlier by just having fun and associating it with field hockey. Look at lacrosse. Hardly any kids under eight can reliably catch and throw with a stick, but they still have four-year-olds running around and laughing while holding a stick and wearing goggles. They associate lacrosse with having fun. Around here, we have to compete with soccer and its well-established recreational programs. Even if kids start playing "fake" soccer at five, they may be completely uninterested in field hockey by the time they are ten. In fact, our attempts at [recreational] programs for younger kids usually do better in communities where travel soccer is out of control and some families are looking for more relaxing sports for their kids. But then it's hard to get fields! The club teams are doing pretty well, but recreational programs

> will only help them expand by drawing more kids to the sport. I'm not sure [everyone] sees it that way, though.

That sentiment was echoed by other people I spoke with throughout the field hockey community, whether they were motivated by commercial interests or simply by a love of the game. Field hockey's youth sports to college pipeline runs directly through the elite and expensive private club system, with high school teams offering a way to stay sharp for college recruiters who will be watching highly ranked teams at the showcase tournaments. A veteran high school field hockey coach reflected,

> FUNdamental Field Hockey is trying to be independent of the elite clubs who control so much of the action. The idea is to have something like a recreational program for kids who simply want to have fun and not necessarily use youth sports as a pathway to college scholarships. It's such a great idea, but they are really starting from scratch, and there is actually resistance from many people within the community! A lot of the premier clubs oppose the program even though it could potentially add to their business in the long run by attracting new kids, including boys, to the game. I think [the clubs] believe it will take away their less serious players who have nowhere else to go. Maybe they are right, but there should still be some low-cost, low-pressure alternatives for kids. A few years ago I was invited to be on a committee about the future of club field hockey. All the other committee members were from these big clubs, and I said something about how the whole conversation seemed to be about making money instead of the future of the game. I haven't been invited back.

TO TRAVEL OR NOT TO TRAVEL?

Figure skating does not fit within the "recreational" versus "travel" paradigm common to many youth sports to college pipelines. There are no figure skating "leagues" where skaters from Club A-Z compete against each other in weekly events by skill category, age, and gender. Kids certainly skate recreationally, and many birthday parties have been held at public and private rinks, but this activity is neither organized nor competitive. More important, competitive figure skating has almost *always* taken place within a somewhat elite club setting and has *always* required a significant financial outlay. Tonya Harding's emergence as a national champion skater in the 1990s was news because her home "club" was a suburban Portland (Oregon) shopping mall that happened to have a public rink. Likewise, Nancy Kerrigan's similarly timed success was a "person bites dog" story, since she learned to skate in the local town rink where her dad voluntarily drove the Zamboni in exchange for Nancy's figure skating lessons (girls were not yet playing organized ice hockey). But these two stories are Pygmalion-esque anomalies within highly competitive figure skating.

Female ice hockey's meteoric rise in the past decade, primarily driven by its growing intercollegiate presence, has created an expensive recreational/travel team system modeled after the long-established (and much larger) boys' system. Kids might still play hockey on frozen ponds, but these games do not figure in the national rankings and are not on the itineraries of college recruiters. There is an unmistakable commercial engine driving this shift away from female figure skating (with no intercollegiate presence) and toward female ice hockey (with an expanding intercollegiate presence). New organizations such as the New England Women's Junior Hockey League seems to be following the ECNL model in soccer. The notable increase in ice rinks, especially multirink facilities, is almost completely hockey-related. More rinks open the possibility for more leagues and teams, be they recreational, travel, or elite. A veteran skating coach commented,

> Hockey is a bonanza for rinks that are able to have it. The economics are completely different. You can have a hockey team come and offer $350 for one hour on the ice. Figure skaters might be interested as individuals buying that same hour of ice time. But their payments as a whole wouldn't come close to that $350. In a figure skating–only club without hockey, it's not the skaters per se who support the club but the membership fees of the skaters. And I know the few figure skating–only clubs around here are barely hanging on. They are always looking for new members. With hockey, especially with girls, the growth is so phenomenal that you don't have to find money. The money comes to you, to the rink. Multirink facilities can better maintain a figure skating program since there is prime-time ice available for all the skaters, and hockey will subsidize any deficits. But it's really tough for a single-rink facility.

Ice hockey is significantly less expensive than figure skating, where it isn't unusual to spend over $50,000 per year for a highly competitive teenage girl.[7] Ice hockey's yearly fees (excluding equipment) can range from about $1,000 per year for a mostly in-house/recreational experience to upward of $6,000 per year for a top-tier travel team. As with other youth sports to college pipelines, this creates significant entry barriers to modest-income families. Intercollegiate scholarships or admissions advantages are available only to girls and families who can afford to enter and remain in the pipeline. And, as mentioned in the last chapter (and as with field hockey), many of these intercollegiate opportunities at US colleges are increasingly offered to players from other countries who may be better able to contribute to a winning record and enhance a school's brand.

Despite the absence of a youth sports to college pipeline, *organized* ultimate has experienced a historical tension between advocates of a local, grassroots league system and supporters of a quasi-elite (i.e., selective) club system that focuses on tournaments, much like soccer and field hockey. A longtime ultimate coach, player, and local league official told me,

> That battle is pretty much over. Most of [USA Ultimate's] strategy is focusing on restricted teams and tournaments rather than local open leagues. It's a visibility thing. They are trying to get more people to notice the sport, not necessarily play the sport, although more people might play if it receives more national attention. I happen to disagree with that philosophy, but many others do not. There's no hostility toward local leagues and local teams who are uninvolved with the club team rankings and tournaments, so long as all the players are members [of USA Ultimate]. Local leagues in the hard-core areas are still flourishing and seem to be very committed to maintaining the spirit of the game. [Mixed-gender] teams have become especially popular, especially with high school and college students. Getting young kids involved has been a little tougher. These local leagues still generally play in a few large central locations with multiple fields, so transportation can be an issue for kids without licenses. And except in certain areas, the sport still has that pot-smoking image.

As mentioned in chapter 1, these competing paradigms for increasing ultimate's appeal emphasize different factors, either a bottom-up, grassroots focus on kids as a whole or a top-down focus on elite players/teams that might receive broad national exposure. A "recreational" strategy would aim to maximize youth participation by creating as much grassroots opportunity as possible, much like AYSO in soccer. A more "commercial" strategy would look to increase the sport's visibility with the help of vendors who could make money from this association.

USA Ultimate's efforts to expand the club system for girls and young women is showing some signs of success. Seven U16 girls' teams participated in the 2015 national youth club championships, up from three teams in 2014. U16 players range from twelve to fifteen, with most at the older end. There are no younger "official" age groups regardless of gender. While this increase in national youth tournament participation is certainly commendable (from US Ultimate's perspective), it pales in comparison to the approximately one hundred club teams competing in USA Field Hockey's regional and national championships (U14, U16, U19) and the 512 girls' club teams participating in US Youth Soccer's regional and national championships.[8]

Officials at USA Ultimate told me they hoped the game's recent recognition by the US Olympic Committee (USOC) and International Olympic Committee (IOC) would help promote the game, stoke youth demand, and lead to more organized league and commercial opportunities. The federation even moved its headquarters from Boulder, Colorado, to Colorado Springs in order to be more connected with other Olympic sports. However, this strategy will likely prove unsuccessful in the absence of college scholarships and/or admissions advantages for ultimate players. Women's field hockey has long been an Olympic sport, and yet its youth club structure is modest and static. Women's lacrosse is *not* recognized as an Olympic sport, and yet its girls' youth sport to college pipeline is growing exponentially. These different youth sports trajectories are due primarily to the changing intercollegiate presence of these sports, not their recognition as current or potential Olympic events. More girls and women in the United States are playing ultimate than are playing lacrosse or field hockey. But they are playing the game in a far less commercialized context. Depending on your point of view, this may or may not be a good thing.

RANKINGS

The five sports highlighted here (and most others) have systems for ranking youth teams and individuals. These rankings play important supply-and-demand roles in the youth sports to college pipelines. On the supply side, a private, commercial, rankings *industry* has emerged in certain sports. In addition to being a commercial force in its own right, other businesses within the pipelines revolve around these rankings. On the demand side, which will be addressed more in chapter 4, players and families often put a lot of stock in these rankings and utilize them to guide their youth sports decisions. Field hockey, ultimate, and figure skating rankings are all coordinated by the sports' governing bodies. Nominally, these rankings help ensure fair seeding at tournaments so that competitors are grouped appropriately. They also serve to identify "national champions" in the various age, gender, and skill categories. However, US Youth Soccer, American Youth Soccer Organization, and US Club Soccer do not overtly rank youth teams. This void, combined with the lucrative appeal of soccer's youth sports to college pipeline, has spawned a commercial cottage industry for ranking youth soccer teams.

GotSoccer is currently the five-hundred-pound gorilla in the youth soccer ranking industry. GotSoccer is the leading source of youth soccer–related software in the United States. The software facilitates scheduling for local league play as well as for tournaments. Around 2003, GotSoccer instituted a ranking system that has since become completely entrenched within the youth soccer world and seems to have become the main focus of its business. Nobody I spoke with in the youth soccer community seemed to know exactly how the GotSoccer rankings became a focal point of youth soccer, but there is no denying its influence. In the GotSoccer ranking system, teams receive a varying number of "GotSoccer points" for participation and success in certain tournaments. To award GotSoccer ranking points, tournaments must use the GotSoccer software. Teams who enter these tournaments do not have to be GotSoccer customers, but having the program makes registration much more seamless and, according to several league officials I spoke with (who dislike the ranking system), the product is quite good. Extra GotSoccer points are awarded based on team performance, but it is possible for a team to receive no ranking points at all for its weekend's work. GotSoccer rankings are based strictly on playing in GotSoccer-approved tournaments. Participating in local or regional league play, within organizations such as Philadelphia Area Girls Soccer (PAGS) or Washington Area Girls Soccer (WAGS), does not count toward your regional or national rankings. Tournaments sponsored by these local leagues, or larger regional organizations such as Eastern Pennsylvania Youth Soccer (EPYSA), may or may not be official GotSoccer tournaments.

The vast majority of the top-ranked tournaments within the GotSoccer world seem to be along the two US coasts, perhaps reflecting population distribution patterns. This would make sense given that most of the teams participating in these tournaments are within the host site's multistate region, although a healthy percentage do come from greater distances. But in the fertile commercial ground of the girls' youth soccer to college pipeline, there is always room for upstart expansion. In addition to ECNL's own ranking system based on participation in *its* sanctioned tournaments, a quick Internet scan reveals at least a half dozen other ranking systems, each claiming that it has the secret algorithm for identifying the best travel soccer teams and players. Some "products" seem to include results not just from tournaments but from local league play as well. Others see goal differentials as very (or not at all) important. The National Premier Leagues (NPL) branch of US Club Soccer seems currently uninterested in rankings and identifies its regional and national championships through a system of league playoffs, although this may be modifying.

This ranking industry also permeates other female sports with significant pipelines. In softball, for example, the US Specialty Sports Association

(USSSA) and Triple Crown Sports offer rankings for club teams based on points accumulated at tournaments sponsored by their organizations. USA/ASA Softball, the sport's official governing body, has no ranking system. Similarly, AES Power Rankings and US Club Rankings evaluate youth volleyball club teams in the absence of formal assessments by USA Volleyball. These rankings are commercial products made available to club teams, players, families, and college recruiters that will presumably help with business (for the clubs and colleges) and intercollegiate aspirations (players and families). Even female ice hockey, which is small but expanding rapidly, has a ranking system independent of USA Hockey. MYHockey is perhaps the premier ranking system within youth hockey. It has many similarities to GotSoccer, only without the software. MYHockey calculates ratings based on participation in its sponsored tournaments but also on independent league play. Access to rankings is free, but premium services are only available for a fee. In contrast to these sports with large or expanding pipelines, there isn't much private commercial interest in team rankings for youth field hockey or youth ultimate. Rankings in these sports are computed and coordinated by USA Field Hockey and USA Ultimate based on participation and success in their officially sanctioned tournaments.

TOURNAMENTS

"There's money to be made here," explained the founder of a company that organizes, hosts, and markets youth sports events across the United States.[9] This entrepreneur was reflecting on his 2008 decision to leave a job with a professional sports team in exchange for working in the burgeoning youth sports event industry. Plano, Texas, hosts many such events each year, and a city official there asserts that they draw millions of dollars to the local economy through hotel stays, restaurant meals, and registration fees. National corporations may pay upward of $5,000 each to help sponsor these events, with the assurance that their brands will be prominently visible among high-income audiences. At the NSCAA convention, several sports-event planning companies had booths in the vendors exhibit, and the conference program offered a panel presentation on planning soccer tournaments. The session was very well attended.

Not all tournaments are created equal. Tournaments run the gamut from local clubs trying to raise a little bit of operating revenue to invitation-only elite "showcase" tournaments where, as discussed in the first two chapters, college coaches are on hand to recruit what are assumed to be the very best players from the very best youth teams. Modest local events might have six or eight teams from within thirty miles of the host club playing in a three- or four-game round-robin on a couple of fields over two days (sometimes only one day). There may be some patronizing of local convenience stores and fast-food restaurants but no overnight stays. At the other extreme, national showcase tournaments (whether invitation-only or open) might include hundreds of teams playing as many as six games in two or three days at multiple sites within a city or county. Players (and their families) could travel thousands of miles and spend thousands of dollars eating and sleeping during the tournament, above and beyond what they might have paid for registration fees and travel. Some premier soccer tournaments have instituted preliminary "play-in" tournaments in order to be eligible for the main attraction.

While higher-education policies *externally* drive the youth sports to college pipelines, multiday, multiteam showcase tournaments are the pipelines' central *internal* commercial component. Again, these showcases permit college coaches to recruit players more "efficiently." They have become the direct interface between youth sports and intercollegiate athletics. Other important commercial enterprises within the pipelines often orient themselves toward these college showcase tournaments. The commercialized and commodified logic goes something like this: join this premier club (with its high ranking) and go to that summer camp (with the famous coach) and wear these shin guards, and use this stick so you can make it to the next level via (for example) the Disney Field Hockey Showcase at the ESPN Wide World of Sports where "magical talent is discovered [and is] the ultimate place for top field hockey clubs to be seen by hundreds of college coaches looking for great field hockey talent."[10]

It is important to distinguish between those tournaments (showcases or not) run by governing federations and those that are run by "private" commercial interests, although generally approved by governing federations. There are no systematic data on the number of nonfederation tournaments in various girls' youth sports, but they seem to be increasing in those sports with large and/or expanding intercollegiate footprints. A seasoned tournament organizer explained,

> The fastest-growing segment of showcases is for girls' soccer and girls' lacrosse. I have heard that volleyball is also growing, but I am not involved in that. Boys' soccer and lacrosse is already big, so there isn't much room for new tournaments, although some people keep trying. I used to do softball tournaments but stopped because I couldn't get big sponsors, especially in [the northeastern states]. [The sponsors] thought there was more "high-end"

> visibility in sports like soccer and lacrosse. I don't know if they are right about softball, but there's plenty of "high-end" families going to soccer and lacrosse tournaments. Not many '82 Datsun pickups in the parking lot.

Among the sports highlighted in this book, soccer has by far the most commercialized pay-to-play tournament system, with hundreds of events each year that are attended by kids as young as six. The bulk of these commercial, for-profit showcase tournaments are not run directly by US Soccer (or one of its affiliates) but will almost always receive its imprimatur. As discussed earlier, the labyrinth of girls' organized youth soccer in the United States is moving toward a tournament-based system that increasingly revolves around intercollegiate recruitment. US Club Soccer's 2009 creation of the Elite Clubs National League (ECNL) was certainly emblematic of this paradigm shift, and its National Premier Leagues (NPL) recently introduced tournaments to complement its primary club playoff system. Philosophies of sport aside, from an economic and organizational perspective, US Club Soccer/ECNL/NPL probably thought it could and should compete in the critical tournament-based component of female soccer's expanding youth sport to college pipeline. These economic and organizational factors were not lost on a regional soccer federation official:

> When ECNL emerged [in 2009], it cemented the centrality of tournament play for girls' soccer and provided more legitimacy for gearing tournaments toward college recruiters rather than identifying players for the national teams. It also weakened [the regional leagues] by shifting resources away from girls who wanted a less-intense travel experience that was more about fun than some future payoff. It also started an ironic escalation of travel team costs. You would think that more competition would drive costs down, but it did just the opposite. Girls started paying higher team fees and attending even more tournaments. Sometimes they played for more than one premier team, which only worked if they were in separate leagues.

The relative organizational and economic success of these different US Soccer affiliates would seem largely dependent on how college coaches view them, which would, in turn, impact consumer demand. So far, there seems to be enough recruiter and consumer interest in showcase tournaments to keep everyone's trough filled. If the many DI and DIII college soccer coaches I spoke with are any indication, they couldn't care less about the US Youth Soccer/US Club Soccer distinctions:

> I'm usually not even aware of who is sponsoring any particular showcase. I pick them more based on location and my schedule. I don't think ECNL or

> NPL has cut into [USYS's] tournaments; there are just more of them. I don't think the talent pool is any different; it's just distributed among more clubs and teams. Lots of the really good players are on both US Club and [US Youth Soccer] teams anyway. I guess they are trying to hedge their bets. But there are also a lot of mediocre teams and players in these showcase tournaments. Any tournament can call itself a showcase.

Field hockey, with its more modest youth sports to college pipeline, has a much smaller tournament system operating more closely with USA Field Hockey (USAFH). The federation itself sponsors the most important tournaments, including the yearly "Festival" attended by some two hundred club teams in the U14, U16, and U19 age groups. USAFH also runs indoor tournaments (NITs) organized around club teams, and a "Futures" program geared toward identifying outstanding individual players (for national/Olympic teams) regardless of club affiliation. Compared with youth soccer, there are almost no nonfederation showcase tournaments. Corrigan Sports' expanded alliance with the National Field Hockey Coaches Association is supplanting an existing tournament (sponsored by Disney) so really doesn't reflect a net increase in commercial products. White Mountain Sports, which began in the 1980s primarily as a field hockey camp, now holds both invitation-only and open showcase tournaments (and other commercial ventures), with prominently available lists of college coaches who will be attending either physically or virtually. There are some small local and regional field hockey tournaments (often called "tune-ups"), but nothing comparable to the commercial intensity of youth soccer. USAFH's former chief operating officer and current executive director, Simon Hoskins, is aware of this commercial vacuum:

> [USA Field Hockey] has started a huge outreach program to try and kindle interest in the sport. We can't rely on private clubs and privately run tournaments, like the lacrosse and soccer models. There is no serious commercial interest from the big sporting-goods companies or private entrepreneurs, since we are seen as a niche sport. Investors think that only girls play the sport and only in wealthy boarding schools in New England. Maybe getting more males involved will help; I'm not sure. But there is a huge perception problem in sparking interest to form clubs and put on multiday national or regional tournaments. So we're going to do it ourselves.

Without genuflecting before the tenets of neoclassical economics, I would argue that this lack of independent commercial interest in national and regional field hockey tournaments accurately reflects the current state of its youth sports to college pipeline. Mr. Hoskins is correct: field hockey in the United States *is* a niche sport played in a localized (although heavily populated) geographic region by a relatively small and static number of (mostly) females from (generally) high-income families. This attracts small-scale niche companies rather than huge corporate conglomerates more able to underwrite showcase tournaments in return for brand visibility. So while US-based corporate powerhouses like Nike, Adidas/Reebok, and Under Armour are commercially entrenched within youth soccer and frequently sponsor showcases, youth field hockey is serviced by the smaller non-American companies mentioned earlier that seem uninterested in sponsoring showcase tournaments in the United States. If field hockey, like girls' lacrosse, had an expanding pipeline, there would almost certainly be more nonfederation showcase tournaments.

USA Field Hockey's "public-private" approach seems to be taking root. The federation has designated that Spooky Nook Sports, located in southeastern Pennsylvania, be the official "home of hockey" through 2022.[11] Spooky Nook will be the base of all USAFH women's national teams and will eventually host most of USAFH's national tournaments for girls and women. Men's national teams will still train in California, which is the geographic epicenter for people playing that particular version of the sport. Creating a "home" for female field hockey in the Northeast, where the women's game is most prominent, coincides with USAFH's mission statement and strategic plan of promoting and providing opportunities for increased participation in the sport. The Spooky Nook facility is enormous, with multiple indoor and outdoor fields designed primarily for field hockey, but also able to host teams, tournaments, camps, and clinics in volleyball, basketball, and lacrosse.[12]

While Spooky Nook is certainly an impressive facility, and USAFH will certainly benefit from shortening the distance between where its young elite players live and where they train, the agreement also accentuates some troubling aspects of youth sports commercialization and does little to expand low-cost recreational options for youth field hockey players. For instance, at the conclusion of the fall outdoor field hockey season, Spooky Nook will host pay-to-play indoor field hockey tournaments every weekend. These are independent of USAFH's official tournaments and seem to be exactly what USAFH's leaders were looking for. These tournaments have not yet been branded as "showcases," but that will probably just be a matter of time given the number of college programs in and around southeastern Pennsylvania. Entrance fees for these tournaments are $360 per team. Those traveling long distances (or who have early-morning games) can stay (and eat) at local motels and restaurants, including an on-site motel/restaurant owned by

Spooky Nook, where rates generally go up on tournament weekends and often require a two-night stay. The nearest off-site motel is about six miles away, as are most restaurants, but staying at the facility allows you to avoid any parking hassles, including the $5 daily fee. Spending money within the facility is also encouraged by policies that prohibit bringing in coolers or water bottles with more than thirty-two ounces of liquid. This restriction applies to the players as well. The sports facility offers two on-site dining options for players and families, one a snack bar and the other a full-service restaurant. Players and spectators can go elsewhere for food, but they may lose their on-site parking spot and upon returning may be required to park in a satellite lot some distance away. Fortunately, if they can reclaim an on-site spot, they will not have to pay another $5! One parent told me after a U14 field hockey tournament, that she loathed the "nickel and diming" at Spooky Nook tournaments, but that they were beginning to be considered a "must-go" even though they weren't official showcases.

NON-SHOWCASE SPORTS

Showcase tournaments are nonexistent in figure skating, since it has no youth sports to college pipeline, and skaters have no reason to show off for university recruiters. As discussed earlier, figure skating does have organized competitions to identify its best athletes. However, unlike in youth soccer, premier figure skating competitions are not profit-making ventures by professional tournament organizers (and ancillary tourism-based businesses), although they are often a fund-raiser for local clubs. There is far less commercial interest in a nontelevised, regional youth skating tournament with a few dozen participants and spectators as opposed to a regional college showcase soccer tournament with several hundred teams, players, and families. Instead, junior skating competitions are often coordinated by and for US Figure Skating, whose official corporate sponsors (e.g., Prudential Insurance, Smucker's, Procter & Gamble) have no direct connection with the sports industry. Mind you, *national* skating competitions, especially when televised, are big-time commercial events with a notable corporate presence that appreciates the income demographic of figure skating fans. But the number of participants (plus families) in these events pales next to the numbers involved in soccer tournaments, or even field hockey tournaments.

USA Ultimate actively seeks local clubs (or other interested parties) to host tournaments independent of, but still sanctioned by, USAU. According to federation administrators, there has been some headway into this but not as much as they would like. They do acknowledge that independent (yet sanctioned) tournaments would increase dramatically were ultimate to become a varsity intercollegiate sport and, thus, eligible for scholarships and admissions advantages. However, they realize this is not likely to happen. As mentioned earlier, though, they believe there is a possibility that the USOC's and IOC's recognition of mixed-gender ultimate might jump-start the commercial appeal of tournaments and even some showcase events that provide a proxy for Olympic tryouts. However, this Olympics-based equation has not been very influential in the expansion of commercialized field hockey tournaments due to its modest (and static) pipeline. Only a large (or expanding) intercollegiate varsity footprint can provide the necessary commercial catalyst for a significant youth sports to college pipeline focused on showcase tournaments.

This may be happening in girls' ice hockey, which seems to be on the verge of a commercial breakout. Currently, most female-specific tournaments are within the organizational structure of USA Hockey (USAH), with a few scattered independent tournaments formally sanctioned by USAH but not run by the federation. This is very similar to the USA Field Hockey tournament model except for the presence of a parallel male iteration that is far more developed. For example, in both the New York and Massachusetts regions, USAH-sanctioned (but independently run) male tournaments outnumber female tournaments by about tenfold. However, clubs are starting to talk more about organizing and hosting girls'-only tournaments, or opening up to girls their historically boys-only tournaments. This makes perfect commercial sense as the sport's intercollegiate presence continues to expand and its corresponding youth sports to college pipeline starts to develop and strengthen. This will only exacerbate the tidal wave of girls moving from figure skating to ice hockey. A figure skating coach commented,

> I teach a few girls who do both figure skating and ice hockey. They are starting to give up local and regional [figure] skating competitions in order to play more hockey, not just in leagues but in tournaments. Usually they are official regional or state championship tournaments, but recently I've heard about more privately run tournaments like the boys have. Even if the girls don't play other sports, they hear from their soccer and lacrosse friends about playing in tournaments in front of college coaches and getting scholarships. It's just a matter of time before that starts in girls' ice hockey. The families can't afford to do both figure skating and ice hockey, or maybe don't have time to do both. The girls are still taking [figure skating] lessons, but I'll probably lose them as soon as one of their hockey friends "goes DI or Ivy." That's what they talk

about. If we were in Minnesota or Massachusetts instead of Maryland, I probably would have lost them already.

COACHES AND CAMPS

Jack recently graduated from a small liberal arts college where he played on the men's soccer team and earned a degree in political science. He spoke about his first postcollege job:

> I worked at a soccer camp during my summers home from college, and my boss asked me if I wanted to coach a U9 girls' travel soccer team in one of the local soccer clubs. [The boss] had expanded her camp business and was going to coordinate the girls' travel team practice sessions for this club and supply the teams with professional coaches. I guess I could be a professional coach since I had my F license after taking an online course last year. Once a week I run a training session for all of the U9 girls' travel players, and then I run a second session just for the team I coach. I certainly don't make enough to live on, but the boss said I might be able to hook up with a second team next year. The club was now requiring that all of the top travel teams in each age group use a professional coach. Then some of the "B teams" decided they also wanted paid coaches instead of parents. So there's more work possible.

Even if Jack gets that second coaching gig and continues working at summer camps, he still won't earn a living wage. But he will have his foot in the door of the expanding youth soccer coaching industry, where job opportunities abound and a living wage is possible if you can land the right gig and, possibly, speak with a certain accent. Although it's hard to earn a living wage as a youth soccer coach, it is increasingly *possible* to earn a living wage in that occupation, not to mention increasing the possibility of someday landing a college coaching job, which does pay a living wage. Coaching a few high-level travel teams and a high school team, combined with summer camp gigs, can almost pay the bills. While hard data on the number of youth coaches are not currently available, the leaders of a regional youth soccer association assured me that it was a growth occupation, especially for girls' teams:

> If you have a [higher-level] coaching license you can practically write your ticket as long as you are affiliated with one of the companies that the clubs contract with for trainers and coaches. It's not really possible anymore to be a free agent, at least not for youth clubs that are part of a community soccer club. But there's such a demand for coaches that clubs and teams are hiring people who

> don't have the proper training. The parents are all thinking about scholarships and the clubs are all thinking about adding teams, raising fees, and saying that "so and so from our club/team is playing DI soccer." It's more intense on the girls' side since the demand is growing faster than on the boys' side.

Speaking with a non-US accent really can be a résumé booster, as we will explore more in the next two chapters. But regardless of any stereotypical assertions of (for example) British soccer prowess, there are a lot of youth soccer coaches who came to the United States from other countries; they are part of an increased *supply* of coaches. Again, while hard numbers are not available, the NSCAA meeting is absolutely awash with British, German, and Latino expatriates. This trend is not lost on a regional youth soccer administrator who has witnessed the trend firsthand:

> American youth soccer is one of the most significant jobs programs ever made available to British men. These guys really love [soccer] and would like to stay in the game somehow after they finish university. Britain has a pretty closed system; you really need to know people in order to get involved with youth clubs. And there aren't as many of them compared to the number of clubs in the States. Plus, you have far more girls playing soccer in the US than in Britain. That means more jobs available. Most of them become citizens and try to make a living as a coach. The lucky ones might actually hook up with a college program, but that's pretty rare. If a Brit gets a college job, it's usually because he went to college in the States.

A few soccer clubs in the Philadelphia area even have specific directions on their websites for British citizens who want to coach in the States.

While the growth of girls' youth soccer in the United States has internationalized coaching opportunities, there are still significant cultural barriers involved with this trend. For one, girls' youth soccer is a new experience for many of these men, since it has a limited presence in their home countries. It can be disconcerting that ten-year-old girls approach soccer differently than ten-year-old boys. Related to this, very few women are able to take advantage of these international coaching opportunities, since there is less homegrown training where they might develop the skills and credentials necessary to get these US jobs (although they do have the accents). The bottom line is that the explosion of youth soccer leagues and travel teams is inexorably intertwined with the male-centered growth of professional coaching opportunities. This will be discussed at length in chapter 5.

Not all of the commercial enterprises linked to coaching are couched in the polite rhetoric of supplying interested players with an appealing product;

of developing an adequate commercial supply to meet consumer demand. Sometimes coaches interested in commercial gain will make players and families an offer that they can't refuse. Many parents of girls involved in different sports related stories about the pressure they were under to buy certain "products" that directly benefited a coach, although it seemed to be more common in soccer. One of these parents was especially explicit:

> The high school coach ran a summer soccer camp and directly told the girls that they would not be on the varsity team if they didn't sign up for at least one session. Most of the high school girls played on at least one premier travel team. I think three of them got some sort of college scholarship. They wanted to be on the high school team for fun, to play with their friends instead of against them since they were all on different travel teams. They wanted to play close to home instead of a hundred miles away. And here was this [coach] basically engaging in extortion. So we signed up for a session. And we didn't dare say anything about it for fear that the girls would be cut or have to play on the JV instead of with their friends. He's like that. I'm so embarrassed thinking about it. How we went along with it. We were all so scared to speak up. About a game, for God's sake. I'll bet we would have made a big fuss if the AP English teacher had required the kids take his AP prep course in order to be in the class. And why did the school hire a coach like that? I don't know if he's still there since we moved out of the area once [our daughter] went to college and her two friends were the last in their families to play. Maybe I don't want to know.

Summer soccer camps probably do not as a rule use extortion to get customers. However, the sheer number of them does create a climate for encouraging "creative" marketing techniques, especially in areas with a lot of competition for young soccer players. In eastern Pennsylvania alone, there are over a hundred summer soccer camps to choose from. Almost all are completely independent from US Youth Soccer and are run by companies like the one Jack works for. They may or may not be affiliated with clubs. The increasing number of camps certainly reflects consumer demand but is also a function of the coaching explosion. These camps provide a necessary income stream, not just to part-timers like Jack but to those (mostly men) who are trying to make a living as soccer coaches. The coaching component of the youth soccer to college pipeline relies on a vibrant summer camp industry.[13]

In youth field hockey, the only way to make a living while coaching (outside of college slots) is if you are a full-time staff member at one of the commercial clubs. A premier club might have ten or more teams in the various age groups, with five or six full-time coaches, each responsible for a few teams. Freelancers might be hired on an as-needed basis or to help with clinics or summer camps. Less prestigious clubs might have half that number of teams and far fewer full-time coaches. In the absence of highly organized travel leagues like in soccer (and increasingly in lacrosse), there simply aren't very many youth coaching opportunities. High school coaching is a part-time seasonal job, with slots frequently filled by existing school district staff. Unlike in soccer, summer camps are far less numerous and are only rarely offered independently of the elite travel clubs. All of the highly ranked intercollegiate programs run camps, and they might hire local coaches for a few hundred bucks per session, but they generally rely on their in-house staff and recent program graduates. One of the constraints facing independent operators is the shortage of field hockey–specific playing surfaces. Kristen, who plays Division I college field hockey, talked about how important that is:

> Most of the top college programs play on Astroturf. It's a completely different game than when played on [multipurpose] turf or grass. If you don't practice full-time on Astroturf, you have a hard time transitioning to it. It's a little easier transitioning the other way since the [non-Astroturf game] is a little slower. Even the DIII programs are looking for Astroturf experience. So you have to join a top club with plenty of Astroturf. Some clubs don't have any Astroturf or enough Astroturf for all of their teams. It's mostly the top clubs and colleges that run camps and clinics on Astroturf. More relaxed camps and clinics will often be on grass, and that's really a waste of time, even if it's in a cool place like near the beach.

Community fields almost always have grass or multisport artificial surfaces, which are amenable to a wider variety of activities. Additionally, the same "accent bias" present in soccer may be expanding within field hockey. Several longtime coaches mentioned to me a noticeable increase in colleagues hailing from Europe and Asia, where field hockey is much more popular and played by females and males. This mirrors to some extent the internationalization of field hockey roster slots discussed earlier, as well as the *masculinization* of female sports that will be explored in chapter 5.

With no youth sports to college pipeline, it is absolutely impossible to earn a living coaching girls' ultimate teams. You can pick up a few extra bucks at summer camps, but they are still fairly rare outside of ultimate's few hot spots. Interestingly, Nike has recently started offering a small number of overnight and day camps for ultimate players (some are not ultimate-only). This may or may not have an impact on ultimate's long-term commercial growth, but it seems that Nike may be showing some signs of interest in a sport that has typically had very little corporate involvement. Ultimate coaching pioneer Tiina Booth considered this:

> There's not quite enough demand yet to meet the increasing supply. I don't know if Nike's camps will be cost-effective. It took us a while for our camp to become viable, and we run it in conjunction with [the local town]. The corporate impact is very interesting. When you used to do a search for ultimate camps, ours would be at the top. Now it's like the eighth listed, because the Nike camps get better placed in the search engines or something like that. Nike sees this as a growth industry. Being on *SportsCenter* has helped. Having college championship games on ESPN helps, even if it's ESPN 12 or whatever. The men's professional league has probably encouraged Nike. But almost all of this exposure is for men, not women. I know that at least one of their camps is for males only. We used to have trouble drawing girls, too. They're all over at that lacrosse camp (points to next field) showing off for the college recruiters!

Figure skating is something of an anomaly since coaches *can* make a decent living teaching high-performing kids (mostly girls), even without any youth sports to college pipeline. Professional skating coaches are really at the heart of the sport. Young girls interested in pursuing competitive figure skating look for the right coach, and will pay upward of $100 for a half-hour lesson. Coaches try to affiliate themselves with skating clubs (often more than one) so they have access to deep-pocketed clients. There is nothing insidious about this. Figure skating has never framed itself as a sport of the masses, and skating clubs are far more interested in having regular dues-paying members than running open public skating sessions. US Figure Skating and the Professional Skaters Association (PSA) have very stringent accreditation procedures for coaches. There is no obligation that clubs and rinks use licensed coaches, but most do, since it makes them more attractive to potential clients, especially young ones (and their parents), and US Figure Skating has strict requirements about who is eligible to coach at its sanctioned events.

Technically speaking, there are "camps" for figure skaters. Those sanctioned by US Figure Skating are primarily for elite skaters who are interested in things like the Olympics. US Figure Skating does not sanction nonfederation skating camps, although it will list them on its website for interested members. Interestingly, most of these camps are very unlike typical pipeline summer sports camps where young athletes spend an all-inclusive five days (and sometimes nights) for one set price. Figure skating "camps" tend to revolve around à la carte purchases of ice time and lessons with coaches affiliated with the host rink or club, although you can bring in your own (nonaffiliated) coach for an extra fee. Overnight accommodations are also à la carte. This arrangement is, perhaps, a more honest and straightforward example of summer sports camps: an opportunity for coaches and rinks to make some extra money during the "slow" season, only without any accompanying promises of possible college scholarships. It would be interesting to see how figure skating's summer camp structure would change if it were to suddenly develop a youth sports to college pipeline.

HOCKEY AS A THREAT

The astronomical recent growth of the girls' youth ice hockey to college pipeline is putting enormous pressure on the occupational viability of figure skating coaches. Kids in general, and girls more particularly, are abandoning figure skating for ice hockey, or never even trying figure skating. As mentioned in chapter 1, PSA leaders are keenly aware of this shift, and executive director Jimmie Santee has written frequently about it in the association's bimonthly publication, *PS Magazine*.[14] This has led to tougher times for figure skating coaches. Ironically, perhaps, the declining occupational vitality of figure skating coaching is being compensated for by a rise in demand for hockey skating coaches, often called "power skating" coaches. Donna Helgenberg is a longtime figure skating coach (from a family of coaches) who recently made the transition to power skating coach. Business is booming, much of it from girls who have left figure skating or who decided not to try it despite being drawn to skating:

> I always made a living as a skating coach. How many industries are there when you can walk out of high school or college and start making over $100 an hour doing something you really like? If you can get the work. I started seeing about five to ten years ago that there was huge drop-off in the number of kids who were sticking with figure skating. They were maxing out, aging out, and moving on with their lives. There were fewer skaters, yet the number of coaches were the same. The ratio of coaches to skaters was just ridiculous. Even with the strong rules against poaching there was a lot of it going on. I had always loved hockey and played hockey, but saw that a lot of hockey players were bad skaters. You could always tell which girls had moved over from figure skating since they were by far the best skaters, even if they didn't know what to do with a puck. So I thought it would be sensible to start concentrating my teaching on hockey players. At first I had about a 50-50 split with figure skaters and hockey. Then it moved to 75 percent hockey and now that's all I do. The demand is ridiculous.

> It's almost an unlimited supply of kids who need to be better hockey skaters. And as the number of [figure] skaters continues to go down and the number of coaches stays about the same, it's going to get ugly. People are starting to struggle making a living as figure skating coaches. Why not supplement your income with some power skating lessons? It's a great side business. I do it as my main business but you don't have to. There's still a battle among coaches and rinks about figure skating versus hockey but it seems to be softening.

Summer hockey camps, generally for boys, have been historically concentrated in cooler climates where hockey has more popularity. That is starting to change, although more slowly than you might think given female ice hockey's growing youth sports to college pipeline. Boys' camps still outnumber girls' camps by about ten to one. A veteran rink manager in New Jersey commented,

> Throughout the industry we are starting to see a slight rise in summer camps outside of the traditional strong spots like New England and the [Great Lakes] region, especially for girls. That's a big help to us since there are a lot fewer skating parties and recreational skaters in the summer. But there aren't nearly as many camps as in dry land sports like lacrosse. I think it's because the [ice hockey] club teams are starting to play all year round and they are using up all of the coach's time, even in the summers. The youth coaches are all working real jobs. You can't make a living coaching bantam hockey, even in Minnesota. Someday, one or two coaches are going to take the plunge and quit their day jobs and do nothing but ice hockey. They can do club teams, high school teams, and summer camps. It's a risk, for sure. But once somebody pulls it off the floodgates will open. It will be more like soccer and lacrosse. I'll bet even some figure skating coaches could pull it off.

WINNING AS A COMMERCIAL PHENOMENON

In the last chapter we discussed the importance of winning for college coaches even in nonrevenue sports where the only substantively intrinsic upside of winning is that you are not losing. Within the corporate university, where budget allocations must be justified in some quantifiably tangible way, winning games or championships indicates that a bureaucratic unit (the team) and its manager (the coach) are performing at an acceptable level. Fully funded nonrevenue sports must perform (win) in accordance with this institutional support. In addition, winning signals to outsiders that a coach excels at her or his job; that the school's brand is solid. Upward mobility within the intercollegiate coaching profession depends on demonstrating competency. In all sports, whether revenue-generating or not, that usually boils down to winning percentages, conference championships, and NCAA tournament appearances.

The same basic tenets inform the youth sports world. Within conventional parameters, winning demonstrates a coach's value. Coaches often receive credit for successful teams (measured by winning) whether it's related to alleged tactical proficiency, recruiting prowess, or the good fortune of being in the same town as a young Carli Lloyd. Other possible measures of success, such as having low injury rates or maximizing players' fun, are largely discounted. Commercially speaking, winning for youth sports coaches increases their cachet of occupational prestige and allows them to secure more or better jobs that can help them increase their standard of living. Since the entire youth sports structure shares this concern with winning, it makes sense that players, parents, teams, programs, and leagues assume that a winning coach is a good coach, and that hiring such a coach will be one of the linchpins for maximizing the chances that girls will successfully navigate the youth sports to college pipelines.

The commodification and commercialization of youth sports coaching is greatly influenced by an occupational hierarchy where college positions command the most prestige and best salary. For many youth sports coaches, working at one job is a means for securing a better job in the future. A relatively young DI college soccer coach reflects,

> College coaching is the gold standard, especially in a DI program where you make a real salary at one job with one team. Some of the [DIII] programs allow this, but you also might have to coach a second team or also teach some phys ed classes. It's so much better than jumping around from team to team and finding extra camp work and clinics. Younger coaches have a better shot at coaching [women's] college teams if they have a thin résumé. Athletic directors want to see that you have been a success and they are mostly interested in your wins, your championships, and the number of kids you send to college programs. They really don't seem interested in philosophy or how satisfied your players have been. Some seem to prefer that you have coached in a school setting as well, but I don't think that's universal, at least not yet.

Thinking about occupational credentials offers a sociological alternative to the primarily psychological reasons we usually employ to understand why certain individuals (or teams or leagues) are so obsessed with winning. These psychological approaches focus on the personality attributes of athletes and coaches. These people are "driven to win" and possess above-average "competitive streaks" and high "intensity levels." It follows that such individuals simply can't help themselves and so might jeopardize a player's health (physical or mental) or enjoyment in order to win games or move up in the rankings. A DIII field hockey coach drove home that point:

> Let's face it. If I want to coach in a more prestigious DIII program or even a third-tier DI program then I have to win games and [conference] championships. Nobody wants to hear about graduation rates and team GPAs. That's the stuff of press releases, not successful job applications. I think some of it is just laziness. Everyone just assumes that if you win you must be good. But that's so superficial. To many of us, it's important that [our players] take something away from field hockey that is more than just trophies and banners. I know it sounds corny, but I always loved playing the game just to play the game. But look at that guy who used to coach all of those great gymnasts. His girls would win a billion medals and he was considered a genius but if you read [Mary Ryan's *Little Girls in Pretty Boxes*] you see that he was a tyrant. He was starving girls, mentally destroying them, making them practice when they were hurt. Anything to win.

We have all seen examples of youth sports coaches screaming at kids. Whether we positively rationalize such behavior as "part of the game" and necessary for player development, or negatively assess such behavior as a personality defect, we fail to appreciate the larger *structural* context that establishes winning as a conduit for occupational mobility and success. Coaches want to win not only because it is the normative standard within organized sports, but because it boosts their résumés. An obsession with winning may be in a coach's best economic self-interest, not just a function of her or his personality. A youth soccer club official who considers herself slightly out of the mainstream offered this story:

> We don't contract with a training academy, so we were looking to hire a head coach for our top-level girls' U10 team. Most of the applicants only talked about their winning percentages, how prestigious their current club was in terms of rankings, and how many girls they knew who went on to college. Remember, we're talking about nine-year-old girls. When I asked them about their philosophies about fun and personal growth, most of them answered along the lines of "winning is more fun than losing." These coaches believed that all [our club] cared about was getting this U10 girls' team into the top 100 of [our regional] rankings. It was just assumed that was our goal. For some of them it was explicit. They would say, "I have a track record of winning and will have this team ranked by the time they are U12." I guess that's what most of the clubs are looking for even though we are pretty well known as a low-key club.

YOUTH SPORTS AS A COMMODITY

The National Council of Youth Sports (NCYS) provides a fascinating metaphor for the commercialized and commodified youth sports to college pipeline. NCYS is an umbrella group whose members include almost all of the US national sports federations such as US Soccer, USA Field Hockey, USA Hockey, US Figure Skating, and USA Ultimate. It also includes youth sports–specific organizations like the AYSO, US Youth Soccer, Little League Baseball/Softball, Pop Warner Football, and Youth Basketball of America. In all, more than sixty million girls and boys play organized sports within these various associations. NCYS has grown significantly since its creation in 1979 and now includes over one hundred member groups. Its self-proclaimed vision is "to enhance the youth sports experience in America," and its motto is "a unified voice for youth sports." NCYS has historically advocated for increased youth sports participation as a matter of health, fitness, and fun. In the wake of Title IX, girls were an especially fertile target for this approach. More recently, NCYS has lobbied for increased training and background checks for youth sports coaches, preventing youth sports injuries, and bolstering K-12 physical education programs.

But the NCYS is not *just* an advocate for children's health and fun via sports participation. It also represents the commercial interests of the youth sports to college pipelines. According to NCYS's mission statement, it "represents the youth sports industry by advancing the values of participation, and educating and developing leaders." Indeed, the NCYS was a creation of the Sporting Goods Manufacturing Association, now called the Sport and Fitness Industry Association. It takes stands on these issues not only for altruistic reasons of childhood health and fun but to increase sales for its member organizations. As explained to me by a person familiar with the organization, NCYS's recent focus on safety and coaching background checks is partly driven by a desire to ease parental concerns about injuries and predator coaches.[15] Easing these concerns means increased participation in youth sports, which translates into more apparel/equipment purchases and more league fees. More kids playing sports is a good thing in and of itself, but it also feeds the commercial appetite of the youth sports to college pipelines.

NCYS's membership base reflects the enormous commercial scope of many youth sports to college pipelines. Among these members are several insurance groups, some concussion specialists, and even an online system for long-term monitoring of brain health ($70 per year). Most interesting, perhaps, are the large number of NCYS members that are part of the youth sports tournament industry, including a motel chain, wholesale food companies, and several regional convention/tourism bureaus. The Foley (Alabama) Recreation Department is one of these members. Foley is a small town of fifteen thousand people about twenty miles from the Gulf of Mexico. The city has created a quasi-independent entity, Foley Sports, to recruit and coordinate large youth sports tournaments such as the 2015 USSSA Baseball World Series and the 2015 Alabama Soccer Festival. The associations were attracted by, among other things, five baseball diamonds and three (lighted) soccer fields that are part of a venue that received the always prestigious "Sports Complex of the Year Award" in 2011 from the Alabama Turfgrass Association. The strong and seemingly accurate presumption is that if you build such a complex, then the players, coaches, teams, and families will come and spend lots of money on fees, lodging, food, gas, side trips, and tournament memorabilia. And they do come, although there is no systematic evidence that Foley is faring better than the hundreds of other towns that have staked their economic vitality on youth sports commercialization. There seems to be a growing demand for entities like Foley Sports. But how does this demand actually get created and transmitted to girls and their families?

4

CREATING DEMAND FOR THE YOUTH SPORTS TO COLLEGE PIPELINE

The pervasive and burgeoning youth sports industry could not exist without consumer demand. Girls are not born with aspirations of playing intercollegiate sports. Parents are not by nature obsessed with getting their kids to the "next level" no matter how high the financial or personal costs. Central to this demand is the culturally misrepresented and exaggerated likelihood of receiving a college scholarship and/or admissions advantage. Mind you, as discussed in chapter 2, the number of women receiving athletics-based scholarships has increased greatly over the past twenty-five years, but the apex of that increase has long passed. Families, though, are still acting as though it's the 1990s during the height of the boom. These exaggerated expectations also apply to admissions advantages not necessarily tied to scholarships. Colleges are responsible for much of this misrepresentation by being less than forthright about the realities of scholarships and admissions advantages available primarily to athletes. Neither schools nor the NCAA publicly list the number of scholarship equivalencies available in any particular school's program or the typical dollar amount of the equivalencies, although the NCAA does generically list the maximum number of scholarship equivalencies allowed in any given sport. However, even this can be misleading since it suggests that most if not all programs in a given sport are maximally funded.

But the corporatized, marketing legerdemain of intercollegiate athletics is only one piece of how demand is created for the youth sports to college pipelines. The youth sports industry itself also participates in exaggerating the quantity and quality of intercollegiate athletic opportunities while reinforcing the social class bias of accessing these opportunities. There are two overarching themes in the socially constructed demand for youth sports industry products and services. First, families think that purchasing the right products and services will increase their daughters' chances of receiving significant athletics-based financial aid or being more easily admitted to highly selective, prestigious colleges. This is probably the most important and commonly assumed undertone of consumer demand, and it pervades the entire industry. However, there is a second theme beyond admissions advantages that is also extremely important: prestige. Parents, especially, think it's cool that their daughters are "being recruited" by a certain noteworthy school, "have committed to" an athletically prestigious school, or are "playing X sport at X school." This is notably different from the more conventional, psychologically based idea that parents are trying to live vicariously through their kids; to capture the athletic glory that somehow escaped them thirty years earlier. A DI coach explained,

> We had a player about ten years ago who was recruited to play, but we didn't have enough money to offer her any kind of scholarship. Not even for books. Even if we did have the funds, we might not have given her anything since she wasn't going to get much playing time and didn't really have many transfer options. She came out of a good club program but was not a particularly strong player at her position. Just before our season began, her dad called and offered me a lump of money that he wanted packaged and presented to his daughter as some sort of partial scholarship that would go toward her attendance costs. She wouldn't know the source. He would be paying more money to the school and wanted the extra money called an athletic scholarship. I was a little stunned, so I asked him why he thought this was important. He said he wanted his daughter to be able to tell her current and former teammates that she was "on scholarship" at [this college]. He also said he wanted to tell his friends the same thing. I don't know if it was a status thing or just trying to justify the hundreds of thousands of dollars he poured into her [sports] training. We turned him down. It has happened a few times since then but never so blatantly. It's more like "is there anything I can do to help her get a scholarship next year?" I usually just say it's against NCAA rules and that's the end of it, whether it's true or not.

Variations of this story were repeated by many of the college coaches and athletic directors I spoke with, all of whom knew other colleagues with the same experiences. It seems that the allure associated with playing varsity college sports goes beyond any financial or admissions subsidy, and beyond any psychological need to fulfill some missed youth sports glory.

CORPORATE MARKETING STRATEGIES

A lot of very smart people are spending a lot of time and resources trying to convince consumers that their products will help young athletes successfully enter and navigate the youth sports to college pipeline. Apparently, people are listening. The NSCAA Conference exhibition hall was the place to go for both creating and fulfilling the soccer-based dreams of players and families, and increasing the profits of those who can exploit those dreams. The most ostentatious presentation was by a niche company touting a revolutionary shin guard retailing for $80 a pair, about twice the price of current top-shelf shin guards and about four times more than a standard pair. This company paid a staggering amount of money to set up shop outside the exhibition hall in one of the main convention throughways, and used soccer legend Pelé as a spokesperson. The looping video on display insisted that protecting your tibias in this fashion could take players to the next level. It was amazing to see how superior soccer skills were equated with having extremely comfortable shin guards that were both flexible and impervious to semiautomatic weapon fire.

Soccer footwear receives the most attention from apparel companies and is marketed as a real difference maker for athlete and club success. Again, this is not surprising given how central feet are to playing soccer. In the NSCAA exhibition hall, there were at least fifteen claims to "revolutionary" designs in footwear technology. Many of these claims revolved around the composition, shape, and pattern of the cleats themselves. Apparently, moving a single cleat one-half inch in either direction is the difference between being a hero or a goat. Next to footwear, moisture-wicking fabrics seem to be the current rage. One vendor told me with a straight face that the extra moisture removed by *their* product could increase an athlete's speed by one to two miles per hour, and that this extra speed was a sure way to get noticed by college coaches, which is good for both athletes and their home clubs. Ninety bucks (per piece) for a space-age base layer is a small price to pay for a supposedly $250,000 soccer scholarship.

But perhaps what is most interesting about these marketing campaigns is that they were not primarily targeted at players and families, but at coaches and league officials, who made up about 90 percent of conference attendees. The underlying assumption seemed to be that coaches held some sway with players' footwear selections; or elite programs might consider standardizing footwear for all their teams. This assumption was confirmed during a completely random encounter with an apparel company representative. This person intimated that coaches or program officials often receive some "excess inventory" (his words) if they can get a certain number of players to use certain products. There was no standard formula of X number of shoes equals Y amount of excess inventory, but apparently some general quid pro quo was in operation. Indeed, as we will see throughout this chapter, many other pieces of the youth soccer industry use coaches (especially) to help market their products in return for some in-kind gratitude.

Expensive field equipment, such as Kwik Goal's $38,000 luxury benches (per pair) mentioned in chapter 3, are also touted as a way for young athletes to successfully navigate the youth sports to college pipeline by identifying those clubs most committed to their success. A representative from a different company told me,

> The soccer clubs look at these high-end purchases in two ways. One is that they think it helps them attract better players who equate expensive amenities with a successful program. It's kind of what colleges do when courting football players and impressing them with weight rooms and player-only cafeterias with endless supplies of steak and ice cream. I don't think it's a matter of charging families more to play on the team, just that they will get a better bang for their buck. The [other reason for this purchase] is to attract teams to their tournaments, especially when they are held during seasons that may have bad weather or hot weather. I have seen brochures from tournament sponsors that highlight their sheltered seating. The subtle message is that kids will perform better for the college coaches if they are dry and comfortable rather than cold and uncomfortable.

As also mentioned in the last chapter, the NCSAA vending exhibition has been shifting from emphasizing apparel to emphasizing equipment and services. These companies' marketing strategies almost completely revolve around increasing the likelihood of players landing that coveted scholarship or admissions advantage. Software packages give clubs and families the ability to track important statistics and package them for recruiters. Agility training systems provide both exercises and computerized analysis to make sure you can dazzle college coaches. One of the more prevalent services was international tournaments and camps that promised teenage players a week of competition against the world's best youth players, plus some interesting sightseeing. The brochures for these programs generally include pictures of both boys and girls, with some even announcing which colleges its former campers now attend without mentioning if they are playing soccer at college or receiving any kind of scholarship. Why such programs would be marketed to coaches became clearer in a conversation with one company representative who said they try to make trips "a little more affordable" (her words) to coaches and their families, especially if they can get more than one team from a club to sign up. It may not exactly be a kickback, but it is fairly close.[1]

Even with field hockey's static intercollegiate presence, equipment sales are not lagging, although there has been a change in the commercial dynamic. A New England–based sporting goods retailer explained,

> Our marketing strategy for field hockey sales is upgrading. We don't really see a net rise in the number of people playing the sport, but we do see people wanting to get higher-end equipment and we do nothing to dissuade them. There might even be fewer girls playing than ten years ago, but those who do play are buying more expensive sticks, and [both indoor and outdoor] sticks, since they are more likely to play year-round than before. Softball is showing a similar "upscaling" trend here, but my colleagues in warmer climates say it is also expanding there in addition to upscaling. Lacrosse sales are through the roof here, especially for girls. More kids playing and what seems to be an arms race for getting the best equipment. They ask me which sticks will get them to the next level and most impress the college recruiters. I don't think there's an answer to that. This is all good equipment and one product will be only marginally different than another. A lot of it boils down to marketing. All the manufacturers have signed up national team members to endorse their [field hockey] sticks. I've even heard a rumor that some clubs receive a "fee" for pushing their players to use certain products. Kind of what they used to do in college basketball during the Sonny Vaccaro era.[2]

LESS-CORPORATE MARKETING STRATEGIES

Competitive figure skating has a far more "personal" approach when it comes to marketing equipment and apparel. The smaller companies making and selling boots and blades do not have a corporate presence or million-dollar advertising budgets. Marketing their products primarily entails convincing coaches and clubs to somehow encourage pupils and members to use them. More publicly, it's helpful when popular skaters use your equipment, and these companies' websites are awash with pictures of successful figure skaters from around the world, but you don't see television commercials during the Olympics claiming that "2014 U.S. Women's National Champion Gracie Gold used Edea skates in Sochi." For one thing, such an ad would be prohibitively expensive for a small company. It's also questionable whether there is a large enough market to make it worthwhile, or if advertising would have any overall impact on sales. One longtime club skating official told me she doesn't know of a single case over two decades where a serious figure skater selected a product based on an advertisement in (for example) US Figure Skating's official magazine. The federation's website does include corporate sponsors on its home page, but none are for skating-specific equipment. Large corporations such as Nike are not involved in making or selling skating dresses. At the highest competitive level, these are almost always custom made and so do not lend themselves to corporate standardization.

Ice hockey, with its expanding intercollegiate presence, has a much more typical corporate approach to marketing. USA Hockey's website prominently displays links to hockey-specific companies such as Bauer and Total Hockey, which claims on its own website to be the exclusive hockey equipment retailer of USA Hockey. But there are also links to Reebok and Nike. As mentioned in chapter 3, Reebok bought the CCM brand in 2004 and now uses that name for all of its hockey equipment except sticks. Few things reflect a corporatized industry more than mergers and acquisitions. CCM/Reebok/Adidas prominently features NHL superstar Sidney Crosby to endorse its products. STX endorsers include nine men (both professional and amateur) and one woman (two-time Olympic silver medalist Hillary Knight). Nike does not yet sell ice hockey equipment or even ice hockey apparel, except for base layers that are not sports specific. It is interesting, then, that they would have a link on USA Hockey's home page. Perhaps Nike will get more heavily involved in ice hockey as participation continues to increase, especially for girls. Given the expanding presence of women's intercollegiate hockey, this is probably a corporate bet worth taking.

Five Ultimate, VC Ultimate, and Savage have tried hard to cultivate an "ultimate-friendly" marketing strategy to set them apart from the corporate behemoths such as Nike. Patagonia, although not officially endorsed by USA Ultimate, supplies apparel to many ultimate teams and markets itself as a socially responsible, noncorporate business that is consistent with the spirit of the game. This overall approach seems to have been marginally successful. Many high school and college players from diverse places told me that they preferred supporting ultimate-only companies over the corporate giants (or even over Patagonia); that it was more consistent with the sport's values. However, USA Ultimate officials were concerned that the increasingly visible men's professional leagues, which fall outside its jurisdiction, might alter the sport's small-scale commercial character. It's also possible that large apparel and equipment corporations would become more interested in ultimate if it actually became an Olympic sport (beyond mere IOC recognition), and it received a little more media visibility at the Olympics than do judo and badminton. But without any varsity intercollegiate presence, it is unlikely that the corporations will become interested, or that the small niche companies will experience staggering growth and expansion. And there remains a palpable schism within the ultimate community about the benefits of intense, corporate-centered, commercial growth.

TEAMS AND SCHOLARSHIPS

Kim, whose daughter Susan endured three knee operations, recalled her first contact with soccer's youth sports to college pipeline:

> When Susie was nine, we started getting e-mails from coaches of elite travel teams in the area who had heard that she was an excellent player and might be looking for a more serious soccer experience. She was a very good player, but we wondered how they knew this. Did they send it just to us or to every family in the league? We were very happy with the town soccer league that had a variety of options, including the travel team she played on with a lot of her friends from school. Her travel team had one practice a week and a game on the weekends, usually within thirty minutes since there are so many teams around here. Then the e-mails started coming. I didn't even know what an elite team was. We must have had a dozen invitations to attend tryouts. Some even offered to waive the tryout and put her right on the team. Almost all of these coaches claimed that playing on their team would increase her chances of getting a college scholarship, and they usually listed the schools that their former players were attending. Susie was in third grade, for God's sake! She had just learned to multiply and divide. College? Really? But we took the bait. We were smitten with the idea of Susie playing soccer at Princeton or North Carolina. Susie learned to think that way eventually. Mostly, though, she just wanted to play.

Susan also remembers this change in her soccer experience:

> Suddenly I went from knowing everyone on the team to knowing nobody on the team. The girls didn't accept me at first. They had been playing together for a year or two. They ignored me when we went for pizza after tournaments. I really missed my friends, but my parents said I should give it some

> more time. Eventually they accepted me, but maybe that was because we moved to the bigger field and needed more players! I tried not to exclude other players who joined after me, but I probably did without even knowing it. I couldn't believe how much more intense our practices were than on the other team. I was becoming a much better player, but all I did was soccer. Soon it was all I wanted to do. I saw more of my teammates and coaches than I did of my family.

Girls can pay to play for hundreds of teams in areas with well-developed youth soccer to college pipelines. Coaches and programs must convince families that their particular product is truly the best, and they can focus on any number of marketable qualities. By far the most prominent marketing strategy is highlighting girls from the team/program who are now attending or "committed to" certain colleges. You can visit hundreds of websites for premier soccer and field hockey programs and very quickly find these names, including players as young as fifteen who may have "committed to" a college program, although the details of that commitment are never stated, especially since the NCAA forbids true commitments until a player's senior year of high school. Indeed, I randomly selected and traced several dozen "committed" players who should have been in their first two years of college at a DI university but were not listed on the team's varsity roster. Others were on the roster but received little playing time (according to available statistics and narratives), usually indicating they received either no scholarship money or a very small partial scholarship.

Listing names of former team/program members who are now "in" college has proven to be a wildly successful strategy at both manipulating the reality of college scholarships/admissions advantages and cashing in on this manipulation. A successful veteran high school field hockey coach commented,

> The parents think that if their daughter is a good athlete then she can get a scholarship. They have no idea about the reality. Yes, they are partly misled, but they are mostly coming from upper-middle-class backgrounds and really should know better. It's like they almost *want* to be fooled into thinking about scholarships or Ivy League admittance. But I understand where it's coming from. Especially the club coaches. They are relentless. I had to sit down with a family the other day and really tell them about the lay of the land. Their daughter, a junior, is just not going to get a scholarship. Even a partial one. But her club coaches keep saying she can if she keeps working hard and, presumably, signs up for a few extra clinics over the summer. That's why they insist on specialization. It's not for the athlete. [This girl] would benefit from cross-training. It's so they can have more girls signing up for more teams, clinics, and camps. It's for the club's balance sheet. It's shameless what some of

> these clubs will do for money. This family drives four hours round-trip two or three days a week so the daughter can train with this elite program. They are always having "special nights" when college coaches come to the practices to feed the myth. In the end, [she'll] be playing club field hockey at a DI school or varsity at a DIII school, but she will have to get admitted with her grades; there won't be a coaches' slot for her. Ivies are out of the question. Her grades are good but not good enough without being a top-shelf player.

Perhaps the most barefaced example of this marketing strategy came during an NSCAA panel presentation titled "How to Talk to Parents," whose participants included coaches and officials from soccer clubs that occupied the middle layer between recreational programs and so-called premier organizations such as ECNL. As a youth sports coach myself, I am always interested in communicating with parents. But the session's focus was quite a surprise:

> You have got to start telling the parents early and often that your team and club will be a ticket to the next level. Don't wait. Start right at U9 or even earlier so they start thinking about travel as an investment in college. Don't just have information on the club website, have it available in nice brochures. The key is identifying recent college players who were in your club. Have a picture of them in their college uniform. If even one family signs up or jumps clubs, it will pay for itself. Have one or two of the college kids come back and do a clinic saying how great the program is in getting you prepared for college. The girls and their families are especially open to this idea. Women's soccer is getting more exposure, and Title IX is opening up new opportunities. You can say how there aren't enough good players to fill these slots and that college coaches will really be looking everywhere for players who have the skills your club can teach. The young girls will be even more impressed if you can bring back a college player who used to play on their very same travel team. It doesn't matter if she's on scholarship or not. Once you get the families thinking about college they will start considering full-year commitments, camps, specialized training, conditioning, and all the other services your club can provide, or should be providing if it isn't yet.[3]

With no youth sports to college pipelines, figure skating and ultimate Frisbee clubs do not recruit members in this fashion. Instead, figure skating clubs are more likely to highlight the success of their affiliated coaches in producing championship skaters at various age and skill levels. Several club officials told me that they didn't think this kind of marketing was particularly effective, but that it was standard operating procedure within the sport. Most new members come through word of mouth or when well-respected coaches expand their affiliations to include more clubs. Elite ultimate clubs, such as Seattle Riot, might mention whether their members do or did play in college, but this seems to be informational rather than promotional. Ice hockey clubs, on the other hand, prominently announce any of their players who are enrolled in or "committed to" college programs. A website review of twenty randomly selected clubs from the MYHockey U19 rankings clearly reflects the centrality of this marketing strategy. Navigation around the website is usually not even required to be presented with the names and college commitments (and often photos) of club players. Interestingly, several of the clubs seem to feature female success stories over male success stories. This could be reflecting the quickly expanding world of women's intercollegiate hockey and attempts by elite clubs to meet the rising demand for youth skaters. Of course, as with soccer and field hockey, there is no indication of whether these ice hockey players are receiving an athletics-based scholarship, how much the scholarship covers, or whether playing the sport even figured into their college acceptances.

TEAMS AND RANKINGS

Rankings are another important marketing tool for elite commercial clubs and teams. This strategy, again, is more salient in those sports with significant youth sports to college pipelines. Whether these rankings emanate from independent commercial enterprises such as GotSoccer or from a sport's governing federation, parents and players take them very seriously. Lila's father, Christopher, had done a lot of research on rankings while searching for her new team:

> Sometimes the rankings contradict the local league placements, so you have to be careful. For instance, one team played in the highest division but had a low regional ranking. Another team played in Division III but had a very high ranking. I've been trying to find out if it's better to look at the short term or the long term and which of the ranking systems are more respected by college coaches. Now I have to think whether joining an ECNL team with its ranking system is better than a regular [US Youth Soccer] team that uses GotSoccer rankings. Lila and I usually check the rankings every week to see how important any upcoming games are, and how much more serious the girls should be. Sometimes their minds can wander.

Remember, Lila and her friends are nine years old, which could explain some of the wandering minds. Even though Christopher doesn't quite understand the ranking system, he is convinced that it will be a crucial part of Lila's journey through the youth soccer to college pipeline. One thing Christopher is missing is the disconnect between these *team* rankings and college coaches' search for *individual* players. The coach quoted in chapter 3 was clear that there can be poor players on strong teams and vice versa; that team rankings are only marginally useful in recruitment. There are no prizes or medals awarded if a team or club has a high ranking, although it may allow for participation in certain top-shelf showcase tournaments. These rankings, then, are important public relations tools for soccer clubs and teams who are in a perpetual hunt for players to help maintain their rankings. It is part of their "brand."

There are youth sports parents who have seen through the madness, but they seem to be minority voices in the dominant narrative about youth sports to college pipelines. Claire, the former Division I soccer player we met in the introduction, has a younger sister, Madeline, who now lives in a youth soccer hotbed where the family moved after Claire went to college. Their mom, Rayna, manages Madeline's travel soccer team:

> I've never seen anything like these parents, even back in [our previous residence], which took youth soccer pretty seriously. They are already talking about scholarships and getting into Ivy League schools when the girls are nine. They get a lot of their information off of this soccer blog that is just filled with nonsense. I tried talking to some of the parents, but they don't want to hear anything. I try telling them about the reality Claire and her friends are facing, but they just sneer and probably assume that she just wasn't that good. They never actually saw her play. One husband and wife team compete with each other to see how many kids they can poach from competing teams. It's like a fantasy soccer league but with ten-year-old kids. I'm the manager of Madeline's team, and the politics are ridiculous. I only stay with it because I want to protect her from the insanity. Switching teams is too much of a risk. I don't like her current team, but better to lie with the enemy you know, or however that saying goes.

Issues with increasing parental intensity, and the misunderstanding that breeds it, are not lost among those youth soccer officials who are trying to keep youth sports in perspective. One commented,

> The GotSoccer rankings have taken on a life of their own. Players, parents, coaches, and league presidents all spend too much time caring about these rankings. Good teams won't go to non-GotSoccer tournaments for fear of dropping in rank. They think that the college coaches are only going to visit tournaments with a lot of GotSoccer points and watch the games played by

> the highest-ranked teams. My god, even the U11s are ranked, and I have seen parents and coaches arguing about whether to travel an extra five hundred miles in order to accumulate more ranking points. They are calculating whether a higher finish in a lower [division] will secure more points than a lower finish in a higher division. For ten-year-olds! I don't think these U11 girls are being recruited by college coaches. But who knows these days.

As the long-serving technical director of the Eastern Pennsylvania Youth Soccer Association (EPYSA), Mike Barr has seen a lot of parents doing a lot of crazy things:

> I was watching an elite U8 club team practice in March. It was 6 p.m. and about thirty degrees with a twenty-five-mile-per-hour wind. The coach, who I know well, was chastised in an e-mail by a parent that there was not enough instruction going on in the shortened hour-and-a-half session. The coach told me he was only trying to keep them moving so they wouldn't get frostbite. My guess is that he thought it would be best to cancel practice for the sake of the kids' health, but the parents might have had a nutty. These kids are seven years old![4]

Field hockey clubs also prominently display the rankings of their many teams, especially when they are high rankings. Remember, though, that these rankings are not themselves commercial enterprises like in soccer. Presumably, the relatively small number of field hockey clubs and teams does not present a viable market for private commercial companies that produce and sell rankings. In a sense, USA Field Hockey provides free to clubs what their soccer counterparts must pay for: allegedly accurate rankings that are useful for marketing purposes. The relationship between rankings and club prestige is very strong among field hockey consumers. Jenny, a Division III college field hockey player, explained,

> Everybody [in southeastern Pennsylvania] just knows that if you want to get a DI scholarship or play Ivy then you better get on a top ["Club A" or "Club B"] team that are almost always ranked in the top five nationally. Even their second-tier teams are better than other clubs' top teams. If you want to play DIII, you'll be OK playing for [the other top twenty] clubs, which aren't quite as intense. ["Club X"] has a lot of good players, but they don't plan to play in college so are mostly looking to stay sharp for high school or have some fun. I knew I wanted to play at a small liberal arts school, or maybe my parents made it clear that I would be going to a small school. Whatever, they didn't see any reason to play for [Club A], which can be pretty crazy and really expensive. You also have to train during the summers, and I prefer going [to the beach]

> with my cousins. A couple of my friends were on second-level teams there, and even that was really intense. They're always pushing you to make the top team so you have to attend more clinics and workshops. I don't know anyone on the top team, but I can only imagine.

Ironically, the impact of rankings may actually hurt smaller clubs/teams looking to expand field hockey in areas where it is relatively unpopular, or to provide less-intense experiences for those who may not wish to get entrenched in the youth field hockey to college pipeline. In places such as western Michigan and western North Carolina, where field hockey is not a recognized high school varsity sport, interested players must join the few club teams spread over thousands of square miles. These clubs have far lower national rankings than most of their in-state counterparts, but their websites remain awash with ranking trends and news about who is going to what college. Despite these clubs' rather modest place within the field hockey pipeline, their marketing strategies still resonate with families looking to get their daughters to that next level and hopefully secure *some* college admissions payoff. A former coach in one of these fringe regions explained,

> Rankings and college placements are everything around here. Kids and families will jump ship in a second if they think the team a hundred miles away will give them a better scholarship opportunity. They don't mind traveling great distances for training since we go that far already just to play other teams. Sometimes all it takes is for a club team to win a game or two at Festival or NITs in order to get new players. Hell, sometimes they only have to be *playing* in Festival or NITs since some clubs, including mine, don't go. It makes it tough to get more players involved in our less-populated part of the state, since these more prestigious teams are usually near [larger cities] and may have relationships with the few DI programs in the state. The FUNdamentals program is great, but it can't compete with the college dreams that some parents have. It's all we can do here to keep afloat. If we could have gotten one girl into a prestigious college program it could have turned things around. Just one, believe it or not. But I won't lie about our placements. Some teams do.

Since figure skaters are ranked as individuals, clubs may only indirectly benefit from boasting that one of their members is a nationally ranked junior at the gold level. Still, clubs are not averse to mentioning these successes, although they are much more subtle about it than are soccer and field hockey clubs. Ice hockey teams seem to highlight college commitments more than rankings, but rankings prowess is certainly not shied away from, especially in areas where there might be several elite teams competing for the small but fast-growing numbers of female players. Ultimate clubs often do feature their USA Ultimate rankings but, as with the announcements of their "college" players, the presentation is decidedly low-key. This may be consistent with the spirit of the game but also could be rooted in the modest size and geographic concentration of elite ultimate clubs. A former Division I college player explained,

> Clubs don't need to boast about rankings or who is playing at what college that may or may not have made nationals. We all know what's going on. The community is so small and concentrated in places like Seattle and Eugene that I knew every [person in my age group] on every high-level club team. We would try out for nationals together, we would play pickup together, we would play with or against each other on school teams, we would take a mixed team to a tournament. The [girls and women] don't need rankings to know which are the strongest teams and which are not quite there. We know. We see. We talk. I mean, if there was no official ranking system we would still rank the clubs in the same way. Besides, winning club championships and tournaments is way more important in our eyes than rankings.

If ultimate ever became a varsity intercollegiate sport with associated scholarships and admissions advantages, the clubs would certainly market their rankings (and college placements) more prominently since new clubs would quickly spring up to get in on the action, and new players and families would eagerly look to maximize their success in ultimate's new youth sports to college pipeline. Currently, though, ultimate clubs barely register on the commercial marketing index compared with soccer, field hockey, ice hockey, and even figure skating. Nevertheless, as discussed in chapter 1, elite ultimate is still increasingly a "pay-to-play" sport even without college scholarships or admissions advantages. It is currently not easy for poorer families to play high-level ultimate, and those financial obstacles would inevitably get worse were ultimate to become a varsity intercollegiate sport, or even an Olympic sport.

SHOWCASE TOURNAMENTS

In terms of creating demand for the youth sports to college pipelines, showcase tournaments operate in two separate but overlapping domains. First, teams and clubs will highlight their showcase tournament participation and success as a marketing tool, adding yet another supposed metric about why players and families should spend money on one club team versus another.

As mentioned in the preceding chapters, showcase tournaments have become *the* interface between youth sports and intercollegiate athletics for almost every activity except football and men's basketball.[5] It's also important to remember that the expansion of these showcases was very much driven by college coaches. Second, the companies (or clubs) who run money-making showcase tournaments must market their products to assure that players and teams attend. This marketing always revolves around the college coaches and programs who will be attending the tournaments to allegedly recruit future players and dole out scholarships and admissions advantages. After all, the "showcase" has to be for someone. Otherwise, it's just a tournament.

In terms of teams and clubs highlighting their prowess at showcase participation, there seems to be a disconnect between team success and individual success. An elite club soccer coach reflected,

> It's utterly amazing how crappy we often play at the showcases. All the girls are trying to show off for the coaches. They almost couldn't care less about the team. I guess I can understand. The college coaches are not recruiting our team. If one of our center backs continually kicks the ball eighty yards downfield with either foot it doesn't do much for our transition game, but it will probably get the attention of some coaches. I think the coaches do want to see how you play in a team setting, not just what your individual skills are. But the girls and especially their parents think they need to show off.

Ironically, this creates a sort of Catch-22 for youth team coaches and officials. They want the team to do well in showcases in order to market that success to future customers. But they also want individuals to do well by getting scholarships so they can use that for marketing. But there may be an inherent contradiction between the team doing well and individuals doing well. After speaking with several soccer club officials and examining dozens of websites, it seems that individual success is more important to marketing strategies than team success. But both are featured in club marketing campaigns.

This marketing preference also seems to be true within field hockey, although there are far fewer clubs involved and a remarkable consistency as to which clubs are highly ranked year after year. Among the most elite clubs and teams, then, rankings are generally ho-hum, since they reflect rather predictable performances in the handful of yearly tournaments sponsored or endorsed by USA Field Hockey. Indeed, clubs seem much more likely to market their successful performance in these tournaments than their resulting ranking; or even (as mentioned above) their mere *participation* in elite tournaments, or how many of their players *participate* in Futures. Soccer club team marketing is more challenging with its myriad of competing tournaments and ranking systems that themselves need to be marketed. Field hockey clubs' tournament-based marketing strategy is far less complex.

Girls' youth ice hockey teams also market their prowess in elite tournaments, although not quite as prominently as they market their college success stories. The relationship, of course, is fairly clear to families, as is the aforementioned irony of team success versus individual success. Maria, a former figure skater and current parent of a U14 female ice hockey player, commented,

> Travel [ice] hockey and high school [ice] hockey in this area are still pretty new. Many of the teams don't seem equipped to get attention from college coaches. Smart parents will do their research and see which of the teams play regularly at high-profile tournaments. Rankings are pretty silly, although people do get caught up in them. I've seen a lot of girls get recruited from bad teams. The college coaches can see who the skaters are, who the players are. But you have to get to the important tournaments. Sometimes being on a losing team can actually help your kid stand out to these recruiters. Someone with the same ability on a great team may not get as much ice time. My advice to families would be get your daughter on a mediocre Tier 1 team that plays in things like the [East Coast] Wizards Columbus Day Tournament, even if they go 0-3 in pool play. The point is to get a scholarship, not to be a bench player on a championship team.

Ultimate clubs will also market their participation and success in elite tournaments but, again, this is treated more as an end in itself in the absence of any youth sports to college pipeline.

Perhaps more interesting than elite teams marketing their participation in showcase tournaments is the actual marketing of the tournaments themselves. Showcase tournaments, especially in soccer, have become a huge part of the youth sports industry. The number of soccer tournaments calling themselves "showcase" expands every year. The tournament organizer we met in the last chapter knows what's important in distinguishing your tournament from the competition:

> Of course it's about landing the college coaches. If just one or two girls get "discovered" at your tournament you could be set for years, especially if it's by a ranked school! Once I would tell other tournament organizers that it was more important spending twenty-five hours getting an Anson Dorrance or Steve Swanson than spending one hour getting twenty-five unknowns from unranked schools.[6] But things are changing, and the girls don't seem to care as much where they play, just that they can get a scholarship somewhere, or

> perhaps into an Ivy or prestigious DIII school like Amherst. I knew someone once who simply said there would be forty DI coaches at the tournament then hired a bunch of locals with clipboards and sunglasses to sit in the bleachers behind some yellow tape. The brochure only spoke about the number of coaches attending, not their names, so it wasn't as big a lie as if it had actually dropped people's names or their schools. The kids came! I would never do that because of the risk, and this guy isn't in the business anymore, but it was actually a clever scam, although highly unethical.

The multifaceted girls' youth soccer to college pipeline, with its myriad of competing commercial alternatives, seems to be cementing a tournament-focused strategy emphasizing college payoffs. This is apparent by the decisions within US Club Soccer, which for years emphasized league play as a pathway to national team selection, not to college scholarships. According to a regional youth soccer association official,

> For many years, US Club Soccer didn't seem to care much about the college stuff. I guess they finally figured out that the [girls] and their families were much more interested in college than in the Olympics or World Cup. I think that explains the creation of ECNL. ECNL's marketing strategy was brilliant. It focused on girls and implied that US Youth Soccer was overly concerned with boys. I don't think that [gender bias] was true, but it was still brilliant. The girls' youth market was real high growth. There are certainly more slots for college players than for Olympians! ECNL's success even encouraged the [National Premier Leagues] into doing showcases now. That's a huge break from their original mission.

It's possible that soccer showcase tournaments will reach a point where the supply exceeds consumer or recruiter demand. In fact, ECNL has now capped its number of teams, which might hint at market saturation. That said, a quick trip on the Internet can identify many more soccer tournaments, such as Copa ESPN, each crowning its own national champion, presumably in front of college coaches eager to identify the next Alex Morgan. As mentioned in the last chapter, this expanding tournament-based youth soccer system is not necessarily identifying or generating more talented soccer players, it is just figuring out different ways to package and market existing talent for eager customers. Kim was one of those eager customers:

> We started to use Susie's showcase tournaments as our family vacations even if they were in unappealing places. We would take the kids out of school for a few days and try to find lots of touristy things to do in addition to watching soccer games. That's not always easy to do when you're at a tournament in

> some suburb where your entertainment options amount to choosing the best local mall. Sometimes we would get lucky and have a tournament near the beach or an amusement park, although [my youngest son] tends to get sick on the rides. Of course, [the Disney Showcase] was often our big trip of the year. We didn't have many home-cooked family Christmas dinners once Susan and her team were in the hunt for scholarships. I still feel like a fool in hindsight for getting sucked into the scholarship fever. But all the college coaches are there. We could have saved all that money and just used it for tuition instead of spending it all on what turned out to be a partial scholarship for a school she would have been accepted to anyway. At least we had a lot of company in drinking the Kool-Aid.

Field hockey's youth sports to college pipeline also revolves around tournaments, but the institutional terrain, and hence the marketing, is far different than in soccer. There are significantly fewer showcase tournaments, and everybody involved in serious youth field hockey knows about them. Even middle school girls I spoke with who had only been playing the sport for a year or two were aware of the Disney Showcase and Festival. Kristen used to be a middle schooler like that, even though she now plays in a Division I college program:

> I mostly played soccer in the fall when I was a kid. I didn't even know what field hockey was until I was about twelve. It seemed really boring, and I couldn't figure out the skirts! I tried it in gym class one day and thought it was OK. I was actually pretty good at it, maybe because I'm kind of short and you have to lean over a lot. I played on a local travel soccer team but wasn't a star or anything. My gym teacher coached the middle school field hockey team and I really liked her, so I tried out. I was suddenly a really good field hockey player instead of just an ordinary soccer player. A coach from a different school came to me one day and asked if I had started thinking about college scholarships. I was like thirteen and didn't even know what college was. She invited me to play for her travel team. She seemed cool, so I joined that team and started playing more field hockey and quit soccer. Then I joined an indoor team that played in the spring. Before you know it, I was playing almost the entire year. I still played for the school, but that was mostly for socializing. The coach was my English teacher. My club teams became way more important, and the coaches there talked all the time about college scholarships and Disney. That was how they motivated us. We wouldn't get to go to Orlando if we didn't work hard enough. And we wouldn't get a scholarship unless we played in Disney. It was nonstop about Disney.

With so few showcases, and with recent additions connected with the National Field Hockey Coaches Association (NFHCA) meetings, it's understood that most college coaches will be at all of these events. Still, it never hurts to be sure when advertising:

> The NFHCA Top Recruit Winter Escape will be held in conjunction with the 2016 NFHCA Annual Convention, meaning hundreds of college coaches will be in Naples, Fla. that weekend. The convention typically draws more than 250+ college coaches annually and with no additional travel expenses, they will be ready to recruit that weekend. The NFHCA Executive Board and Corrigan Sports have created their recruiting tournament series with you, the prospective student-athlete, and college coaches in mind.[7]

Interestingly, these joint NFHCA/Corrigan ventures also offer individual players the opportunity to join "house teams" if they are unaffiliated with a club or high school team (unlikely), or if their team has chosen not to attend the event (more likely). For a $150 registration fee, they will be placed on an appropriate squad where their talents can be displayed before 250-plus college coaches *and* they can keep their tournament pinnies. Such house teams are not currently available at Disney, Festival, or NITs, which primarily resemble club championships. An idealistic assessment of this would be that it gives some girls an opportunity to get a college field hockey scholarship or admissions advantage (or just play highly competitive field hockey) without having to join a prohibitively expensive club program; or perhaps it is a way to stay sharp for Futures tryouts (which cost $485). A slightly more suspicious assessment would be that it attracts some extra bodies to these commercial ventures by suggesting that anybody with some talent or initiative can get to that "next level" if they can scrounge up $150 in addition to paying for transportation, lodging, and food. It would be interesting to monitor the future trajectory of these house team players.

In the absence of any commercial youth sports to college pipeline, figure skating's highly centralized and regulated competitions have no need for sophisticated or deceptive marketing. Some of these competitions are part of an intricate qualifying system for USFS's national championships while others are independent of the qualifying system but still part of the USFS umbrella. Host clubs do not produce and distribute glossy brochures for skating competitions that tout their brand-new Zamboni, how the entire family can enjoy itself while in town, or the number of college coaches who will be in attendance. There are no figure skating equivalents to Corrigan Sports or White Mountain Sports that must create demand for their products by insisting that it is a sure route to that ever-elusive next level of the pipeline and, eventually, a college scholarship. The competitions are there, and you do need to participate in them in order to move to skating's "next level," but that advancement is an end in itself rather than a commodified means to securing a college scholarship or admissions advantage. The same is true with ultimate. USA Ultimate acts as a clearinghouse for all "sponsored" tournaments and, without any intercollegiate incentives, there are very few independent operators that need to convince girls and parents that *their* tournaments are the best way to become a varsity college athlete at a prestigious university. Girls' youth ice hockey's nonfederation tournament system is still in its infancy, so there is currently very little effort to cultivate consumer demand for attending them. This will very likely change drastically in the next five years as the showcase tournament sector of the girls' youth ice hockey pipeline starts piggybacking on the sport's 300 percent increase in college scholarship equivalencies over the past decade.

COACHES AND CAMPS

The steady growth of paid coaches in many girls' youth sports cannot happen without a corresponding growth of consumer demand from players and families. Not surprisingly, this increased demand for paid coaches is most prominent in those sports with the largest or fastest-growing youth sports to college pipelines. Youth sports camps, many affiliated with college programs, are also multiplying rapidly, as are other commercial enterprises that promise consumers a successful trip through the youth sports to college pipeline, assuming the sports have such pipelines. A community soccer league official remarked,

> The pressure to hire so-called professional coaches is coming from lots of places. The regional and national soccer associations continually push the advantages of using licensed coaches. Sometimes they push the competitive angle, but for the lower-level teams their pitch is more on safety. They insist that professional, licensed coaches know how to run a practice and make sure kids don't get hurt. That resonates with the parents in addition to many thinking that their eight-year-old daughter can play DI if nurtured correctly. I'm a little torn on the issue. Some of these paid coaches are very good. But so are some of the parent volunteers. And sometimes the paid coaches are juggling so many jobs that they can't really focus on, say, the second-tier U10 girls' team in our club because they are also coaching a premier U14 team that plays in showcases. Ten years ago we had basically no paid coaches for our girls' travel teams. Now we have them for all of the top-level teams and most of the second-level teams.

Parents may be concerned with a professional coach's expertise on safety issues, but it is more likely that they believe a professional coach will better equip their daughters to successfully navigate the youth sports to college pipeline. Lila's dad, Christopher, said,

> I see where a lot of my friends are coming from. Their kid was on the B team in Lila's age group, but they feel that a nine-year-old probably hasn't reached her potential and is more likely to reach her potential if she's coached by a professional rather than by some [parent volunteer] who has some free time on the weekends but doesn't really understand the game's intricacies. Why shouldn't Amanda have the same chance to make the A team next year? It's the A-team kids who get recruited by ODP teams. Believe me, as parents we don't want to eliminate any future options for our kids. We don't care how much it costs or how many extra miles we have to drive. Well, we might care a little, but not that much.

Christopher was a first-time parent, so it was especially interesting that he knew so much about the youth soccer world, although not always very accurately. Most of his information came from coworkers and neighbors who had older daughters with more youth soccer experience, or from blogs like the one Rayna referenced earlier. Naturally, these coworkers and neighbors are upper-middle-class suburbanites, and almost all are light-skinned. Christopher and his friends are also among those who seem impressed with foreign accents, or with what these accents allegedly represent:

> Some of us at the U10 level were a little irked that the U11s were getting the better coaches for their A teams and their B teams. Don't get me wrong, I really liked [Lila's coach], but these other guys have all played in England or Germany. One of them was with a club affiliated with Manchester City. They have been eating and breathing soccer since they were born. Their understanding of the game is beyond that of [Lila's coach], who probably grew up playing a lot of baseball and lacrosse in addition to soccer. But these European guys are all soccer all the time. I think they can give the girls some more intensity.

When pressed, Christopher admitted he had never met these European chaps or seen them interact with the ten-year-old girls, although he had heard them speak at soccer club board meetings. His assumptions about their talents were based strictly on cultural stereotypes about soccer. As we will discuss in the next chapter, assumptions about gender were probably also on his mind. These stereotypes about non-American soccer prowess are not lost on the players either. Claire recalled,

> When I was going into U14, I was invited to tryouts for this really exclusive club team that was always ranked in the top ten [where I lived]. I was excited because all of the coaches in this program were from Britain. I think the club was started by a British guy, and they were always talking about the British way of doing things and how it was so much better than the American way of doing things. I certainly believed them, and my parents believed them. In summer training they brought in more British guys to run the camps and clinics. I think my friends and I started to talk in British accents. Looking back, we really did get good instruction, but it probably wasn't any different than other clubs with fewer British guys. Our team did really well, but maybe that was because all the good players joined the team.

Interestingly, the same non-American preference also seems to be on the ascent in field hockey, in addition to the interrelated masculinization that will be discussed more in chapter 5. Since teams from smaller countries are far more successful in international competitions than teams representing the gigantic United States, many assume this is due to better coaching. Kristen remembered,

> One of our U19 coaches moved, and I was so happy when the club hired a [non-US] coach for my last year. [She] had won an Olympic medal and was filled with energy and ideas that were new to us. They seem to have a different approach there, and [she] had been through a lot as a kid and still managed to play in the Olympics and World Cup. Her family moved [there] when she was young, and they were really poor. Her dad had played field hockey in [their original country], so she eventually took it up and made the national team in every age group. We had a lot of new players at tryouts the next year who wanted a chance to play for [her].

Three years after this coaching change, Kristen admitted that her former club team was faring no better than when it had a US coach. Her story also touches upon a more important reason why US field hockey may not be internationally successful: its expensive pay-to-play system excludes potential stars such as Kristen's former coach, whose family could not have afforded to enter the youth field hockey to college pipeline. It is interesting to wonder how much stronger the US national teams would be if poorer families and players had the same opportunity as richer families and players to recognize and develop their talents. There are people within the field hockey community, including some of its federation leaders, who recognize this, but the entrenched commercial interests (buttressed by consumer demand) are resistant to change a very lucrative system that is being driven by a seemingly intransigent intercollegiate athletics structure.

The figure skating world has long revered coaches and skaters from outside the United States. Accents mattered here far earlier than they mattered in soccer or field hockey. The success of skaters from European countries and, more recently, from East Asian countries has increased the strong demand for the best coach in a sport that is already very coach-centric. A longtime figure skating coach (US born) commented,

> It is actually kind of hilarious to see how gaga some of the parents and girls get when they can work with a foreign coach. It's usually the ones with really high aspirations. Some of the coaches are certainly excellent, but some of them are only average skaters and teachers. But those accents are marvelous at seducing people. So are the stories of skating on frozen rivers in the "old country" with used skates. I kid around with some of my friends that we could double our business if we all changed our names to Olga or Dmitri and worked on our Russian accents. Maybe used a little more Tchaikovsky in the program music.

I would resist dismissing this perspective as the coach's xenophobia or ethnocentrism since she is merely reflecting on existing consumer stereotypes that have been forged by multiple social sources. If the skaters and their families believe (for instance) that Russian-born coaches are better than US-born coaches, then those beliefs will be real in their consequences. The same is true in field hockey and soccer, only with different cultural stereotypes. In each of these cases, the "consequences" are reinforcing certain commercial elements of the youth sports industry, whether or not they are part of a pipeline leading to college scholarships. The existence of a pipeline only alters how this stereotype is contextually presented.

There is no shortage of sports-specific summer camps marketed explicitly for aspiring college athletes. As mentioned in the last chapter, the proliferation of these camps is heavily intertwined with the proliferating supply of youth coaches. There are two different types of summer camps: those that are run by youth clubs or independent businesses and those that are an extension of an intercollegiate program (see chapter 2). Both are part of the youth sports to college pipeline, but they cultivate consumer demand in slightly different ways. Summer soccer camps are usually offered by companies that have been hired by local clubs. Sometimes these camps are restricted to club members, but not as a general rule. Their marketing pitch is a more subtle variation of those strategies used to promote showcase tournaments: this camp will help you develop skills that are important to college coaches. There are no promises of college coaches coming to visit the camps, but the camp literature always includes the names of former campers now attending certain colleges. Again, it seems to be an effective marketing strategy. Maryann, who plays soccer at a small Division III school, explained,

> After my sophomore year of high school, I really wanted to go to the [XYZ camp] even though it was in a different state and would mean living in the dorms instead of doing the soccer day camp near my home. I thought I was too good for the local camp and it wouldn't really help me reach the next level. Some really good players from [a nearby ECNL team] raved about XYZ, and they were probably going to get college scholarships. My parents tried to talk me out of it, but I pleaded with them and promised to do more chores and not buy any new clothes for school and maybe even skip junior prom. The camp was interesting. It really wasn't that much different from my local camp. The drills were all the same. The games were a little more challenging since there were some better players, but that also meant I played a position I didn't really like and would never play on my club or high school team. I'm not sure if I liked it or not. Looking back, it might have turned me off from looking at a DI program. Everyone was so serious. The following year I went back to my local camp and worked as a counselor. That was really fun.

Given the shortage of premier playing surfaces discussed in the last chapter, field hockey summer camps (not linked to a college program) are almost always affiliated with a local club and are just one piece of the club's overall marketing strategy that features its successful pipeline to intercollegiate programs. The ultimate camps mentioned in the last chapter market themselves in terms of fun and personal development. That might change if Frisbee was ever to become an official Olympic sport, and would definitely change if it became a varsity intercollegiate sport.

Every highly ranked DI intercollegiate soccer and field hockey program offers one or more summer camps (usually five days) for young girls aspiring to reach that next level. Many, but not all, highly ranked DIII programs offer similar camps or shorter clinics. Contrary to conventional wisdom, these camps are not primarily a recruiting mechanism for specific intercollegiate programs but a standard way for college coaching staffs (and sometimes players) to make some money, and for highly corporatized universities to generate income from "assets" that go unused during the summer. The standard marketing approach for these camps is to speak more generally about getting ready for college soccer (the next level). A fairly typical brochure from DIII women's soccer powerhouse Williams College advertises,

> This clinic is designed for high school student-athletes who have an interest in playing collegiate soccer. You and your family will get a glimpse into the life of a collegiate women's soccer player by interacting with current players and

> coaches. You will train with the Williams College coaches in a daily schedule much like preseason for a college program. At the end of the clinic, our hope is that you will have gained technical and tactical awareness that is essential to play college soccer. The ultimate goal of the clinic is that you will gain a better understanding of what it takes to play at the next level.

But even though these summer camps rarely claim that girls can get the inside track on eventually playing for that school, girls and their families still believe that this will help. Almost every older soccer and field hockey player I spoke with thought at one point that attending a certain camp (usually between sophomore and junior year) would help them be recruited by a specific school. Patricia, a high school senior, was pretty typical of this group:

> [DI powerhouse] was my dream school. Who wouldn't want to play for [highly successful coach] and always be in the NCAA tournament? [The coach] had been at one of my showcase tournaments, but there were like a million other girls there and it's sometimes hard for a defender to stand out. I wanted to get on [the coach's] radar, so I thought the summer camp was the best option [laughs]. Me and about a thousand other high school girls. The camp was camp; I mean, how many different drills can there be? But everyone was trying to show off for [the coach]. The forwards were dribbling like crazy and taking stupid shots. I would receive a long ball and juggle it for five or six seconds even though I could have brought it to my feet much more quickly and started advancing. The funny thing was that [the coach] wasn't even there. He gave a speech the first day of camp and the last day of camp but otherwise wasn't around. It was all assistants, college players, and I think some local high school coaches. But we all got a great T-shirt with the camp's name. I wore that to every high school practice! But I think the camp really changed my mind about college. I am going to play DIII or not play at all. I don't think a single one of my high school or club teammates went to college at the same school where they went to camp.[8]

Patricia's observation was borne out by a DI athletic director and former women's team coach:

> Some programs and coaches are starting to use summer camps for recruitment, but doing so restricts your pool of players. Sure, some kids travel hundreds of miles to attend a certain camp but 85 percent of them live within fifty miles. No coach wants to limit their player pool that much, even in field hockey, where the high-quality players are already concentrated on the East Coast. That's why we started to encourage the showcase system in the first place. But yes, the kids do believe it will help them out. When I was still coaching I would get e-mails from girls letting me know how much they loved

the school and that they would be at the second session of camp and staying in the dorms so they didn't miss a single chance to improve. They really had no idea that there were a hundred girls trying to get five freshman slots and divide up two or three scholarships.

As mentioned briefly in the last chapter, if the NSCAA vendor exhibition is an accurate reflection, there is a growing commercial presence of what might be called "pipeline consultants" within youth soccer and, presumably, other sports as well. Without exception, the common thread running through all of the marketing for these products was how they could help players maximize the possibility of securing a college scholarship. An Internet search uncovered an amazing number of companies that guarantee to optimize a player's successful navigation through the youth sports to college pipeline. Rayna, Claire's mom, did not use one of these consultants, but several of her friends did:

> Claire's club team coach told us about this consultant, and some of her teammates paid for his help. We didn't. As far as I could tell, he was just repeating information that was available for free all over the Internet and even at the NCAA website, which was quite helpful and actually said how hard it was to get a scholarship. When I told my friends, they said that was why it was important to have [the consultant] helping them, since he knew where the hidden money was. There was no hidden money. Those girls had the same college opportunities as Claire: partial scholarships the first year with no guarantees beyond that. Frankly, we were all equally surprised at how little scholarship money there really is. At least we didn't have to pay [the consultant] an extra $1,000 to find that out. It's even worse in [our new hometown] with Madeline's teammates. I keep telling them they are wasting their money, but they don't want to hear it.

In addition to accurate (if very limited) information available through the NCAA, players and families can obtain free, unemotional advice from US Soccer, USA Field Hockey, USA Hockey, and most of the other federations representing sports with intercollegiate footprints. The advice from these federations is the antithesis of the message promoted by the commercial elements of the youth sports to college pipelines: families must temper their expectations of receiving significant college scholarships and admissions advantages; parents and players should resist specializing in a single sport to reduce the risk of overuse injuries or emotional burnout; players should to take a few months off from their primary sport to recover physically and psychologically; parents should not purchase a lot of products and services that promise to help kids strike scholarship gold. But this sober approach seems no match for the marketing juggernaut offering products and services guaranteed to whisk girls through a sport's pipeline and into intercollegiate heaven. This marketing message is augmented by the overall exaggeration of organized sports' importance transmitted by schools (at all levels) and the media. In terms of sports-based college scholarships and admissions advantages, things are not as they appear to be. But that reality does not seem to be affecting consumer demand in the youth sports to college pipelines.

5

FEMALE SPORTS ON MALE TERMS

Highly commercialized and commodified female sports are increasingly being played and organized on male terms. This "masculinization" of female *sports*, though, is not equivalent to the masculinization of female *athletes*. When talking about the masculinization of female athletes, we might focus on things like body types, sexuality, or the very meaning of what it means to be male or female. For instance, the ongoing controversy surrounding South African runner Caster Semenya reflects the relationship between certain biological hormone levels and the very definition of what it means to be a "male athlete" or a "female athlete."[1] Far less attention, though, has been paid to how, beyond the athletes themselves, organized female *sports* are increasingly defined within conventional male parameters reflecting patriarchal cultural norms. As mentioned briefly in the introduction and in chapter 1, certain ways of playing sports—"masculine" ways—are seen as more legitimate and, hence, more likely to be emphasized at all stages of the youth sports to college pipeline. Thus, we have "regular" ice hockey and "girls'" ice hockey; "regular" soccer and "girls'/women's" soccer. Highlighting the "masculine" elements of a female sport, and those who play it, is intended to give the activity more legitimacy; to make it more of a "real" sport. Within the youth sports to college pipelines, the masculinization of female sports has become a marketing point for those selling products and services, including coaching services. Girls have a better chance at successfully navigating the pipelines if they play more like males, train more like males, and are coached by males. This creates significant problems, including the astonishing increase in serious injuries to female athletes, and the increasingly formidable barriers to qualified women who may wish to coach female sports teams. Indeed, these negative outcomes can be viewed as the unintended and somewhat ironic consequences of Title IX, which while creating more opportunities for female athletes and making female sports more culturally legitimate, has also been the unwitting catalyst for other forms of patriarchy.

It is vitally important here to reemphasize the notion of "irrelevant essentialism" explored in chapter 1. Identifying and acknowledging that male and female sports (and athletes) are *different* does not mean that one is *superior* to the other, even though our cultural default is to presume that male versions *are* superior. It is even hypothetically possible (albeit unlikely) to define female sports as superior to their male counterparts! The commercialization, commodification, and corporatization of sports is a serious social issue regardless of an athlete's gender; it's just especially interesting to examine these processes within female sports, since they have been changing so rapidly over the past few decades. Similarly, the masculinization of sport is not only about gender. As the economic, political, and organizational stakes of organized sports (especially youth sports) continue to grow, there has been a corresponding growth in a "win at all costs" ideology. This leads to increases in cheating (broadly defined), using performance-enhancing drugs, ignoring (or masking) minor injuries until they become more serious, and even denying the connection between sports activity and afflictions like traumatic brain injury. In the seemingly inevitable quest to mirror the structural dynamics of organized male sports (college and youth), organized female sports (college and youth) seem to be adopting their primary ideological tenet: male sports, athletes, and coaches are better than female sports, athletes, and coaches.

MALE-CENTRISM AND MALE IDENTIFICATION

Male-centric and male-identified aspects of sports (both organized and nonorganized) have long been part of the social scenery. High school and college team nicknames are often some name and the "lady" version of that name. So we have Lady Volunteers, Lady Aggies, Lady Wildcats, and Lady Pioneers, but never "male" variations of the name. Could you imagine the shock at high school pep rallies if the football team was introduced as the Boy Lions? Would *Sports Illustrated* treat us to a cover photo of the college football champion Gentlemen Crimson Tide? In addition, games themselves are judged by male standards. This is especially true of games where there are different male and female iterations. In lacrosse, for example, the male version includes far more physical contact. Rather than just seeing this as different (or even inferior), we afford the male version more prestige and legitimacy; there is lacrosse and there is "women's lacrosse," not vice versa. This is reflected even by the women/girls who play the sport and claim they can be just as good as the men/boys at full-contact lacrosse. Never, though, do we hear players (or observers) insisting that men should play lacrosse more like women. The same male-centric phenomenon takes place in basketball, where the "standard" version of the game is played above the rim while the "watered-down" female version is played below the rim (and with a smaller ball). There is even recent chatter about lowering the basket height in female basketball to allow more high-powered dunks and, thus, improve the sport's mass appeal.[2] Never, though, do we hear pleas to *raise* the rim in men's basketball in order to emphasize teamwork, passing, and defense. This male-centrism is deeply embedded in our patriarchal society and gets reinforced by social institutions both inside and outside the sports world. From inside, we often hear a constant defensiveness from coaches and players about the skills and "toughness" of girls and young women. A Division III soccer coach (female) explained,

> I'm really tired of people saying that these girls can't play at the same level as the guys. That's nonsense. I've had players who could kick the crap out of most guys. Maybe not a whole team of them, but at least three or four at a time. They play just as hard and sweat just as much. They run, they lift weights, and do planks better than most guys. They play physically and don't cry when they get hit. When [one of my players] saw the New Mexico thing, she said she would have decked the kid, and I don't doubt it.[3]

Players also may internalize this male-centered definition of how a sport should be played. It is unclear whether they develop this perspective on their own or because of the constant cultural reminder that male versions of sports are superior. These messages are not limited to sports with large intercollegiate footprints. Hallie, a middle school ultimate Frisbee player, remarked,

> Everyone thinks the boys are better because they can throw the disc farther. But there's more to the game than that. You have to be creative and run good patterns. You have to check the wind. You need to know who is throwing and how far they can throw it. You need to look at the defense. There is thinking involved. But when I go to camp, most of the counselors try to teach us how

> to [throw] longer and harder. Even the girl coaches. I wonder if they are just trying to show the boy coaches how far they can throw it.

Not all athletes internalize this male-centric definition of sports excellence, and there are probably different patterns of internalization depending on the sport. For instance, athletes in more individual (rather than team-oriented) sports may be more resistant to this trend:

> One reason I quit figure skating [in middle school] was because the coaches and judges all wanted bigger jumps and more jumps, [but] I always loved the creative side of skating. It was like dancing on ice. Listening to music that I liked and dancing to it. The music was so important to me. So I started playing hockey [the next year] since I missed skating and a bunch of my friends were doing it, but I missed the music. But my coach tells us it's not real hockey since we don't get to check like the boys and we can't skate as fast. Why does it always have to be about speed? Or hitting?

Kinesiologist Mary Louise Adams echoes this male-centrism in her detailed exploration of (primarily) Canadian figure skating.[4] She argues, among other things, that there is nothing inherently more important or worthwhile about jumping, and yet all singles figure skaters, male and female, are increasingly judged by that metric. Adams believe this reflects both patriarchy and homophobia, since men who cannot master (for example) quad jumps often have their masculinity questioned. Conversely, female figure skaters who do master (or attempt to master) difficult jumps do not have their femininity questioned, since they are just conforming to figure skating norms that reward power and strength, despite it being far more popular among females! This is similar to Barrie Thorne's (1993) idea that females who "cross over" into male domains of play are far less stigmatized than males who cross over into female domains.[5] Adams and many people within the organized figure skating community believe that the newer ISU (International Skating Union) scoring system exacerbates the masculinization trend within female figure skating. A longtime figure skating coach explained,

> Every technical skill has been reduced to its most microscopic pieces. You can get a mandatory deduction for the slightest thing, even if it doesn't affect your whole program. It seems to encourage skaters doing harder jumps, since falling on a hard jump is better for your overall score than [making a minor error] on an easier jump. It also benefits men, since they can do harder jumps and thus have higher overall scores than women. The [old scoring system] looked at the entire program as more than the sum of its technical parts.

Field hockey's recent participatory malaise and its modest commercial footprint are almost certainly tied up with male-centrism. Interestingly, this gets reflected through other sports in other countries, depending on the particular cultural landscape. The chief operating officer of USA Field Hockey observed,

> This gender exclusivity is particular to the United States. [Field hockey] is played in 144 countries where it is primarily a male sport, although women also play it. The US is really the only exception to it being a male sport. That's through culture and the way the sport came into the country. It started at more prestigious colleges. It was seen as an appropriate sport for women. They wore skirts and all that. Couldn't hit each other. But that gave it a stigma as being *just* for women. Those elite colleges were in the Northeast, so that's why it also became an appropriate high school sport in that region, even before Title IX. Ironically, in England, lacrosse is seen as the "girls'" sport and is the "appropriate" thing for girls to be doing at their fancy boarding schools. The boys are all playing cricket and wouldn't be caught dead playing lacrosse. But this stigma can be overcome. Look at California, where most of the US men's national team comes from. Almost all of them are second- or third-generation immigrants from Australia and New Zealand. Their fathers and grandfathers and uncles all played [field] hockey, and they don't think it is inferior.

It's certainly possible that the male-centric stigma about field hockey could be overcome, but this is unlikely given the status of intercollegiate field hockey and its correspondingly modest youth sports pipeline. Commercial interests searching for profits, and colleges looking to fortify their brand presence, see the more masculinized, less stigmatized, lacrosse and ice hockey as better avenues for reaching those goals. Women and girls often internalize this male-centric social norm, eschewing a "girlie" sport for something more masculine and, hence, legitimate.

I'M TALKIN' ABOUT ETHICS

The masculinization of female sports also has an ethical component. The University of Idaho's Center for ETHICS has been studying moral reasoning and moral education since the mid-1980s, relying on a longitudinal database of approximately seventy-two thousand individuals. Its 2006 comprehensive report shows that athletes score significantly lower on moral reasoning scales than do nonathletes; athletes in revenue-producing sports score lower than in non-revenue-producing sports; scores decline the longer someone is involved in organized sports; female athletes score higher than male athletes; and female scores are dropping and may soon converge with male scores.[6] In short, assuming these moral reasoning scales are valid, serious female athletes are becoming more like male athletes when it comes to cheating. Female sports are becoming ethically masculinized. This is a natural corollary of male-centrism and male identification. If male sports themselves are more legitimate than female sports, then the ethical parameters of male sports participants must also be the norm. Historically, men have been more willing to "win at all costs" than women. But that has been changing and, if the Center for ETHICS data are correct, there should now be far less measurable difference between male and female athletes' willingness to win regardless of moral parameters. This convergence is by no means an inevitable pattern in human evolution or a social Darwinist selection of superior values. Rather, it is a social construction reflecting the normative patterns of a patriarchal capitalist society built around an unequal distribution of class-based and gender-based power. Hypothetically, the ethical convergence of male and female sports (and athletes) could go in the opposite direction. Male sports (and athletes) could become more like female sports in eschewing the desire to win at any price; to put more emphasis on sports activity itself rather than on the outcome. In reality, of course, this is next to impossible in a cultural framework rooted in the logic of patriarchal capitalism, where accumulating wealth and "relevant" gender essentialism are seen as part of a valuable social meritocracy.

This socially constructed, gender-based convergence of ethics is perhaps another unintended consequence of Title IX and the increasing economic and organizational potency of female pay-to-play youth sports pipelines. The *stakes* in organized female sports are far higher than they were thirty years ago, so it is no wonder that players, coaches, and others are willing to employ any means possible to achieve the culturally defined prime objective: winning. For female athletes, winning games and generating impressive statistics could lead to coveted slots on premier teams or attract the attention of college coaches bearing scholarships and/or admissions advantages. Cheating (broadly defined) can get them to that ever-important next level. For parents, the ends justify the unethical means since nothing is more important than ensuring their daughters are afforded every possible opportunity for success. For coaches, winning is a conventional source of professional pride but, more importantly, a conduit of occupational mobility. Both amateur and professional coaches are more likely to get "better" jobs based on winning percentages than on how much their players enjoyed themselves or experienced personal growth. Before Title

IX and the emergence of female youth sports to college pipelines, the stakes were much lower and the consequences of not winning were more modest. Winning at all costs is consistent with a commercialized, commodified, corporatized philosophy of sport that minimizes the importance of participation, social relationships, physical activity, and having fun. A DI field hockey coach reflected,

> It's really not so bad at [this school]. Our overall record for the past ten years is way below .500, but my job has never been in jeopardy. Everybody graduates, there are never any academic problems, the parents don't complain, and our away games are never too far away, so we're pretty inexpensive. But my colleagues at most other schools aren't so lucky. You would think the whole university rises and falls with the on-field success of the field hockey team. One of the advantages of field hockey being considered a "girlie" sport was that we had some immunity from the craziness around male sports or women's sports like lacrosse that have a male counterpart. Sure, we wanted to win, but not at any cost or any price. [My coaching colleagues and I] would often share "secret" information with each other in order to have better games. Once, one of my friends who was coaching a vastly superior team rested some of her best players so we would have a better game against them. That could never happen now with all the pressure to win big and have the stats to prove how good you and the team are. And I doubt a male coach would have ever done it.

All five female sports examined in this book are exhibiting a masculinization of ethics. When discussing this topic, interview subjects would generally accompany their statements with a "tonal shrug," which indicated disapproval of this trend, accompanied by a "what can you do?" resignation. It was similar to their responses concerning "recruiting babies" at a U10 showcase tournament or sacrificing academic integrity in order to land some hot-shot center striker who reads at an eighth-grade level as a high school senior. These crocodile tears were not limited to college coaches. A youth soccer coach admitted,

> I don't exactly tell them to cheat, but I encourage them to see what they can get away with [smiles]. Steal a throw-in even if it went out off of us. Move the ball up ten yards on a throw-in until the ref calls it. Take a flop when hit, just don't be too dramatic. When I first started coaching I told the [U10] girls to "thumb up" on corner kicks.[7] My high school coach taught me that fifteen years ago. The girls thought it was disgusting. By [U13] they were all doing it without being asked. This is the kind of seriousness college coaches are looking for. The girls have to show their commitment to winning if they are going to make it to the next level.

At U13, Elizabeth also exhibited this sort of resignation when queried about what she would do in order to win:

> I always thought that stalling with a lead was rude, but my mom said it was just like any other tactic. At first we were just told to play long balls to defensive corners, but as I got older, we were told to kick the ball out of bounds as far as we could or to REALLY take our time on throw-ins and restarts. My new coach is really into this. I guess it's OK since everyone was doing it and why should we penalize ourselves? The dirtiest player I ever saw got picked for the league all-star team because I guess the coaches all thought she had what it took to be successful even though she wasn't that skilled. I heard that she quit but [don't know for sure].

Interestingly, among sports with a college footprint, the field hockey players I spoke with seemed far less inclined to "cheat" than soccer players. This could have something to do with the game itself, which has an astounding number of technical rules that make infractions more the norm than the exception. Or it could be related to the moribund intercollegiate status of field hockey, or that it is still primarily played and coached by women, such as the one quoted earlier.

Even ultimate is experiencing these ethical changes that challenge the "spirit of the game" (SOTG) ostensibly central to its existence. Essential to this is the ever-present argument discussed in earlier chapters about whether the game's players should identify infractions or whether there need to be nonplaying referees or observers to mediate activity. A USA Ultimate executive reflected,

> All of us here really believe in the "spirit of the game." It's one of the reasons we originally got involved with ultimate and are now spending our lives promoting it. But it's easy to see how this is always under attack, even at the high school level. It's more of an issue on the men's side because of the professional leagues who have paid referees and since we get a lot of crossover players from other sports like lacrosse where players are, let's just say, not discouraged from cheating a little bit. But it's not absent on the women's side, where we have had to employ far more observers during the national tournaments. I've even heard of some elite women's teams who won't play in [certain regional tournaments] if there are no observers, since they believe other teams are purposefully cheating against them in order to improve their ranking. It's always the other team.

Considering SOTG's normative weight within ultimate, eliminating self-policing would be a staggering change in how the sport is played and how it is perceived. Ultimate's increasing commercialization and commodification is also intertwined with its masculinization, just like in more "mainstream" sports such as soccer and field hockey. It's almost as if the sport cannot be considered serious (or seriously marketable) if it isn't played in a relatively masculine fashion.

YOU LOOK LIKE A MAN

The physical expectations of female athletes have also become masculinized. To some degree, as mentioned earlier, this phenomenon has been examined by sports sociologists and gender studies scholars, but usually in terms of the cultural backlash against those women who try to "look like men." Often this backlash is connected with conceptions of sexual orientation or other elements of "hegemonic masculinity." In terms of youth sports to college pipelines, however, it is also important to explore the commercial elements of physical expectations and physical appearance. Physical training and strength development is yet another commodity that is purported to help girls and young women make it to the next level. And, as with many of the phenomena explored in this book, cultural changes within sports that seem to level the gender-based playing field may unintentionally harm women and girls. Looking like a male may be the new female, but this is not necessarily a good thing.

One manifestation of this masculinization is the training regimens increasingly employed to improve female athletes' performance and/or team success. This has amplified the "strength and conditioning" component of the youth sports pipeline that used to focus strictly on men and only in specific sports such as football and wrestling. A college athletic director explained,

> We have probably increased our expenditures for strength and conditioning more than for anything else. All schools are doing this, so we have to keep looking for better trainers and more beneficial programs so our [athletes] can stay competitive. Title IX has forced us to figure out what we should have known anyway: that [female athletes] can also benefit from this training. And also men beyond the football team. Most off-season work now consists of strength training rather than unofficial games and scrimmages. Many of the players have had strength coaches for years through their high schools or travel programs and are looking to bring their physical conditioning to the next level while playing in college.

However, these programs may be especially harmful to women. They have generally been designed by men and for men, with the assumption that women can use them also. But women on the whole are physically different from men, even though there is far more variation in physical characteristics *within* genders than there is on the average *between* genders.[8] Large or small, the physical differences of women and girls are not inherently (or "essentially") inferior, although our cultural norms often treat them as inferior. In our well-meaning, Title IX–driven attempts to provide equivalent athletic opportunities for males and females, we may have become too accommodating in accepting male-based standards as the ultimate measuring stick for female athletes and female sports. DI field hockey player Kristen explained,

> Squatting is just one of our [field hockey] weight-training exercises. Intensified workouts with increased weights. I would get incredibly sore. I sometimes would go back to my room and just lie there for hours. My friends would have to help me to dinner. Even studying was a challenge. But then the soreness would lead to other muscle strains because our running form would change to compensate for the soreness. The weight training made me stronger but it also made me slower, less agile, and more tired. I started noticing these changes at the beginning of my sophomore year when not a single upperclass player could outrun a [first-year] player. But I'll bet we could have picked them up and thrown them!

There is a certain irony when a training regimen for a sport that emphasizes speed actually makes you slower. A growing body of research suggests that this sort of conditioning affects males and females differently.[9] Our insistence that what's good for male athletes should be good for female athletes may be contributing to (rather than preventing) the cataclysmic rise in female sports injuries, documented by Michael Sokolove, Mark Hyman, and others.[10] Kristen continued,

> It happened spring of my freshman year. Our strength coach put the same weight on everyone's bar [for dead lifts] not realizing it was too much for many of us. He is also a trainer for the football team and is constantly telling us how many thousands of pounds they can lift, and that we can do it too. Not to be afraid of pushing our bodies. Well, on the second set I felt a sharp pain in my back. My back has never been the same since. I was nineteen years old and having back spasms every day. I had to be diligent taking ibuprofen, using a heating pad, and applying Biofreeze every day. I was in the training room every day. The only thing that ever really helped was rest. But I could never rest. If I took some time off I might fall behind, and it simply wasn't

> acceptable to fall behind. I had spent all that time preparing to be a college athlete; how could I just throw it away? It wasn't the money. I was only on a 40 percent scholarship. This was my dream. But I came here to play field hockey, not be a weight lifter.

Interestingly, Kristen's conditioning-based injury occurred in the off-season. This may be the new norm as year-round strength and conditioning regimens become more central to the alleged success of female athletes and teams. Even female college ultimate players are finding themselves enmeshed in male-centered assumptions about the game's legitimacy and about physical conditioning:

> We have a lot of arguments about whether we should or shouldn't practice with the men's team and if we should adopt their lifting program. Many of us think we can only get better if we play against the guys, but others think that it is prepping us for a style of play we will never see. It's the same with lifting. Many of us believe we can be just as strong as the guys, but some think our bodies aren't built for that. I like doing the training, but a bunch of my teammates have gotten hurt trying to muscle up. The trainers insist that they won't get hurt in games if they build up their strength. The problem is they're getting hurt in training and then can't play the games.

As with most aspects of the youth sports to college pipelines, intercollegiate programs are the genesis of pushing female strength training beyond what might actually be healthy. And, as with most things connected with the pipelines, the effects are directly impacting the youth sports world. Caroline explains,

> Half of my new travel team practices are dedicated to conditioning. It's really exhausting, especially when we have to do it before any ball work. The coach says we have to be able to play three hard games each day of the tournaments and the college coaches are looking for stamina and strength. He talks a lot about showing college coaches how tough we are. And we're just starting high school. Even my younger sister is starting to do some weight training on her [U10] squad. My friend on an older team says the club is going to hire a full-time weight-lifting [coach], probably because [a competing club] has one and they won a regional tournament and have two girls getting scholarships. I haven't seen any difference in my play since I started working out, but I am a lot more sore.

It's almost as if merely surviving a two-day, six-game tournament is proof that a youth program is valuable, and that its players are worthy of consideration by college coaches. Premier youth soccer teams may play upward of fifty games per year, usually bundled in four- to six-game weekend tournaments. Such a grueling schedule is associated with increases in both small and severe injuries, especially to females. In contrast, college teams play twenty games per year and Major League Soccer teams play thirty-five. World Cup and Olympic teams never play on consecutive days, much less multiple games on the same day. There has even been a movement among college soccer coaches to lengthen the primary season in order to provide more rest and recovery time between matches.[11] This unhealthy movement toward overplaying seems to be dictated by the commercial dynamics of showcase tournaments and the college coaches who are at the heart of their existence. So the expectations to look like a man and play like a man are rooted not strictly in patriarchal assumptions about males' essential superiority, but are a by-product of highly commercialized female youth sports pipelines that are responding to changes in intercollegiate athletics. A perspective rooted in irrelevant essentialism would allow us to accept the physical differences between most men and most women without automatically privileging what men (in general) happen to be better at. Instead of wondering why female figure skaters can't land a quadruple toe loop in competition, we could be asking why male figure skaters can't better coordinate their skating and music, and maybe smile a little more at the crowd.

THE COACHING LABOR MARKET

Beyond the ideological insistence that certain ways of playing sports are superior, masculinization also impacts the occupational structure of both youth and intercollegiate athletics. At the professional level, nine of the ten teams in the National Women's Soccer League have male head coaches. Within youth sports, there has been very little systematic analysis of gender-based trends among girls' team coaches at either the recreational or elite levels, although anecdotal and experiential observations strongly suggest that most girls' youth teams are coached by men even though there is an entire generation of post–Title IX women who have actively participated in organized sports. Among the more interesting studies, Michael Messner has ethnographically documented the gendered division of labor among soccer teams, with men normally doing the coaching and women being team managers chiefly responsible for bringing snacks and organizing end-of-the-year parties.[12] Messner's analysis might actually underreport the extent of this gendered division of labor since his ethnography takes place within an American Youth Soccer Organization (AYSO) league in Southern California. As discussed throughout the book, AYSO has a decidedly recreational, low-key approach to youth sports, with scrupulous attention paid to maximizing fun rather than preparing kids for that all-important next level in the youth sports to college pipeline. There are few if any paid professional coaches within the AYSO system, unlike the rampant increase of professionals within the more elite US Youth Soccer and US Club Soccer systems. The same patterns are evident at the college level, which has been systematically explored far more than youth sports. Increased professionalization and increased prestige within women's intercollegiate athletics have led to a simultaneous masculinization that, ironically perhaps, seems to be growing more entrenched despite the Title IX–based explosion of female sports participation.

MASCULINIZATION OF WOMEN'S INTERCOLLEGIATE ATHLETICS[13]

Since 1977, R. Vivian Acosta and Linda Jean Carpenter have been tracking a variety of gender equity issues within college athletics.[14] Every other year, Acosta and Carpenter send questionnaires to the Senior Woman Administrator (SWA) at every NCAA member school that has a women's athletics program. In 2014, the number of such institutions was a bit fewer than 1,100. The NCAA mandates that every member school designate someone to hold this title. This designee need not hold a top-level managerial position such as athletic director, associate athletic director, or assistant athletic director. However, it is expected that this person be involved with high-level decisions within the intercollegiate program. In fact, though, only about 30 percent of the SWAs (as of 2010) held a top-level position, a mere 3 percent increase from fifteen years earlier.[15] Acosta and Carpenter report a high response rate among the SWAs surveyed, but do not provide a precise number.

Similar data are available through the US Department of Education's Office of Postsecondary Education. This information was mandated by the Equity in Athletics Disclosure Act (EADA) and applies to all postsecondary institutions that participate in federal financial aid programs and have intercollegiate sports programs. Its main purpose was to allow oversight for Title IX compliance within college varsity sports. Presumably, the information reported by SWAs via the Acosta-Carpenter surveys should be identical to the EADA, which is reported to the Department of Education by a school's

SWA or some other designee. The following discussion of college coaching trends relies more on EADA data, since they allowed for more customized analysis. The EADA data are mostly, but not totally, consistent with the Acosta-Carpenter survey results.

Figures 5.1 and 5.2 show the masculinization trend among women's college soccer head coaches and assistant coaches in select divisions and conferences. Only soccer is being highlighted here. Data on other sports can be found in tables 5.1 and 5.2. At the most aggregate level, women's intercollegiate teams are increasingly being coached by men. Across all DI women's college sports, the percentage of male coaches has increased from 51 percent to 55 percent between 2003 and 2013. Amazingly, just before the enactment of Title IX, only 10 percent of women's teams' head coaches were male. In DI soccer, male head coaches have increased from

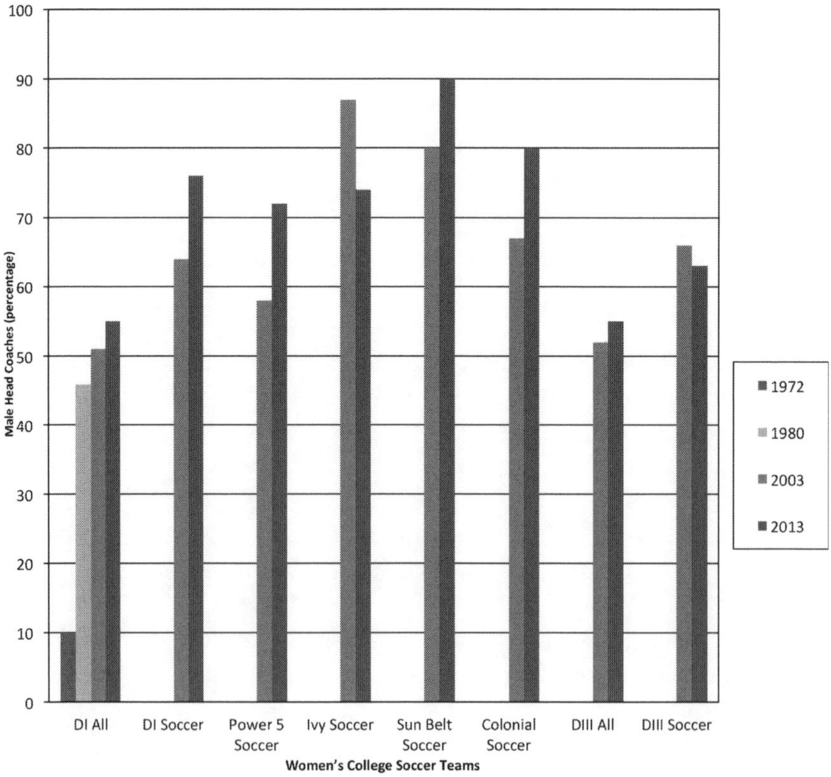

Figure 5.1. Percentage Male Head Coaches of Women's College Soccer Teams, 1972–2013

Source: US Department of Education Office of Postsecondary Education

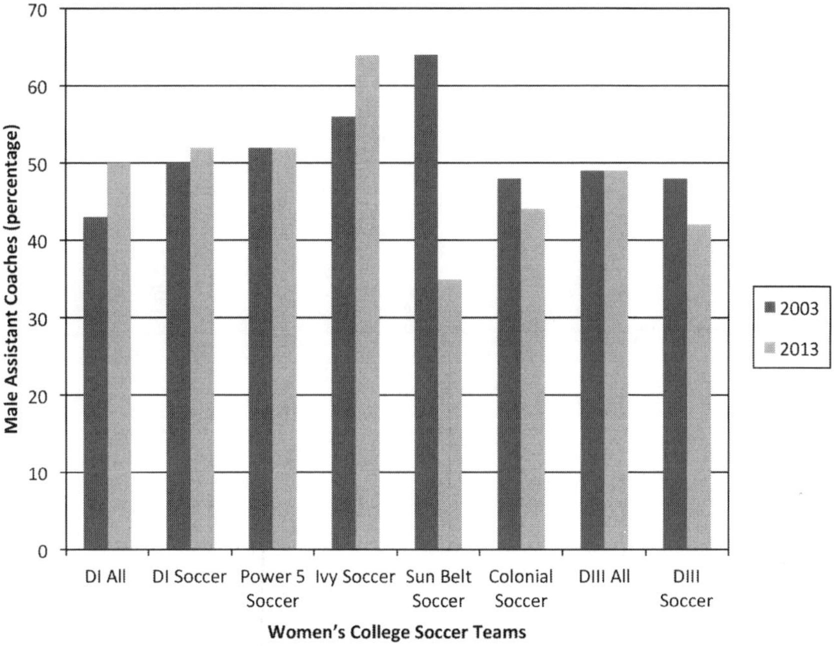

Figure 5.2. Percentage Male Assistant Coaches of Women's College Soccer Teams, 1972–2013

Source: US Department of Education Office of Postsecondary Education

64 percent in 2003 to 74 percent in 2013. This overall masculinization trend is consistent across all types of DI conferences except for the Ivy League, where the percentage of male head coaches has declined, although only two out of its eight current women's head soccer coaches are female. Among DIII schools, there has been a more modest overall masculinization across sports (from 51 percent male to 55 percent male) and a slight decline in the percentage of male head coaches of women's soccer teams. The same general trend holds true for assistant coaches, with masculinization trends being more prominent in DI schools than in DIII schools. Soccer itself is a mixed bag depending on conference, even at the DIII level. My interpretation of the EADA assistant coach data is a little less sanguine than Acosta and Carpenter's interpretation of their similar (although not identical) survey data. They believe that great strides have been made toward equity in coaching, especially among paid assistant coaches. They accurately note that opportunities for women in coaching and other athletics-related occupations (i.e., strength and conditioning) have never been greater and that there are more female paid assistant coaches than ever before.

Table 5.1. Percentage of Male Coaches of Division I and Ivy League Women's College Teams, 2003 and 2013

	Head Coach			*Assistant Coach*		
	2003	*2013*	*% Change*	*2003*	*2013*	*% Change*
Division I						
All	51	55	+10	43	50	+16
Ice hockey	40	86	+115	40	53	+33
Soccer	65	76	+17	50	52	+4
Volleyball	50	60	+20	50	53	+6
Basketball	26	39	+50	32	33	+3
Softball	20	28	+40	22	28	+27
Lacrosse	0	7	+7	N/A	12	N/A
Field hockey	0	7	+7	29	41	+41
Ivy League						
Soccer	87	74	−15	56	64	+13
Field hockey	0	12	+12	12	22	+83
Ice hockey	34	67	+100	46	41	−11
Lacrosse	0	0	0	7	10	+43

Source: US Department of Education Office of Postsecondary Education

But the increased raw number of female coaches does not negate the falling percentage of female coaches in many sports, even those like field hockey that are female-dominated. In addition, given the sheer number of post–Title IX women who almost certainly have the skills and experience necessary for coaching, we should assume that the coaching labor market would be flooded with competent women, and that the percentage of men coaching women's sports (especially) would be dropping precipitously rather than slowly rising. We might even expect to see an increase in the

Table 5.2. Percentage of Male Coaches of Division III Women's College Teams, 2003 and 2013

	Head Coach			*Assistant Coach*		
	2003	*2013*	*% Change*	*2003*	*2013*	*% Change*
All	51	55	+6	49	49	0
Ice hockey	67	54	−19	41	40	−2
Soccer	66	63	−5	48	42	−13
Volleyball	32	32	0	35	38	+14
Basketball	31	33	+6	35	35	0
Softball	31	32	+3	36	31	−14
Lacrosse	13	14	+8	21	11	−48
Field hockey	5	1	−80	2	6	+200
NESCAC (all)	45	55	+22	46	45	−2
MIAC (all)	63	67	+6	50	55	+10

Source: US Department of Education Office of Postsecondary Education

percentage of women coaching men's college teams.[16] Other masculinization patterns are consistent with the commercialization, commodification, and corporatization of college and youth female sports. Four of the "first-tier" women's college sports have seen a notable decline in the percentage of female coaches.[17] More specifically, sports like soccer, ice hockey, and volleyball, which have only minor differences between the female and male iterations, have the most significant levels of college coaching masculinization. Softball, women's lacrosse, and field hockey have seen much less male infiltration, possibly because the first two are significantly different than baseball and men's lacrosse, and there is no male version of intercollegiate field hockey. However, while youth and collegiate field hockey in the United States is played almost entirely by women, the current Women's National Team is coached by a man of British descent.

Masculinization trends seem especially strong in women's college soccer. Even seemingly silver linings within the sport call for tempered enthusiasm. As mentioned earlier, for instance, even though there has been a "doubling" of women head coaches in the Ivy League from one to two, the other seven head coaching positions are occupied by men. The same is true in the relatively low-key, DIII Minnesota Intercollegiate Athletic Conference (MIAC), where a tripling of female soccer head coaches still leaves only 40 percent of these positions occupied by women. DI ice hockey trends are also not surprising due to the recent growth in its intercollegiate footprint and high scholarship levels. Interestingly, the trend is moving in the opposite direction within DIII ice hockey, although women are still coaching less than half of the teams at that level. This trend is evident even in the relatively noncorporatized and noncommercialized world of ultimate. For example, perennial women's DI ultimate powerhouse Oregon has a male head coach, as do many of the top women's college teams.[18]

MASCULINIZATION OF GIRLS' YOUTH SPORTS COACHES

Figure 5.3 examines masculinization trends within the world of girls' travel soccer between 2010 and 2015. Data were collected from the websites of organized leagues and teams in four different metropolitan regions across the country. All of these leagues were suburban-based but included a few teams from the local anchor city. I examined three age groups (U10, U12, U14) to try to capture different parts of the youth sports pipelines. I also wanted to consider the intensity level of teams to see if that had any impact on masculinization trends. Age groups are normally divided into

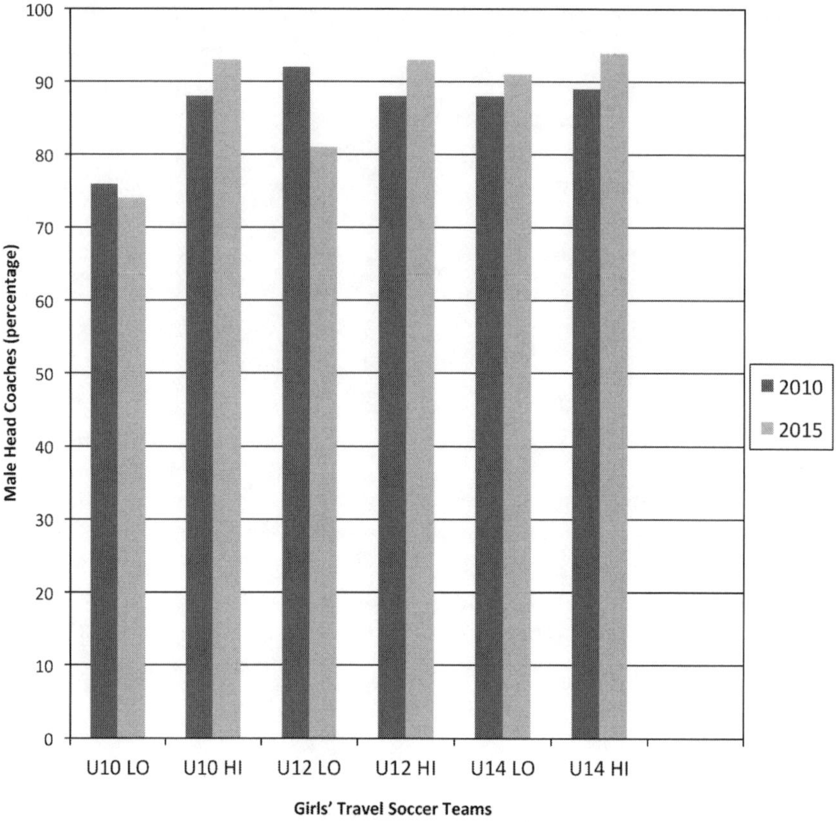

Figure 5.3. Percentage Male Head Coaches of Girls' Travel Soccer Teams
Source: Author's analysis of youth sports league data

approximately ten divisions, roughly corresponding to the quality of players and teams (self-identified). Teams playing in the top two divisions were designated as "high intensity" while teams in the bottom two divisions were deemed "low intensity." All of these leagues play under the USYS umbrella since ECNL does not offer "low-intensity" soccer, and AYSO does not offer "high-intensity" soccer. The White Stallions and Hurricanes from chapter 1 both played in division five (medium intensity) of their respective age group. Elizabeth's new team, FC Manchester, plays in division one. After U14, travel soccer leagues change dramatically, with many girls simply dropping out of the sport (or only playing for their high schools). Those who remain in the pipeline are increasingly playing in a more elite (and expensive) ECNL-type setting. Presumably, these more serious female players will also begin gravitating toward US Soccer's new elite Development Academies.

Assuming these four leagues are representative of girls' travel soccer throughout the United States, the overall percentage of male head coaches is truly astounding. In the aggregate, well over 80 percent of these head coaching slots are occupied by males. It is impossible to know how many of these people are paid professional coaches and how many are parent (or other) volunteers. High-intensity teams within each age group have slightly more male coaches. The only decline in the percentage of male coaches between 2010 and 2015 was among low-intensity U10 teams. Clearly, males dominate the world of girls' soccer head coaches, with only a slight hiccup in increased masculinization during the past decade. The masculinization of girls' youth soccer coaching is even more startling than the masculinization of women's college soccer coaching. You could imagine that youth sports might be immune from this masculinization trend since, hypothetically, there is far less at stake both for the coach and for the players. However, it seems that the ubiquitous forces of commercialization, commodification, and masculinization within intercollegiate women's soccer have trickled down through the pipeline and impacted girls' youth soccer. With all of the competent and experienced post–Title IX women available to coach young girls, it is quite amazing that almost 90 percent of these coaches are men.

EXPLAINING MASCULINIZATION

There are both supply-side and demand-side components to this occupational masculinization. On the supply side, this is another example of the "glass escalator" that often revs up when certain jobs start paying more and gaining prestige.[19] Female organized sports are no longer perceived as a feeble imitation of male organized sports. They are a significant economic, organizational, and occupational entity in their own right. As discussed in chapter 3, you can now earn a living wage as a women's college coach in almost any sport. You can also make a living coaching youth teams in sports with a large intercollegiate footprint and correspondingly robust youth sports pipeline. A longtime Division I athletic director (male) explained,

> It has really been the last ten to fifteen years when coaches of female teams can make something similar to what male team coaches make. That was probably one of the slowest changes after Title IX, although I'm not quite sure that Title IX actually caused it. Scholarships evened out, resources and facilities evened out to some degree, access to trainers and conditioners is the same, but the salaries were always lower for the women's team coaches. I really

> didn't think about it much. They eventually started coming around mostly in response to the increasing pressure for women's teams to do well. I'm sure it was in the backs of some people's minds that only male coaches could get these new women's college teams to the next level, and that men would not be interested unless salaries increased. Hell, it was probably in the back of my own mind. I'm not sure if men would have applied for these jobs even with the lower salaries, but once we did start offering more, the men came out of the woodwork. They were usually very qualified and only sometimes felt like coaching women was beneath them.

The masculinization and professionalization of youth coaching is a little more complicated because of the generally lower wages and salaries available, and the lack of opportunities in those sports without expanding youth to college pipelines. Girls' youth soccer, of course, is something of a poster child for this masculinization, professionalization, and, as discussed in the last two chapters, internationalization. A *female* DI women's soccer coach reflected during the NSCAA convention,

> I have seen it at these conventions during the past ten to fifteen years. Even with the increase in female coaches, there has been a larger increase in male coaches. Yes, a lot of them do have accents! How about that. I also see this when I am recruiting. The travel team coaches and tournament coordinators are almost always men and so are the directors and coaches at the first-tier camps and clinics. You know, I'm not even sure why they are considered first-tier, but that's the thinking we all go with. [My athletic director] tells me that every year there is a larger number of men applying for women's team coaching jobs. I'm not sure they are better qualified, but a lot of people think they are better qualified. Many of us, even the women, seem to subconsciously buy into the idea that male coaches and camp directors are producing better products. That's pretty disturbing.

Males comprise 100 percent of the approximately sixty members of the NSCAA Hall of Fame. Only five of the sixty-eight NSCAA presidents (7 percent) have been women, although all five have held that position since 1999 (28 percent), including Amanda Vandervort, director of social media at Major League Soccer.

This belief that male coaches are better than female soccer coaches also permeates the demand side of occupational masculinization. Female players and their parents *believe* that male coaches are better. This is not necessarily limited to male-associated sports like soccer but even female-associated sports like field hockey. The alleged male superiority in coaching sports is deeply embedded within our collective conscience, internalized even by many women and girls, although not always purposefully. A staff member with a regional youth soccer association commented,

> There's a definite preference among the elite female players, or at least their parents, to seek out premier teams with male coaches. I see it mostly within the higher divisions, but the preference seems to be trickling down as even the lower-placed teams think they have a shot at making it to the premier tournaments. And it's getting easier to find male coaches since there are so many of them being hired by the clubs. That goes along with the preference for accents that I mentioned earlier. Usually British, but sometimes other European or Hispanic is OK [laughs]. It depends on who won the most recent *men's* World Cup [emphasis in original].

Claire and her family faced these sorts of decisions as she was making the move from recreational soccer to travel soccer at age eight:

> There were so many clubs to choose from in [this area] we weren't sure what to do. Yes, there were a few clubs with women coaches, but I think my parents wanted me to have a male coach since they thought it would make me tougher. I agreed with them, but there was no reason for me to think that way, since I never even had a female coach except in [pretravel soccer] when I was six. Wow. In all my years of playing club and in high school, I didn't have a single female coach. I don't think there were any at the showcases. In high school, there were only a few women coaches of other teams. I've only seen a couple during college. I never really thought about that until now. You would think there would be more. I always thought I would make a really good coach, but now I'm wondering if that's even possible. It's pretty funny that my own stereotypes about gender may come back to kick me.

Claire's self-reflection was mirrored by many other female players I spoke with, even those not yet in college, but only when coaxed to address it. Parents, on the other hand, seem to be more willing endorsers of the alleged superiority of male coaches. Elizabeth's mom, Rebecca, commented,

> Women's college soccer is a rough game, especially in DI. I don't want Elizabeth learning that girls' soccer is somehow different than what the boys do. So yes, I want her to have male coaches whenever possible since they will be more likely to teach a male approach to the game. To not be afraid of contact. To go after every [loose ball] as if her life depended on it. Female coaches stress fun a little too much. Not that [she] shouldn't have fun, but she has so much potential to reach the next level. I think male coaches will help her get there better. I wish I had more male coaches growing up.

The masculinization of female sport is also evident beyond the intercollegiate and youth coaching ranks. Within intercollegiate athletics, high-level administrative positions such as athletic director have been and continue to be heavily dominated by men, with only a slight movement toward equity in DIII programs.[20] Youth leagues and clubs are almost completely run by men, even those exclusively for girls. For example, while the ECNL has a female executive director, the board of directors is almost completely male. A similar lack of female leadership is evident within US Soccer, where two (of five) female youth national teams are coached by men, and World Cup team coach Jill Ellis has two male assistants. Are there similar numbers of women coaching high-level male teams? The US Soccer Board of Directors is mostly men, as are its Diversity Committee (five women, thirteen men) and its Task Force on Youth Issues (four women, seven men). In the professional National Women's Soccer League, two of the three primary league officials are men, as are nine of the ten team general managers. Elsewhere, despite American field hockey being primarily a female game, three high-ranking executives at USA Field Hockey are men, although this may be driven more by internationalization than by masculinization. USA Ice Hockey's Olympic team recently named its first-ever female coach, but the youth national team has a male coach with three male assistants. USA Ultimate's national U23 mixed team and U23 women's team are both coached by men. In figure skating, females comprise 72 percent of USFSA's membership yet account for only seven out of sixteen board positions (albeit all three vice presidents) and five of thirteen administrative positions at or above the "director" level. US Lacrosse's leadership, on the other hand, is very gender-balanced.

Organizations such as the Alliance of Women Coaches are doing what they can to fight the overriding masculinization of coaching opportunities.[21] The group sponsors regular workshops where women coaches can share experiences and establish useful professional networks that might aid their occupational success. In conjunction with the NCAA, it frequently offers a Women's Coaching Academy. The Academy is four days of "educational training open to coaches of all experience levels that offers non-sport-specific program management strategies, with a special focus on philosophy development and building your skills and knowledge about planning, communication, legal issues, ethics, hiring, supervising staff, conflict resolution, learning styles and achieving success."[22] The Women's Soccer Coaches Committee (formerly the Women's Committee) within the NSCAA has also tried valiantly to address both the structural and the ideological masculinization within organized soccer. The University of

Minnesota's Tucker Center for Research on Girls and Women in Sport is an interdisciplinary research center leading a pioneering effort to examine how sport and physical activity affect the lives of girls and women, their families, and communities.[23] The Tucker Center holds valuable symposia and encourages new approaches to gender-based sports research. While the masculinization trend in female sports still seems to be going strong, it would probably be much more severe without the educative and activist work of these and other organizations.

MASCULINIZATION IN A GLOBAL CONTEXT

Despite the enduring patriarchy and hegemonic masculinity within US organized sports, these cultural phenomena may play a far more constraining role in other societies. Even socially progressive countries are not immune from the power of patriarchy in limiting girls' and women's access to sports participation. For example, Dutch women faced significant resistance when trying to establish professional soccer leagues, despite the sport's huge popularity among females.[24] As mentioned in earlier chapters, girls and women sometimes have problems playing field hockey in countries where, unlike the United States, it is primarily played by males. Elsewhere, journalist Timothy Grainey has detailed some of the systemic social obstacles to female soccer in various countries.[25] In most cases, elements of religion, cultural machismo, and blatant hypocrisy interact in various combinations to limit the participation opportunities for female players. Although not systematically studied, the same limits undoubtedly exist in many other sports. There is, quite simply, nothing quite like Title IX in the rest of the world. But even something like Title IX would not have an impact in countries where organized sports are not thoroughly intertwined with formal public education. Remember, Title IX only addresses gender-based opportunities in educational settings. Organized sports only fall under Title IX's jurisdiction because of the United States' serendipitous combination of sports and education. Title IX does not directly impact the world of commercialized, pay-to-play youth sports outside of formal education. Thus, as currently constructed, Title IX could not be exported to other countries looking to ease gender-based barriers to sports participation. There might be other policy initiatives that could address this discrimination, but they would have to be crafted much differently.

In the United States, patriarchal biases within organized sports are perhaps less important than class, racial, and geographical biases. There are plenty of opportunities for American females to play organized sports *if* they can afford it and *if* there is enough physical space to play sports such as soccer and field hockey. Imagine if Brazilian-born Marta, considered the finest female soccer player in the world, had been born in the United States. Marta's family was extremely poor, and yet there were still outlets (albeit mostly male) where she could develop her innate soccer skills and eventually be noticed by Brazilian professional teams, who are the financial backbone of the youth soccer system. If Marta had been born in the United States under similar economic circumstances, it is quite likely that she never would have reached these sporting heights. Instead, she may have never taken up organized soccer at all due to lack of opportunity. Or she might have started playing but eventually faced the financial constraint of continuing her development in the pay-to-play system. Perhaps she would have been able to play in largely invisible public school programs. But she would not have been selected by the US Women's National Team since she would not have traveled far enough (if at all) through the youth sports to college pipeline. In the United States, with a population of 330 million, 45 million of whom are officially poor, it's worth considering how many potential Martas are out there, where class, racial, and geographical barriers are perhaps more important than patriarchy in limiting access to sports participation.

TOWARD A MORE IRRELEVANT ESSENTIALISM

Despite Title IX or, perhaps, because of it, a rigid and patriarchal essentialism is omnipresent within organized sports in the United States. This reflects both structural and ideological factors. Structurally, organizational dynamics such as professional network composition, job descriptions, hiring practices, and working conditions all combine to ensure male domination of key occupational positions even as the supply of qualified females increases exponentially. The huge influx of non-native men into the US coaching labor market has altered any potential balance between coaching needs and the gender composition of the available labor supply. Quite simply, there are a lot more men looking for US work in female sports than was the case twenty-five years ago. Ideologically, there seem to be only minor challenges to a belief system insisting that male athletes are not just different from but superior to female athletes; that male versions of sports are not just different from but superior to female versions; that male coaches are not just different from but superior to female coaches. Importantly, these ideological beliefs are instilled at a very early age and do not exclude women and girls, at least those who are enmeshed in the youth sports to college pipelines. These socially constructed hierarchies get reflected in the paucity of so-called co-ed sports, especially at the youth level. There is absolutely no inherent reason why males and females cannot compete together in most sports except that we have culturally convinced ourselves that it is wrong or "unnatural." Even in sports like ultimate that have challenged conventional gender norms, patriarchal essentialism still thrives. A former Division I college player explained,

> I get so thoroughly pissed off sometimes during mixed games. The guys are unbelievable. Even the ones that are cool off the field turn into morons when we play, especially in prestigious tournaments. They will only pass to each other, even if it's a stupid play. On one team we had two women who had made Nationals. They were by far the best players on the field. One of them could [throw] the disc a hundred yards on the fly. But the guys would stop running their deep patterns when she was handling. Then they would try to pass it to a guy who was triple-teamed while I'm standing wide open screaming for the disc.

The masculinization of female sports is important in its own right, but also interacts with the overall commercialization, commodification, and corporatization of college and youth sports. Female athletes (or their guardians) *believe* that acting more like male athletes will help them reach the promised land of intercollegiate athletic scholarships and/or admissions advantages. This augments the already overwhelming pressure to purchase commercial products and services supposedly guaranteed to get girls into and through the pipeline's many levels. Any reduction in the commercialization and commodification of female youth sports, then, must simultaneously address the masculinization of female sports at the youth, college, and even professional levels. In this regard, the logic of patriarchy is just as important as the logic of capitalism for challenging the girls' pay-to-play youth sports pipelines that are draining the fun from childhood. In many respects, the masculinization of female sports is an unintended and unforeseen consequence of Title IX. The drive toward participatory equality has been accompanied by a latent belief that men's sports (and athletes) provide the normative standard to which women's sports (and athletes) should aspire. As a result, women's college sports and girls' youth sports place a premium on male-centric models of success and prowess. It should be no wonder, then, that our dominant patriarchal ideology pushes us to believe that male coaches are better equipped than female coaches to help players reach this male-centered Nirvana. Only by embracing a position of irrelevant essentialism can we hope to break this connection between commercialization and masculinization. We have to stop comparing female athletes and female sports to male athletes and male sports. Each should be recognized and applauded for its own intrinsic worth and value. Perhaps this irrelevant essentialism will contribute to making girls' youth sports more about fun. Male sports can then aspire to that!

6

SAVING GIRLS' YOUTH SPORTS BY CHANGING HIGHER EDUCATION

It is not easy challenging conventional wisdoms, and attitudes about sports are among the most resistant to critical reflection and actual change. As mentioned in the book's introduction, many people (not just students) are extremely reluctant to critically assess our social sacred cows about sports. There seems to be far more open-mindedness (to a degree) about the social construction of traditional gender roles, the very existence of racial categories, and whether poor people deserve their fate. Given this genuflection before conventional wisdom about sports, there will likely be great resistance to even small changes within intercollegiate athletics, interscholastic athletics, or the youth sports to college pipelines. Even when people acknowledge, as they often do, the negative aspects of organized sports, they believe that the problems are acute rather than systemic. This is especially true at the intercollegiate level. With just a wee bit more administrative oversight, with just a tad of tinkering, with just a few more workshops on balancing athletics and academics, we can fix any problems and ensure the taken-for-granted positive attributes of college sports. However, I think it is legitimate and necessary to confront the very premise that intercollegiate, interscholastic, and organized youth sports are, by definition, positive. I'm certainly not implying that they are inherently negative either. Rather, the social and personal value of organized sports should be approached as a blank slate; as an empirical question that needs to be answered. Organized sports can take positive forms or negative forms, depending on a host of factors. This book clearly leans toward a negative assessment of the current state of women's intercollegiate sports and girls' youth sports, and how the former is hurting the latter. I do not see the pay-to-play pipelines as a good thing. But underlying that empirically based conclusion is an acknowledgment that organized female sports *could* be much more positive. Organized sports *can* have wonderful personal and social benefits, especially for kids. In many cases, we can plainly see these positive outcomes. We should try to make sure these positive outcomes become the norm rather than the exception.

REFORMING HIGHER EDUCATION AND INTERCOLLEGIATE ATHLETICS

It bears repeating that the United States is the only country in the world with something akin to intercollegiate athletics. This is somewhat rooted in the unique history of American higher education, which evolved in one century from an exclusive conduit of social prestige to a less-restrictive source of practical knowledge and exposure to the liberal arts and sciences.[1] While higher education was certainly not accessible to people from all social strata in the beginning of the twentieth century, far more people outside of the economic and social elite were able to obtain college degrees than before. As the population pool of potential students expanded, so did the number of higher-education institutions, resulting in increased competition among schools not just for paying customers, but for other financial benefactors. This was the cultural context for the corporatization of higher education discussed in chapter 2 and the accompanying noneducational elements of higher education often used to attract these customers and benefactors. After 1973, Title IX more or less forced universities to expand athletic opportunities for women, roughly doubling the size and scope of intercollegiate sports. Within a society heavily informed by capitalist logic, it is no surprise that this growing institutional appetite for women's intercollegiate athletes has spawned a multifarious for-profit industry aimed at satisfying this hunger, with a corresponding cultivation of consumer demand (often highly masculinized) for its products. In the wake of this commercialized, commodified, and corporatized offensive, fewer girls are participating in youth sports and those still standing (if they can afford it) increasingly suffer serious physical injuries, bear enormous emotional pressures, and come to despise previously enjoyed activities. It is, in essence, a higher education–led betrayal of childhood fun.

Thus, attacking the problems associated with girls' youth sports *must* first address higher education and intercollegiate athletics. Merely focusing on youth sports themselves will not alleviate the tremendous influence of intercollegiate athletics on the pay-to-play pipelines that now dominate the landscape. Many fine organizations are currently working on easing the financial barriers and other structural impediments to youth sports in order to increase participation for kids of all social classes and abilities. These include but are not limited to the Aspen Institute's Project Play, America SCORES, the JT Dorsey Foundation, and the National Youth License movement within US Youth Soccer.[2] Project Play has been an especially active and visible advocate for physical activity among an increasingly dormant generation of kids. The organization's yearly summits bring together a wide array of knowledgeable people and groups who have constructed creative strategies for understanding and addressing the decline of childhood play.[3] However, I firmly believe that even these outstanding and well-meaning approaches will not transform the youth sports landscape unless greater attention is also paid to changing intercollegiate athletics, which is driving the problematic pay-to-play youth sports pipelines.

The following reform proposals run the gamut from completely revolutionary to moderate tinkering. They share a premise that we can only make youth sports more about fun and play by dismantling the youth sports to college pipelines. And dismantling the pipelines will require seismic changes in the structural and ideological landscape of intercollegiate athletics. Girls' youth sports will stop being primarily a commercialized and commodified pipeline to the "highest level" only when the exit portal of the pipeline is closed off or drastically reconstituted. And while girls' and women's sports remain the focus of these proposals, boys' youth sports would also benefit from them, although that will be a far tougher nut to crack given the professional possibilities available to aspiring young male athletes (and their parents) and the commercial behemoth of certain men's college sports. Many scholars and social observers have championed intercollegiate athletics reform but rarely with an eye on how that might directly benefit younger kids.[4] It may seem odd to argue that childhood fun is being held hostage by an increasingly corporatized American higher-education system, but that's the connection I have tried to make throughout this book. What are we collectively willing to do so that current and future kids can reclaim part of their childhoods?

The Nuclear Option: Eliminating Intercollegiate Athletics

The most effective and enduring way to return the fun to youth sports is to completely eliminate intercollegiate athletics. Completely. From the largest DI football machine to the smallest DIII bowling team. Not only would this immediately shut down the expensive, exclusive, and harmful pay-to-play girls' youth sports pipelines, but higher education itself would benefit.[5] Universities could redirect the disproportionate amount of resources currently commanded by varsity sports toward an almost infinite number of areas: increasing library acquisitions; updating classrooms and dorms; raising salaries for those more directly involved with teaching and learning; and boosting financial aid without the quid pro quo of playing a sport for thirty hours a week. There are also the many indirect costs of intercollegiate athletics that don't always show up in the budget under "varsity sports." These could include facility overhead and maintenance, alumni and advancement efforts for keeping up with the college sports arms race, university PR resources dedicated to athletics, library space expropriated by teams with "mandatory" study halls, and participating in league and NCAA structures. Or universities could simply pass the savings on to customers in the form of lower tuition or higher nonathletic financial aid. With all of the recent political chatter about soaring college costs, it is astounding that the high cost of intercollegiate athletics is never identified as a direct cause of these high prices.

If universities decide that participating in *organized* sports is a good thing, resources for intercollegiate athletics could be redirected to club and intramural sports that serve far more students than do varsity teams. These might include activities specifically tailored to those with physical challenges or other special needs who are normally excluded from the world of intercollegiate athletics. Currently, with limited facilities and growing varsity footprints, existing club and intramural sports often find themselves without a place to play, or having to play and practice at 3:30 a.m. In many ways, intramural sports and varsity sports reflect very different philosophies about the role of organized sport within an educational framework. Intramurals emphasize participation and player-centered activities. The students themselves form teams, organize practices (or not), and take charge of any in-contest decisions (such as substitutions). If referees or officials are necessary they are almost always other students trying to pick up a few extra bucks. Often, although not inevitably, playing time is relatively balanced among teammates, and strategic decisions are often reached consensually rather than by one person. The overriding goal of the activity is to have fun and build friendships. Winning may be important, but not necessarily at the expense of fun and friendship. In this sense, college intramural sports are more akin to the notion of "play" referred to earlier. Their value is primarily intrinsic.

Conversely, the dynamic of intercollegiate sports is increasingly extrinsic. It is less about the actual experiences and personal growth of the student participants, but about the commercialized, commodified, and corporatized meaning of these activities. Intercollegiate sports are more adult-centered than student-centered. There are coaches, athletic directors, administrative support staffs, officials, sponsors, alumni, benefactors, apparel manufacturers, and local businesspeople who all have a stake in the system. Colleges increasingly use sports to build and maintain a public persona that has little to do with the nuts and bolts of teaching, learning, and research. A successful and visible varsity sports program, even if it operates deeply in the red, is presented as proof of a university's organizational competence, even if the students playing in these programs don't take real courses, fail to graduate, suffer debilitating injuries, or grow to despise a game they once loved. Athletes in nonrevenue, low-visibility sports are not immune from these outcomes.

Completely eliminating intercollegiate athletics is not usually on the list of options for either improving higher education or reducing youth sports commercialization. However, it should not be unilaterally dismissed from conversation just because it is unusual or will face monumental resistance. Intercollegiate sports programs' drain on university budgets is often justified by insisting they are a source of community pride and "school spirit." There are two problems with this argument. First, is "school spirit" really an important part of higher education or is it just a mechanism for establishing a long-term financial relationship with alumni? True, a strong sense of school spirit might make college more interesting for students, but it has little impact on teaching, learning, and research. In fact, school spirit might actually interfere with the educational aspects of college by legitimating the "beer and circuses" orientation that revolves around certain varsity programs. As discussed in chapter 2, this may well be a concerted attempt to distract students (and their families) from the diminishing resources targeted for the educational component of higher education.

Second, all but a very few varsity sports play no role in building community cohesion (for better or worse) and are merely a ferociously expensive pastime serving a small percentage of students. They are of little concern to anyone besides the players, their families, their significant others, and (maybe) the players' roommates who have to suffer through early-morning alarms or late-night leg cramps. How many community members attend a squash match or walk the links with the varsity golf team? How many students paint their faces in school colors when the field hockey team is playing for the conference title? Even football and basketball are not necessarily the epicenter of a campus community as commonly argued by defenders of intercollegiate athletics. We hear a lot about the 102,000 people at a Penn State home football game and 22,000 screaming fans at Duke's Cameron Arena, but far less about the 782 spectators watching Duquesne play Wagner in football on a fall Saturday in a geographic region where the game is quite popular.[6] Where are the other 5,000 full-time Duquesne undergraduates (assuming all of the 782 are students)? Why aren't they participating in this rite of solidarity? Duquesne is one of those midsize schools discussed in chapter 2 that is employing a "Flutie Factor" strategy by ramping up its visible DI sports programs, especially football, which only recently added athletic scholarships and switched to a slightly more "prestigious" conference (because it allows more scholarships). Even Duquesne's men's basketball team, which is probably considered more "elite" within the school's culture, averages only 1,800 attendees at home games in an arena seating 4,400. Of course, few if any campus community members attend tennis matches or soccer games. This lack of spectators was not lost on Claire:

> Nobody comes to the games. Even last year when we had a great team and almost won [our conference] the stands were mostly deserted except for the parents who live close by and some guilty boyfriends. We had way bigger crowds in high school. Most of our parents and siblings would go. The JV would usually stop by. Lots of times the younger kids in the local travel program would be ball girls, so their parents would be there also. I don't mean there were a thousand people at a game, but we might have had a hundred some nights. It made it more fun to play, even when we were playing away games. Now, it's like playing in a morgue. Someone in my English class didn't even know we had a women's soccer team and had no clue where the field was. It is tucked away in a corner of campus, but it's not like we're playing on the moon. We're so immersed in [the soccer team] we forget that most people just don't care.

The point here is to challenge the idea that colleges and universities would inevitably disintegrate if they eliminated intercollegiate sports, even those often considered "elite" and that generate some community involvement beyond the players, coaches, and support staff. At Duquesne (and elsewhere), it's possible that more students (ten thousand full and part time) attend the school's jazz band performances and read the student-run newspaper, *The Duquesne Duke* (circulation four thousand). Yet the school does not subsidize those popular activities to the same degree as its varsity teams; it does not bestow special titles on its participants such as "student-trumpeter" or "student-journalist" even though young men and women spend countless hours on these activities that may positively impact the campus community. If Duquesne were to eliminate its soccer teams overnight, nobody would likely notice the next morning except for the sixty players on the teams plus a few coaches and support staff. Far more people would notice if *The Duquesne Duke* closed down.[7]

It's quite likely that subsidies for musicians and journalists would cost far less than subsidies for athletes. Duquesne's intercollegiate footprint, while expanding, is still relatively modest by intercollegiate standards. In 2014, it spent about $18 million (gross) on varsity sports. Roughly $3 million of that went to football. Given the university's overall operating budget of $278 million, direct spending on varsity sports accounted for 6.5 percent of total spending, with 1 percent for football alone. Duquesne has 415 total varsity athletes on 18 teams, or about 7 percent of the total undergrad population.[8] Football alone has 97 players (1.5 percent). With very little gross income from either football or basketball, the athletic programs must be financed primarily by the university's general operating budget. In addition to tuition and (if applicable) room and board, full-time Duquesne students are charged a $2,500 fee, some of which goes to pay for intercollegiate athletic programs that directly benefit only 7 percent of the students. On the other side of Pennsylvania, Villanova University has 15 percent more full-time undergraduate students than Duquesne, but an intercollegiate athletic footprint more than twice its size.[9] In 2014, Villanova spent about $37.5 million on 24 varsity teams with roughly 500 athletes. This amounts to about 10 percent of the school's overall operating budget directly targeted for about 7.5 percent of the undergraduate student population, on top of the resources already being spent on all students for things like instruction. Despite a successful, visible, revenue-generating men's basketball program, about three-quarters of Villanova's intercollegiate athletics program is financed from the university's general operating budget or student fees.

Defenders of intercollegiate athletics could argue that other sectors of the university also "lose" money but are not subject to the same criticism as athletics. This is a fair point within the traditional "not-for-profit" rhetoric. Naturally, this logic goes, we should not expect athletic programs to be self-sufficient. They are part of the school's overall educational mission. It is one of many important facets of higher education, not unlike the library or most academic programs. We don't demand that the library or sociology departments be self-sufficient, so why should we expect it from athletics? Should the library start charging $100 a day for overdue books and $1 per page for photocopying just so it can be economically self-sufficient? Should the sociology faculty charge $100 per hour for meeting with students outside of regular office hours, for advising independent studies and senior projects, or for writing recommendation letters?

Of course, within an increasingly corporatized approach to higher education, such seemingly ridiculous strategies are no longer just fictional. Different "units" and "sectors" of the university *may be* judged using such a rudimentary cost-benefit analysis. How many people check out or use certain library books or periodicals, and how does that weigh against their cost? How many individuals actually use the library's physical space on a given day, and does that justify staying open and providing amenities such as light and heat? How many students are enrolled in sociology classes, how much of their tuition is reflected in these classes, and how does this balance with departmental salaries and operating expenses? Do sociology classes need to average a certain enrollment level each semester in order to be fiscally responsible? Should the department try to fill every available classroom seat regardless of how it might impact teaching, learning, academic standards, and faculty workloads? Will there be a bonus for signing up majors? Will faculty with positive income-expense ratios share in the surplus? Will those with a negative ratio be terminated or required to perform other tasks such as issuing parking tickets or mowing the grass? Is it acceptable to ease academic standards in order to offer a more desirable classroom product?

However, there seems to be a lot more tolerance for intercollegiate athletic deficit spending than, say, library deficit spending. Over the past two decades (at least) university spending for varsity sports and for libraries has gone in opposite directions. According to aggregate data from the Association of Research Libraries, university spending on libraries declined from 3.7 percent of operating budgets in 1982 to 1.8 percent in 2012.[10] University spending on varsity athletics, as we saw in chapter 2, is trending in the opposite direction. Duquesne spends almost five times more of its budget on athletics (6.5 percent) than on the library (1.4 percent). Table 6.1 shows that this trend holds true at other schools as well, regardless of their NCAA division and the presence (or absence) of big-time FBS football. These particular schools are not being presented as a representative sample of intercollegiate programs, but to highlight a few interesting patterns. First, reflecting some of the Knight Commission's conclusions, schools with more modest FCS football teams may actually have larger overall athletics programs than schools with "big-time" FBS football teams. Second, schools

Table 6.1. Select University Spending on Athletics and Libraries, 2015 (in millions of dollars)

	Operating Expenses ($)	*Athletics Expenses ($)*	*Athletics (%)*	*Library (%)*
University of Idaho	368.2	18.9	5.1	1.7
Idaho State	222.0	11.9	5.4	2.4
University of Southern Mississippi	328.1	21.3	6.5	2.0
Duquesne	278.0	18.0	6.5	1.4
Villanova	373.8	37.5	10.0	2.6
James Madison	458.8	38.8	8.5	2.0
St. John's	507.0	39.7	7.8	1.7
Fordham	534.3	31.9	6.0	3.2
Bucknell	200.8	22.8	11.4	2.5
University of Indianapolis	98.9	13.2	13.3	1.3
Quinnipiac	291.8	24.2	8.3	1.0

Sources: Association of Research Libraries; US Department of Education

with no football at all (e.g., St. John's, Quinnipiac) can still spend a hefty amount of money on varsity sports. Third, Division II schools such as the University of Indianapolis often have very large spending differences between athletics and the library. A random sample of twenty schools each from Division II, Division I-FCS, and Division I-FBS showed an athletics: library budget ratio of 5:1, 3:1, and 2:1, respectively. Smaller schools with more modest intercollegiate footprints actually spend far more on intercollegiate athletics (as a percentage of their overall budgets) than on their libraries. In many cases, a Flutie Factor–based ideology is probably justifying these fiscal priorities.

Imagine how youth sports priorities could change if colleges and universities eliminated their varsity sports programs and redirected those significant resources to other areas, or simply reduced the cost of attendance. The pipelines would probably disappear overnight, at least the female version. Perhaps they would be replaced by a "youth band to college pipeline" with an entire industry on hand to help aspiring young brass players reach that next level of musical success. Just attend this band camp, use this slide oil, and perform in certain elite showcase concerts where university band directors will be on hand to identify the next Miles Davis. Parents would constantly be searching for the right instructor who could help their daughter or son reach that high C necessary to land a college scholarship or admissions advantage. Rather than seeking out British expatriates as mentors, parents enmeshed in the youth band to college pipeline would search for New Orleans–based African American musicians with long résumés performing in smoky Greenwich Village bars to help get their kid to that ever-elusive next level. Of course, given the nature of the United States' advanced capitalist economy, *any* commercial pipeline promising some ultimate payoff, be it for sports or music, would likely exhibit significant biases against those who could not afford to enter or navigate it. Any pipeline can be pay to play if left to the political economic forces of modernity.

The Less-Nuclear Option: Eliminating Athletic Scholarships and Admissions Advantages

Short of completely eliminating intercollegiate athletics, we could just significantly scale them back. The starting point for this slightly less drastic approach would be acknowledging, but not exaggerating, that intercollegiate athletics *do* offer certain unique and desirable personal and social benefits. Participants can find new and exciting ways to expand their physical and mental capacities. Spectators can enjoy and appreciate the excitement and, perhaps, form some community bonds around a particularly successful or interesting team. Coaches can find creative ways to help athletes discover hidden talents and recognize formerly untapped athletic potential. Sports information directors can find creative ways to package and present sporting events that might provide a welcome temporary respite from studying for (and grading) final exams, or expose the larger local community (beyond the school) to the fun of a raucous water polo match. Admissions officers can find creative ways to show prospective students how intercollegiate sports seamlessly integrate with academics to provide a splendiferous college experience worthy of a $70,000 yearly expense.

I am reluctant, though, to include offices of alumni affairs or university advancement (i.e., fund-raising) as worthwhile beneficiaries of a scaled-down approach to intercollegiate sports. The function of these offices is almost purely financial and reflects some of the worst elements of corporatized higher education. These offices are the foot soldiers for the captains of solvency. It is actually quite odd that *former* consumers of a product or service would be asked to continue paying for it long after it has been used. Do we make financial contributions to hospitals years after having our tonsils removed there? Do we continue offering cash payments to music teachers and physics tutors long after we stop playing the saxophone and studying quantum mechanics? But higher education has developed a business model addicted to revenue from former students, forcing it to convince these students that a positive school "brand" will help them throughout life. The modern university *needs* alumni contributions and hopes that the amount collected from them exceeds the amount spent on securing them. But this fiduciary relationship breeds a host of problems, besides its resembling a Ponzi scheme. First, alumni financial loyalty is often courted with expensive, noneducational things (like varsity sports), and alumni contributions often go only toward those very items that are used to court them. It is something of a vicious cycle where alumni contributions are often being used for the gratification of alumni so that they keep contributing. If a school spends a few million dollars more on its visible sports programs, perhaps alums will give a few million dollars more, which will largely be targeted for these visible sports programs. Second, alums often think that making donations gives them some influence over university policy. This is especially likely from large donors. There is no shortage of cases where alums have influenced graduation speakers, academic offerings, and most notably, athletics.[11] In some ways, intercollegiate sports programs are mostly about cultivating alumni relationships or, more accurately, not irritating alums into misplacing their checkbooks. The spending "arms race" in college sports is largely fueled by the needs of *former* students rather than *current* students. What do former students care about the library, innovative programs, student theater, faculty development, or the habitability of dorms and classrooms? They are far more interested in how many of their friends are returning for homecoming weekend, which parking lots will be open for tailgating before the game, and how many port-a-potties will be available in those lots. With their addiction to alumni donations, colleges must appease these concerns, often at great financial and organizational expense. Universities must also have a ready supply of merchandise available for alumni purchase, even if this merchandise was manufactured by sweatshop labor in southeast Asia. But alums only care about these things because the captains of solvency provide them. Which is greater, the amount of money collected in alumni donations or the amount of money spent creating an organizational infrastructure (including intercollegiate sports) to generate and collect alumni donations?

Philosophically speaking, the first step in reducing higher education's disproportionate emphasis on intercollegiate athletics is to treat it similarly to other extracurricular activities. These activities, whether based in the arts or other milieu, are also purported to be part of a well-rounded college experience for both participants and the nonparticipating community. Why is the field hockey team considered more important than the jazz ensemble? Why does the water polo team with twelve players and maybe fifty total spectators receive more university funding (including a paid coach) than the student newspaper with thirty-five staffers and thousands of weekly readers (and a volunteer faculty advisor)? Why are varsity soccer players eligible for academic support services but not campus Habitat for Humanity volunteers? You could argue that building homes for local low-income families is more personally worthwhile than kicking a ball (or spiritually worthwhile at a religiously affiliated school), and that the time spent on the former is more socially beneficial than the time spent on the latter. Assertions that varsity athletes spend more hours on their extracurricular activities completely beg the question of whether athletes *should* spend more hours on them. Who would suffer if the soccer team cut its practice hours in half? Perhaps the team would have a worse won-loss record. But so what? In contrast, it is clear who would suffer if there was a 50 percent decline in campus Habitat for Humanity volunteers.

Eliminating athletics-based scholarships would be the practical application of this less-nuclear approach to changing intercollegiate athletics, and beginning to liberate childhood fun from the insatiable clutches of the youth sports pipelines. For DI and DII schools with scholarships (and corresponding admissions advantages), millions of dollars would now be available to expand educational programs, increase need-based financial aid, or subsidize other extracurricular activities that have taken a historical backseat to athletics. Or, again, schools could just lower their prices! Ivy League and DIII schools without official athletics-based scholarships would have to eliminate the institutionalized admissions advantages offered to recruited athletes. No more coaches' lists. No more early reads. No more allowing overwhelming athletic prowess to compensate for underwhelming academic credentials. No more creative financial aid formulas that purport to have no relationship to athletic skill. Admissions officers would treat an applicant's sports participation as just another extracurricular activity. Individual schools could feel free to weigh these activities differently, but there would be no inherent bias in favor of sports accomplishments. As a safeguard, schools could be required, by either the NCAA or the Department of Education, to provide aggregate data on the academic credentials of their incoming students to see if there are any notable patterns among varsity athletes. Or saxophonists, for that matter.

Recruiting future players would also have to be reassessed under this less-nuclear model. Without actual scholarships and tangible admissions advantages, college coaches really wouldn't have much to offer a potential player except the promise that they will be on the team IF they get accepted through the school's regular channels. Coaches might suggest that applying "early action" might give them a better shot at admissions, but they will not be able to use the charade of an early read to semiguarantee acceptance. If too few players receiving such "promises" actually get accepted, teams would have to conduct actual tryouts open to all members of the campus community in order to fill their rosters. Many schools currently hold tryouts, but they are largely a masquerade to fill some "walk-on" slots that might expand their squads and allow for better practices (and help with Title IX compliance), or for a higher team GPA.[12] In a true tryout system, many young women and men who have already been sifted out by the pay-to-play pipelines might have a chance to play intercollegiate sports.

Schools might even choose to completely eliminate all recruitment and select teams exclusively through open tryouts. For this to be successful, all schools within a conference should agree to the approach so that no team has a real or perceived advantage over any other by actively seeking future stars. Teams would be successful (in the traditional sense) because they performed well or had excellent coaching guidance, not because of some strong connection with a few high-powered showcase tournaments or some elite private high schools that can afford (for instance) rowing or equestrian programs. Eliminating recruitment would save colleges significant amounts of money through a reduction in travel costs and possible reduction in nonessential staff. As discussed in chapter 2, college programs, even small ones, spend a lot of time, energy, and resources on recruitment. Perhaps those resources are better used elsewhere, both inside and outside of athletics. It is quite possible that this nonrecruiting, tryout-only model will be wildly successful at making the reality of intercollegiate athletics more consistent with the rhetoric surrounding it. It might even catch on. All that's needed is a few bold and brave schools or conferences to take the initial plunge. It could even help build an interesting and newsworthy front porch!

Any downsizing of college recruitment would almost immediately have a shocking impact on the pay-to-play pipelines by reducing the importance of showcase tournaments, the prime interface between youth sports and intercollegiate athletics. Since so much of the pipeline is geared toward these tournaments, disrupting their real or perceived importance would cause them irreparable damage. College coaches might be mildly impressed that a player attended an elite showcase tournament, but merely creating such a vague impression may not appeal to people like Christopher, who is about to push his daughter Lila to the next pipeline level. Just as the pipelines expanded when college coaches started recruiting at certain tournaments, they would contract if the coaches stopped showing up. This contraction would impact every commercial inch of the pipeline, including the rankings industry. Naturally, this revolutionary shift in filling college rosters would have to be accompanied by a changing philosophy that deemphasizes winning as the primary goal of intercollegiate athletics. In this new intercollegiate athletic model, young women and men will play college sports not because they had the personal resources necessary to navigate the youth sports pipelines, but because they enjoy it. Rosters will be stocked by the best players, not those who have accessed and survived the pipeline due to deep family pockets. Many people give lip service to this less-competitive perspective, often heralding it as the "pure" model of college sports. But their actions often contradict their lips.

Nuclear Fallout: Football and Men's Basketball

The most likely opposition to these "nuclear" proposals would center on football and men's basketball. Whether these programs are seen to be direct or indirect revenue generators, a central part of university life, or an integral piece of the school's branding campaign, it is unlikely that university leaders would support either their eradication or the elimination of scholarships or related admissions advantages. In fact, only a small handful of schools have successfully downgraded or eliminated their football or men's basketball programs over the past few decades.[13] Athletic directors and presidents might start reducing the footprints of so-called nonrevenue sports if not for the NCAA's mandate that schools field a minimum number of teams (which varies by division). Those reductions might face resistance at schools that depend more heavily on recruited athletes to influence acceptance rates and overall brand recognition, and from the NCAA, which would have to revise its dominant narrative about intercollegiate athletics being only incidentally commercial. Scaling back intercollegiate athletic footprints would be more likely at schools that do not "need" recruited athletes to help influence acceptance rates, that could easily fill their incoming class with people uninterested in playing intercollegiate sports, and that believe their public brand can withstand having fewer varsity teams.

In order to accommodate the financial and cultural addiction most schools have to marquee sports such as football and men's basketball, sociologist Howard Nixon II (reflecting ideas from Duke University men's basketball coach Mike Krzyzewski) has suggested a "partition model."[14] Nixon's partition model would have separate local and national structures for revenue and nonrevenue sports. For nonrevenue sports, things would continue pretty much as they are except for a drastic cutback or elimination of athletics-based financial aid at DI and DII programs. These resources would be redirected to need-based aid available to both varsity athletes and nonathletes. At most schools, regardless of current NCAA division designation, all varsity teams (including football and men's basketball) would operate on the "noncommercial" side of the partition since they do not generate any net revenues. The overriding philosophy driving these programs would be parallel to the current conventional wisdom about all college sports: it is an integral component of higher education that seamlessly augments academics. The NCAA would now oversee and regulate only these nonrevenue sports, staying more consistent with the organization's official mission of educational enhancement through athletics.

Under Nixon's proposed partition model, revenue-generating football and men's basketball programs would be considered "super sports." At some schools, both sports would fall into this category. At others, only one might. Schools in the so-called Power Five conferences would almost certainly have both sports included. These more commercially oriented programs would be regulated by a new system of super conferences independent from the current NCAA structure. This would end much of the transparent hypocrisy surrounding revenue-producing college sports by acknowledging the participants as "athlete-students" rather than student-athletes.[15] The local administration of these super sports would be formally connected with university governance structures, but operate autonomously from them (except in egregious cases). In Nixon's view, super sports would employ the university name, utilize university-owned facilities, and rely on athlete-students admitted by the school and subject to its rules and regulations, both academic and nonacademic.[16] Commercially, the super-sport programs would need to be completely self-sufficient. As a result, there would be far fewer regulatory or ethical constraints on generating revenue. Part of this revenue would go toward leasing university-owned stadiums and arenas, although commercially successful programs could probably just build such facilities on their own. Another part of this revenue would go toward compensating athlete-students since there will be no more sports scholarships.

Maximizing the Impact on Youth Sports

Nixon develops his partition idea very thoroughly in *The Athletic Trap*, and I do not wish to repeat all the details here. While I agree with his overall approach to reforming intercollegiate athletics, I would change a few pieces so that these reforms have maximum impact on taming the youth sports to college pipelines. For revenue-generating activities, which really have not been addressed much in this book, I would completely sever the "super sports" from the organizational structure of the university. The supposedly educational ship of big-money college sports has long sailed. All the rhetoric and pedagogical acrobatics in the world will not get this ship back to port. College football and men's basketball far beyond the Power Five conferences have become a primarily commercial enterprise that often contradicts and suffocates the fundamental academic mission of higher education. It is time to stop the charade. A completely independent revenue-sports system will benefit higher education directly by reducing the resources needed to subsidize most DI football and men's basketball programs. In turn, this could reduce college costs and remove a critical element driving families into the clutches of the youth sports pipelines. If higher education were less expensive, or even *perceived* as less expensive, families might be more resistant to the pipelines' siren songs of subsidized college costs.

In this intensified partition model, universities would be free to align with "independent" football and men's basketball teams "representing" their schools. These teams must be not only economically self-sufficient but also organizationally independent from the university. They would pay a fee for using a school's name and its stadium/arena, guarantee free admission to a certain number of students (negotiable), and be responsible for paying appropriate taxes on any revenues. Players, who must be high school graduates and under twenty-five years old, would have the option of receiving a market-based salary (taxable) or receiving in-kind vouchers (nontaxable) subsidizing the cost of attending that school. The amount of the voucher could also be market-driven but must be used prior to age twenty-six and be nontransferable. Players using vouchers would also be eligible for other forms of institutional financial aid. Whether being "paid" in cash or vouchers, players could not be on a "college team" for more than four years within a six-year period. Voucher recipients would be free to use them concurrent to their time playing, after they are done playing, or both. Players could even mix and match their compensation by, for instance, taking two years of salary and two years of vouchers. Certain teams affiliated with certain schools might actually find that vouchers are more appealing than a salary to prospective players. Since the value of these vouchers would likely exceed the salaries paid most players, teams would receive a tax credit for the difference between a voucher's value and the median income of players on a given team. Players would receive no admissions advantage to the school being represented by this independent team. They would have to be selected from the same applicant pools as all other prospective students. If accepted to the school, players (current or former) will receive no special forms of academic support apart from what is available to the entire student body.

Establishing a truly independent system for revenue-generating sports would offer an unintended advantage to universities: it would decrease the role of Title IX in constraining the allocation of resources. This would be especially relevant for football and its ninety-plus roster spots, which must be balanced by an equal number of slots on female teams. With football and men's basketball removed from their current educational domain, and thereby not subject to Title IX imperatives, schools would only have to provide gender equity among nonrevenue sports. Some universities without football teams, and/or with non-revenue-generating men's basketball teams, already operate this way, and those numbers could improve greatly. Eliminating the already specious claims that big-time football and men's basketball are part of a school's educational mission, athletic programs could cut down on the legerdemain necessary to achieve Title IX compliance. There would be no more need to establish ghost players on two-hundred-person women's rowing rosters. Male practice players on the women's basketball and volleyball teams would no longer need to be counted as female. And if Title IX compliance ever starts to include resource allocation, schools would be immune from trying to balance the outsize coaches salaries and recruiting costs of marquee men's sports.[17] The NCAA (or its proxy) would need to immediately end its minimum team requirement. Schools and conferences would independently determine whether they want to offer seventeen programs or seven programs.

Nixon's partition model also doesn't pay much attention to the admissions advantages currently offered in nonrevenue intercollegiate sports. As mentioned above, eliminating these advantages at every divisional level is absolutely crucial to taming the economically restrictive youth sports pipelines and their detrimental impact on many kids and families. *All* sports at *all* divisional levels must end admissions advantages for *all* recruited athletes, not just those receiving tuition vouchers. For this to happen, an almost revolutionary philosophical shift would need to precede what has become standard practice. Higher-education leaders would have to firmly challenge the conventional wisdom that varsity sports inevitably accord significant advantages to the university community, above and beyond the utilitarian manipulation of acceptance rates, alumni wallets, and brand construction. Intercollegiate athletics must be treated like any other extracurricular activity if they are ever to lose their luster at the end of the youth sports to college pipelines. Even though these admissions advantages are largely exaggerated by both universities and the youth sports industry, they do exist and are indispensable to the pipelines' existence.

The NCAA would have three choices under any of these revolutionary changes in the structure of intercollegiate athletics. First, it could morph into a less duplicitous version of what it already is: a coordinator and overseer of the college sports business enterprise, leaving nonrevenue sports oversight to some new organization, perhaps in the model of the old Association for Intercollegiate Athletic Women. Second, it could create a hybrid organization, one part dealing strictly with the commercialized sports and another part dealing with nonrevenue sports. These different organizational domains would have to be very carefully separated from each other. In this scenario, the money-making element of the NCAA would financially support the nonrevenue element, but there would otherwise be no operational overlap. Third, the NCAA could completely abandon commercialized "college sports" and align its actual behavior more consistently with the rhetoric of pursuing excellence in academics and athletics. Nixon's partition model suggests that the NCAA should follow the third option and return to its alleged roots of assisting universities in realizing an intercollegiate sports system rife with true "student-athletes." However, since 80 percent of the NCAA's revenue comes from the men's basketball tournament, the third option seems unlikely unless colleges and universities were willing to contribute money via a dues structure, prorated by things like school size, number of teams, and overall financial status. Ivy League universities, with their gargantuan endowments and large number of teams, might be asked to pay a little more while small, independent colleges might pay a little less. From each according to their ability (to pay). In any case, a more honestly operating NCAA (or alternative) would have a notable impact on dismantling the disingenuous pay-to-play youth sports to college pipelines.

A GENTLE STARTING POINT: TRUTH IN ADVERTISING

These radical suggestions will undoubtedly be met with great skepticism and resistance from both those with a financial stake in the pay-to-play pipelines and those who truly believe that it is a worthwhile system for offering social mobility to those normally denied a college education. But even with these revolutionary changes to intercollegiate athletics, girls (and boys) could still feel free to participate in more intensive forms of organized sports either as ends in themselves or as an apprenticeship to a professional sports career. But without the holy grail of college subsidies, the overall youth sports industry would be much smaller and less nefarious, especially for females who have very few sports career options. There is no substantive reason why a college degree or college attendance makes a person better qualified to play professional sports, qualify for a national team, or participate in the Olympics. Professional leagues and national sports organizations should feel free to subsidize these new self-sufficient "college teams" or other nonrevenue intercollegiate programs in the so-called Olympic sports (under the less-nuclear option). This would be much more honest and transparent than the current system where universities largely subsidize the preparation of future professional and quasi-professional athletes. Indeed, this would align the United States with the rest of the world that manages to stock its professional (domestic), Olympic, and international teams without demanding that higher-education institutions subsidize much of these athletes' training, and only after kids have survived the socially exclusive youth sports pipelines. Imagine the (especially female) talent that never makes it to national or Olympic teams because a huge swath of the population cannot afford or access these restrictive pathways.

In the meantime, while we await these more dramatic structural changes in higher education, there are more modest changes that can immediately ease the pipelines' many injustices. These changes revolve around transparency and truth in advertising. I would suggest that the NCAA could better align its actions and rhetoric by offering to become the primary watchdog of this expanding honesty in all stages of the youth sports to college pipelines. Within higher education, all NCAA member schools would need to prominently publish real data about their intercollegiate programs. At DI (non–Ivy League) and DII schools, this would mean truthfully disclosing the actual number of varsity athletes receiving any scholarship money (by team), the percentage and amount of the athletic scholarship received by each pertinent player (by team), and the typical out-of-pocket costs incurred by these so-called scholarship athletes.[18] In terms of admissions advantages, all schools in all divisions must report the aggregate GPA and standardized test scores of all incoming recruited athletes (by team) and compare them to the academic credentials of the overall student body. In essence, schools would be institutionalizing the same data collected by the Mellon Foundation's College and Beyond study (see chapter 2, notes 44 and 45). Schools would also be required to report the percentage of varsity athletes (by team) who participate in study abroad programs and internships compared to the student body at large.[19] To protect the anonymity of athletes on smaller teams like golf and tennis, the last three years of admissions data could be combined. DIII and Ivy League schools would also be required to explicitly announce how many athletes (by sport) were admitted via a preferential coaches' list or through an early read. The aggregate academic credentials of these particular students would need to be identified and compared with the overall incoming classes. Any attempt to falsify or manipulate this information will be treated as a Level I NCAA infraction.[20]

The NCAA could also exercise oversight of the youth sports pipelines. Showcase tournaments and premier clubs could be randomly inspected for truth in advertising. Lists of coaches who are supposed to be attending tournaments will be checked against those who actually did attend, either by visiting the tournament or contacting the coach. There will be periodic fact-checking of elite clubs' prominent lists of former members who are "attending" certain colleges or current members being "recruited by" or having "committed to" certain programs. People and organizations within the youth sports industry who in any way mislead consumers about their products will be placed on a publicly prominent "blacklist." The NCAA will also announce an honor roll (perhaps with a financial or in-kind reward) for industry representatives who purposefully subsidize the cost of their products and services in order to increase accessibility to low-income families and children with special needs. The US Department of Education could also contribute to truth in advertising by changing the reporting guidelines for its Equity in Athletics database so as to better reflect the actual expenses and revenues of each varsity program at every university, especially the amount of money from the general operating budget and student fees used to finance intercollegiate athletics. This would provide a much clearer picture of the actual amount of money spent at schools and could be a first step in corralling the intercollegiate athletics arms race and its starring role in the pay-to-play youth sports pipelines. In the long run, however, these incremental changes will be little more than Band-Aids. Dismantling the pay-to-play pipelines and returning youth sports to the kids who play them will necessitate a much more radical transformation or elimination of intercollegiate athletics as we know it.

HIGH SCHOOLS CAN ALSO HELP

High school interscholastic sports occupy a very interesting and somewhat contradictory niche within the pay-to-play youth sports to college pipelines. On the one hand, schools spend significant resources on organized sport and, mirroring the larger society, place it on a social pedestal that exaggerates its importance compared with other high school activities.[21] Within the status hierarchies of a typical American high school, being on the soccer team is more prestigious than being on the newspaper staff; being a "jock" is more prestigious than being a "band geek." As discussed in chapter 1, high school athletes planning to play sports in college are the beneficiaries of special school ceremonies heralding their sports successes. Their on-field exploits receive designated space on the morning announcements and in the local newspaper, which also dutifully reports game/meet scores while ignoring, say, the interscholastic jazz band competition, where participants exhibit exceptional skills rooted in focused practice and dedicated mentors, just like their athletic counterparts. High school athletes get their own administrator and sometimes their own end-of-the-year picnic. Morally questionable behavior by players and coaches is tolerated far more liberally than similar behavior by students and teachers. Imagine the community reaction if a teacher screamed at a student for "making an error" on an algebra exam or "showing no heart" on a research paper. Imagine an AP physics class where the seniors coordinate a "bonding" ritual for the juniors that requires hooking electrodes to various body parts and measuring the impact of different voltage and amperage.

On the other hand, high school interscholastic sports, at least within the domain of public education, are increasingly anachronistic to the pay-to-play youth sports pipelines. College coaches in most sports rarely recruit in public high school settings, although they might do so more in private high schools for expensive niche sports such as rowing. Instead, college coaches attend pay-to-play showcase tournaments featuring exclusive elite travel teams that are independent from the interscholastic system that often (although not always) subsidizes participation costs in traditional team sports like soccer and field hockey. Many premier programs within the youth sports industry actually forbid their players from participating on high school teams, making travel teams that much more central to successfully navigating the pipelines. Prospective players at even the smallest DIII programs with tiny intercollegiate footprints are asked to identify their travel team experience. Young women and men who did not participate in this pay-to-play system, either by choice or due to financial barriers, must somehow justify this résumé lapse to future coaches. Less than one generation ago, public high school sports were still central to college recruitment. This somewhat mitigated the social class biases of a pay-to-play system where relatively wealthy families have a huge advantage in securing the real, if exaggerated, fruits at the pipeline's exit.

Private high schools are a whole other matter and, in many ways, are much more fully intertwined with the youth sports pipelines. To many college coaches, pay-to-play private school sports programs are a reasonable facsimile of premier programs not connected with schools. A DIII field hockey coach explained,

> Private school teams can be helpful gatekeepers in identifying talent. Some schools actively recruit players so the ones on the field are probably more reliably skilled than most public school teams. There are "field hockey schools" out there just as there are schools known for basketball or rowing. If you get a game between two of these schools, it's almost like a mini showcase tournament. It's also a pretty good bet that kids who can afford private schools can also afford the best club teams and the best instruction, with access to great conditioning facilities and programs. Many of them even have regular sessions with sports psychologists.

Private high schools are much more likely than their public counterparts to prominently display on their web pages those players who have "committed" to an intercollegiate program. This is largely identical to the marketing activity by elite club programs and driven by the same need to recruit customers by quasi-promising a successful ride through the youth sports pipeline.

Within the domain of public education, though, high school interscholastic sports' contradictory niche actually offers an opportunity to chisel away at the unjust pay-to-play system rather than reinforce it as a reluctant coconspirator. If those overseeing public high school sports realize that it is mostly tangential to students becoming intercollegiate athletes, they might be more likely to tone down its seriousness and better integrate it with overall educational philosophies geared toward the personal and social benefits of developing the "whole" person. In short, high schools could put interscholastic sports into perspective; to make them more about fun and about learning to work well with colleagues in a collaborative yet sensibly competitive setting. High school sports could become a respite from the commercialized and commodified pay-to-play sports pipelines rather than a vestigial replica of them. It could reorient itself around fun and education instead of around wins, league championships, and state titles. This unconventional approach might also allow financially challenged individuals to develop their talent if, for whatever reason, they were interested in playing intercollegiate athletics. It could level the playing field for those financially (or physically) excluded from the pay-to-play pipelines and offer an alternative model to kids who want to play organized sports, but not quite so intensely. If enough kids and families abandon the commercialized system in exchange for a less intense and more intrinsically rewarding interscholastic (or even intramural) format, the pay-to-play pipelines might start to corrode even without drastic changes in higher education.

How would high schools accomplish this? First, they would need to consciously address sports' almost universal position atop the school's status hierarchy. Why not have the marching band perform at a different sporting event each week instead of strictly at the football games? Field hockey and soccer games also have halftime breaks. The band could even play at nonathletic events like a regional chess club competition. Assuming that things like pep rallies are an important part of community solidarity, schools could also highlight activities and accomplishments other than sports (or other than football and boys' basketball). Why not focus pep rallies on different teams each year, including girls' teams? Why not hold a pep rally for the school band before it flies off to compete in a national competition sponsored by Disney? Why not hold a pep rally for the Model UN before it buses to New York for an elite competition against the best high school teams in the country? And why not offer the students a half-day off from school if the band returns from Florida with a "superior" rating or the Model UN returns from Manhattan with a bunch of delegate awards and position paper awards? Many schools currently offer this bonus if a sports team performs admirably in some designated event. Schools will even grant excused time off if a local professional team wins the Super Bowl or World Series. What makes sports so important?

Public schools could find other ways to tone down their contribution to the social exaggeration of organized sports. For example, athletes would no longer be automatically excused from late-day classes so they can spend an hour getting to and preparing for contests at distant locations. Players will not wear their jerseys en masse on game days. There will be no practices the day after games in physically grueling sports, and games in these sports will never be scheduled on consecutive days to allow the players appropriate recovery time. Teams would be *prohibited* from practicing or scheduling contests during official school breaks when students should be resting and rejuvenating their brains. Players are rightfully skeptical when a coach says some practice or unofficial scrimmage during a school break is "optional," since there are always examples around of people who have been reprimanded or have lost playing time for skipping "optional" practices. Model UN advisors do not schedule optional practices during break, and chemistry teachers do not schedule optional labs. Students, on their own, are free to work on their debating skills or memorize the periodic table. Sports teams, however, get a free ride on this encroachment, which elevates their perceived importance compared with other school-based activities.

Public high schools could stop embellishing and exaggerating the "National Signing Days" discussed in chapter 1. In addition to being outright misleading about the future intercollegiate "commitments" of high school athletes, it gives interscholastic sports a public platform not offered to other important activities, thereby contributing to its superior status within the school (and to outside observers). Why no press conferences for those who have received significant merit-based college aid or preferential admissions due to academic prowess or talents having nothing to do with sports? Why no ceremony for financially challenged students who have "committed" to colleges ranked in the top ten of some arbitrary *U.S. News and World Report* category? Why no press releases to local papers about the "Princeton-bound" captain of the school's quiz bowl team or the outstanding pianist "being recruited by a number of DI conservatories"? The current status quo of high schools highlighting sports achievements is not much different than the "branding" campaigns increasingly central to higher education. It's almost as if public school officials think families will move to their areas and start paying taxes if their sports teams are visibly successful.[22]

High schools could also be more careful in hiring team coaches. They should be especially hesitant to employ professional coaches who are looking to make a living or augment their incomes with a high school gig. As discussed in chapters 3 through 5, the expanding youth sports to college pipelines often generate a robust labor market for professional coaches, a disproportionate number of whom are male, even in female sports. Schools may be excited about hiring such professionals in order to take their programs to that ubiquitous "next level." While certainly not inevitable, these professionals are less likely to embrace a holistic "educational" view toward interscholastic sports and more likely to view winning as the main purpose of athletic competition and an important credential for their own occupational success and mobility. A strong emphasis on winning will likely be correlated with demands that students prioritize sports among their many responsibilities. Since coaches (but not teachers) are permitted to scream at students, publicly question their personal desire, and restrict participation, it is no wonder that young women and men might choose attending an unnecessary weeknight practice or "voluntarily" raising money for the team booster club rather than completing a lab report or going to drama rehearsal. Schools could mitigate the institutional exaggeration of sports by trying whenever possible to hire coaches who are also teachers. While this would not be a panacea, educators might be more sensitive to the cornucopia of expectations facing high school students and to encourage a more tempered perspective toward sport. This might be especially likely for those who teach in the same school (or the same school district) as they coach, since informal social networks often serve as a check on behavior. A teacher/coach may be less likely to act like an idiot if she or he knows that her or his colleagues are likely to hear about it the next day.

Putting high school sports into a more appropriate perspective would be aided by explicit, written guidelines about how teams and coaches should and should not behave. At the heart of such guidelines would be a clear philosophical mission statement about the importance of *physical* education in complementing *intellectual* education. The goal of school sports teams, and the behavior of coaches who direct these teams, must be consistent with this philosophy. If the mission statement preaches a balanced approach toward academic education and physical education, then coaches cannot insist that their players prioritize sports over studying or other extracurricular activities. If the mission statement asserts that specializing in a single sport is ill-advised for the physical and emotional health of young adults, then coaches cannot establish explicit or implicit out-of-season expectations for their players. To assure this, there should be no off-season sports-related contact between coaches and students until two weeks before official tryouts for any specific team.[23] This would lessen the likelihood that certain players might receive an unfair advantage (or disadvantage) in making the teams or securing (or losing) playing time. It would also eliminate the sort of egregious situation referred to in chapter 3 when high school coaches actually extort players and families into buying certain sports-related products and services they are associated with.

To help ensure that these guidelines are followed, schools should establish athletic advisory committees consisting of students, teachers, parents, and a school administrator not directly involved with the hiring and firing of coaches. Representatives of each constituency could be selected by the appropriate representative body, be it a student government, a parent-teacher association, a faculty senate or union, or some amalgamation of these groups. The committee would be advisory to the school's athletic director and/or principal, and work in both proactive and reactive ways. Proactively, it would regularly administer anonymous surveys to sports program stakeholders and peruse the results for anything that might warrant further exploration. Reactively, it could provide a completely confidential forum where players, parents, and coaches could raise problematic issues in-season. If a player thinks she is being hazed (even gently) by her teammates, she can bring it to the advisory committee's attention. If a parent objects to a coach continually shifting practice times, and fears that discussing it with the coach might be held against their child, they could bring it to the committee in complete confidence. If a coach is continually berated by a parent for her tactical decisions, the coach can bring the issue before the committee and be guaranteed that her or his identity will not be revealed. This committee would make recommendations to the appropriate school/district administrators who, ultimately, would have the final say in responding or not responding. In all honesty, it is a sad state of affairs, and reflective of our social exaggeration of sports, that young adults and their parents are afraid to identify a coach behaving inappropriately. Yet this culture of fear is the current lay of the land.

Even if high school interscholastic sports were less serious and more consistent (in praxis) with a holistic educational philosophy, it would not completely dismantle the influence or persistence of the commercialized youth sports to college pipelines. Parents and kids would still pour boatloads of money into the pipelines in hopes of reaching the Valhalla of a college athletic scholarship or admissions advantage. And, like Robert and Rebecca, the intense sports parents we met in chapter 1, they might also decide to spend $30,000 a year more to send their daughters to private school, where there are fewer illusions that youth sports should be about having fun. However, if correctly designed and implemented, high school sports could actually become a welcomed alternative to the exclusive, high-pressure world of pay-to-play sports rather than a cheap facsimile. High school sports can become an end in themselves rather than another commodified way station heading toward intercollegiate athletic glory. Kids, especially girls, who might normally drop out of organized sports after age thirteen because they are getting too serious (mostly because of adults) or too expensive, can stay involved in activities they might truly enjoy. Those who might want to try certain sports for the first time, maybe because they look like fun, can participate in a collaborative setting and work toward achieving personal and team goals. Even young women who, for whatever reason, are embedded in a youth sport pipeline might also appreciate playing a long-loved game with longtime friends in a less-intense atmosphere. Schools, school districts, counties, and other governmental levels would have to be sensitive to issues of affordability and access (including physically challenged children), but nothing could be more unfair and unjust than the current pay-to-play system that is metastasizing throughout the youth sports world. Grounded in a philosophy of well-rounded learning rather than winning at all costs, public schools could probably do more with less and provide an enjoyable and worthwhile activity for kids who are increasingly being asked to act like adults at ever-earlier ages.

PUTTING THE FUN BACK IN YOUTH SPORTS

The pay-to-play girls' youth sports to college pipeline is robbing many kids of their childhood. Girls (and boys) who want to participate in organized sports may find their access blocked due to financial barriers that have turned youth sports into a cash cow for a plethora of individuals and organizations. Those able to gain access and sustain participation increasingly experience a highly commodified and commercialized system geared toward preparing kids for some esoteric and amorphous "next level" rather than enjoying the intrinsic elements of sports as a form of play. Parents enable this system as they accept the commodified promises of commercial entities while harboring prestige-driven dreams of their daughters' sports prowess generating admissions advantages and full scholarships to prestigious (and unnecessarily expensive) universities. The masculinization of female sports is thoroughly intertwined with its commercialization, commodification, and corporatization.

Higher education is the driving force behind commercialized pay-to-play youth sports pipelines in the United States. The corporatization of higher education has led to an increased emphasis on visible and expensive intercollegiate athletics. Due to the undeniable impact of Title IX (and other factors), female sports have been the prime beneficiary of this increased emphasis over the last twenty-five years. These increased intercollegiate opportunities, while significant, are highly exaggerated by a plethora of social forces leading families to make decisions that are financially imprudent and that may risk their daughters' physical and emotional health. Ironically, perhaps, the immense cost of intercollegiate athletics programs has contributed significantly to the high costs of higher education, which fuels the misperception among families that successfully navigating expensive youth sports pipelines will remedy this financial challenge. Again, the growing price tag of intercollegiate sports is rarely indicted in the many social critiques of higher education's skyrocketing costs.

Despite expanded intercollegiate opportunities and a more omnipresent youth sports industry, fewer kids are playing organized sports than twenty years ago. This trend is somewhat alarming, assuming that participation can be intrinsically fun and healthy. These participation trends are inexorably intertwined with social factors such as family income, race, ethnicity, and residential location. Fewer kids play organized sports, but a greater percentage of those who do play are participating in the expensive pay-to-play system rather than, say, a less-intense township-sponsored program. After the age of thirteen, a decreasing number of inexpensive (or free) recreational options are available for anyone who has not already left organized sports for financial reasons or because it was no longer (if ever) fun. The youth sports to college pipelines have become an institutionalized affirmative action program for relatively richer families to subsidize the increasing costs of a higher-education system that is devoting more of its scarce resources to varsity sports programs. Contrary to conventional wisdom, youth sports excellence provides virtually *no* social mobility for low-income families, except in weak pipeline sports such as football and boys'/men's basketball. But even in these two domains, the alleged Horatio Alger impact of sports is greatly exaggerated by the cultural focus on a small number of highly visible college programs and highly visible rags-to-riches stories. All of these exaggerations are rooted in the neoliberal corporatization of higher education that focuses on developing a school's "product" and its "brand" in appealing ways to potential customers and benefactors, including alumni. Thus, any attempts to make youth sports an intrinsically rewarding part of childhood rather than a commodified means to an end must ultimately focus on changing higher education.

Mike Barr, director of coaching education for the Eastern Pennsylvania Youth Soccer Association (EPYSA), tells a great story about how parents sometimes lose their focus on what kids like about sports. Mike had recently asked his own now-grown kids about their best childhood soccer memory. He was expecting to hear about high school state championships or travel team MVP awards. Instead, his children reminisced about some obscure tournament where one of the kids' teams played poorly, which made Mike (the head coach) really upset. By itself, that sounds like a strange favorite memory, but there's more. It seems that on the way home, while Mike was still fulminating, his two kids (the other was dragged along for the day) complained about being hungry since, after all, they hadn't eaten in about five hours. Mike snapped out of his postgame coaching funk and realized he had forgotten his wallet. No money. Hungry kids. On a lark, he pulled into a newly constructed gated community that was featuring open houses and tours of the complex. Mike and his kids found lots of free food in the model homes and then got to drive a golf cart around the community to see the pool, clubhouse, and proposed golf course. The kids did the driving. The three of them had an absolute ball infiltrating this future bastion of the rich and not famous before returning to their upper-middle-class split-level home. Missed headers and untimely fouls seemed very far away. So did sitting in the stands for half a day watching your sibling play soccer. This was his kids' best soccer memory. Getting to drive a golf cart and eat food while pretending to be interested in buying a house they could never afford. Parent and kids collaborating in subtle class warfare.

It is these meaningful personal relationships that often suffer from our collective obsession with reaching the next (and possibly ultimate) level in the youth sports to college pipelines. It's Caroline remembering the food-court antics of her teammates far more vividly than what happened in a game five minutes earlier. It's one of Elizabeth's former teammates wondering not who is going to play left wing next year but where the post–Labor Day tournament pool party is going to be, since it was always at Elizabeth's house. It's Claire recalling when she and three teammates used their entire meal allowance on ice cream during a particularly unenjoyable road trip. By overemphasizing youth sports as a means to an end, we are increasingly denying kids the opportunity to have fun doing something that *should* be fun. We are, to a great degree, betraying our kids' childhoods by turning youth sports into a human capital investment project.

In many regards, organized youth sports have become "high-stakes" in much the same way as standardized testing. Colleges and universities have constructed absurd, soul-deadening admissions procedures designed to maximize their marketing appeal to future customers.[24] People are convinced that if their kids do not get into a certain sports program or have a certain British-accented coach (or get certain SAT scores), then they will never get into a "decent" college and avoid a life of destitution. Slews of individuals and organizations are extraordinarily happy and well equipped to exploit this social exaggeration of sports' importance, just as others have been exploiting standardized test anxiety. Hundreds of colleges have made standardized test scores an optional admissions requirement, recognizing their lack of predictive value, their class bias, and their creation of commercially exploited test anxiety in a generation of kids (and their families). Why couldn't colleges do the same with intercollegiate athletics? It's time to stop this exaggeration of sports at every level, but especially within higher education due to its hurtful impact on youth sports. If we can't agree on any deep philosophical reasons for dismantling the pay-to-play youth sports to college pipelines, then let's just do it so kids can be kids, not simply pint-size apprentices for college varsity teams who are caught up in the corporatized university's quest for brand visibility and fiduciary prestige. Let's do it so girls and boys can enjoy sports for what they are, not for some apparition of what adults think they are. Kids like Susan deserve a childhood free of knee surgeries and rooted in fun and friendship, not one betrayed by parental misconceptions and commercial interests. There's plenty of time for this betrayal when they are adults.

APPENDIX

The Challenges of Ethnography

I have gone back and forth about including this appendix on methodology. What finally pushed me over the edge was a recent conversation in the spring 2016 issue of *Contexts*, a public-oriented journal published by the American Sociological Association. The conversation focused on some of the pitfalls faced by ethnographers both while conducting their research and presenting their findings. Many of these issues struck close to home, and I thought contributing to this discussion would be beneficial to current and future social scientists (including students), while simultaneously clarifying my research strategy in this project. While important in its own right, this conversation might also be helpful to those who wish to replicate this or similar research. I make no assertions that my research strategy is the best or only one available. But I believe it has helped produce an interesting piece of social science research that is accessible to those who are not professional social scientists.

One of the major issues facing ethnographers is the confidentiality of our sources and subjects. Almost all of the adults I spoke with or observed gave me written permission to use their names. However, I have chosen to disguise most of them just in case my interpretations of their words/actions are different from how they might have intended them. There is nothing unethical about this. It is at the heart of what is sometimes called the "emic" versus "etic" debate within anthropology and other observational-based social sciences. An emic perspective gives primacy to an actor's "definition of the situation." Reality *is* the subjects' actions and, more importantly, their explanation for those actions. From this perspective, the social scientist is merely a recorder of actions and explanations and does not subject them to any "outside" analysis. In contrast, an etic approach contends that sometimes a subject's actions, and the explanations of these actions, do not tell a complete story of what they are doing; that their actions have a larger social meaning than what is readily apparent to them. The social scientist's mission, then, is to tease out these deeper meanings and patterns; to provide a more "objective" rather than purely subjective perspective on people's behavior. Of course, different observers employing an etic perspective may generate different explanations for "native" behavior. That's not a bad thing! Some explanations may be more persuasive than others, and it's possible a consensus may eventually form around one view. Or not.

Regardless, though, these "objective" views may be disturbing to the subjects being studied, who prefer their own culturally embedded subjective explanations (or myths) for their actions and beliefs. The research strategy in this project employs both an emic and etic perspective, with slightly more use of the latter. So when college soccer and field hockey coaches explained to me their rather whimsical view of what goes on at showcase tournaments, it in no way detracts from the larger nonwhimsical meaning of these showcases within the youth sports to college pipeline. Similarly, when university athletic directors sincerely assert that athletic scholarships provide a means for low-income families to afford college, the sincerity of that assertion does not make it true in light of other information at my disposal. In such a case, I am not particularly interested in the motive for this disconnect between personal (emic) perspective and more objective (etic) reality. The athletic directors may be uninformed or they may be consciously trying to perpetuate a popular myth about intercollegiate athletics that they know to be false. The social scientist's challenge is to highlight this contradiction without impugning anyone's intentions. But just in case there is some unintentional impugning, it may be best to leave people's names out of it.

Another similar topic of debate among ethnographers is whether to disguise demographic information about our subjects. I have regularly employed such "deception" in this project, also with the intention to protect people's confidentiality (especially the kids'). Arguments against this practice are sound. They include the obstacles to replication when factors such as gender, geography, and organizational membership are critical to developing an analytical model for understanding the social situation at hand. These obstacles are magnified when the ethnography is in the form of a single case study. Checking the validity of this model, or even just using it to understand a different case, is greatly hampered without knowing its finest details. Thus, in altering certain factors to protect subjects' confidentiality, social scientists may find themselves on a slippery slope where more and more factors need to be disguised just in case some clever reader will put a name on these anonymous faces. In protecting our subjects' identities, we detract from the long-term social scientific prowess of our ideas and arguments.

I believe there is much merit to this critique when the disguised factors are truly central to any analytical model being developed or to our ability to make sense of the subject. However, the "youth sports to college pipeline" model developed in this project is not dependent on factors that are frequently disguised in ethnographic research. Geography, for instance, really does not matter to the form and function of youth sports pipelines, and disguising where subjects live will not impede using the pipeline model to guide future research on, say, a different array of sports or to challenge the veracity of the model itself. It is largely irrelevant if Caroline and Elizabeth live in suburban Detroit, suburban Dallas, or suburban Baltimore, as long as it is clear that being in a suburb *is* important. And while certain locations are clearly "hot spots" for youth soccer or "fringe areas" for youth field hockey, precisely identifying the exact hot spot or fringe area adds nothing substantive to the data. The hot spots and fringe areas are almost identical to each other except for their zip codes. Likewise, it doesn't matter that a NCAA Division I coach works at a university in the Big Ten Conference, the Atlantic Coast Conference, or the Southeastern Conference, since conference affiliation really doesn't impact how youth sports pipelines work. It's really not even important to know if the coaches (or players) are affiliated with "major" Division I conferences or "mid-major" conferences since I found no empirical evidence that people think and act differently based on this status. Conversely, there *was* notable empirical variation between the perspectives and actions of Division I–based subjects and Division III–based subjects, so it would be inappropriate to disguise that particular characteristic in order to protect confidentiality.

Finally, some researchers are wary about creating composite characters to represent certain "genres" of ethnographic subjects, whether to make for a more compelling narrative and/or to further protect anonymity. Again, this is a valid methodological criticism but one that should not be cast too widely and too absolutely. There are different degrees of appropriateness when employing this technique. It is, I believe, relatively appropriate when there is a strong convergence among the actions and voices within a genre, and there are enough representatives of that genre to provide some assurance that the composite is not an overgeneralization. In terms of convergence around significant issues, I only saw it strongly among the players and parents whom I observed and interviewed. For instance, the "prestige" factor of having a daughter play college sports was very strong among almost all pipeline parents. Since that issue was decidedly *not* on my radar when the project began, it caught me a little off-guard when first uncovered but soon became a standard line of inquiry during interviews. Parents were certainly not "monolithic" about this topic, but the pattern was clear. Did enough subjects mention it so that I was sure the pattern was not a spurious result of deliberately leading questions or "sampling to the dependent variable"? Did I put my words into the mouths of parent and player interviewees? Did I misinterpret the hundreds of casual sideline conversations I overheard while doing naturalistic field work? How many interviews or observations does it take to establish an empirically verifiable pattern? These questions are mostly impossible to answer definitively and, more importantly, are a misguided application of quantitative methodologies to qualitative research. Instead, this "theory" about parental motivation for participating in youth sports pipelines needs to be falsifiable; it needs to be disprovable. I believe that it *is* falsifiable and would encourage other social scientists to also study this general topic to see what they discover, either similarly or differently.

In addition to meeting certain methodological requirements, composites should only be used when they truly contribute to a more compelling narrative that helps readers better understand important underlying behavioral patterns. Again, there is no "secret code" that tells a researcher when composite characters will benefit a story. It is a judgment call. In this book, I decided that highlighting the form and function of youth sports pipelines was better served using representative composite characters rather than repeating the same general idea from eleven different subjects, or defaulting to a more quantitative orientation and stating, for instance, that 83 percent of college soccer and field hockey players felt significant amounts of physical and emotional burnout. In fact, that *is* the percentage of interview subjects who indicated they practically hated playing a sport they once loved. But that factoid is far less interesting than hearing the actual voices of players (Susan, Claire, Jenny) and parents (Kim, Rayna) talk about the girls' physical trauma and emotional turmoil while playing a game that was supposed to be fun. I believe the use of composite characters in this project is defensible since it does not impede suitable replication and/or falsifiability. Another ethnographer examining girls' youth sports to college pipelines might find very little evidence of stage four burnout or disdain among older players, and few if any younger players like Caroline and Elizabeth (or the sixteen girls they represent) who are in stage one. Reconciling competing narratives about, in this case, burnout within the girls' youth sports pipeline is part of the fun of doing social science research. I welcome and encourage others to replicate this study (IRB willing), using similar or different sports, and see what they come up with. Other ethnographers may find little or no evidence of any Carolines, Elizabeths, or Susans. In the meantime, I offer this good-faith research as a way to start the conversation about a cultural practice that may have devastating personal and social consequences. This is a subject that we *should* be talking about.

NOTES

INTRODUCTION

1. Rick Eckstein, Dana Moss, and Kevin Delaney, "Sports Sociology's Still Untapped Potential," *Sociological Forum* 25, no. 3 (September 2010).

2. Karl Marx, *The Eighteenth Brumaire of Louis Bonaparte* (New York: International Publishers, 1969). The original phrase was "[people] make their own history, but they do not make it as they please; they do not make it under self-selected circumstances, but under circumstances existing already, given and transmitted from the past."

3. C. Wright Mills, *The Sociological Imagination* (New York: Oxford University Press, 1959); Alfred McLung Lee, *Toward a Humanist Sociology* (New York: Prentice Hall, 1973).

4. The research was approved by Villanova University's Institutional Review Board.

CHAPTER 1: THE FEMALE YOUTH SPORTS TO COLLEGE PIPELINE

1. Many youth sports are organized around age groups consisting of kids "under" the indicated age, although many are actually the same age. In reality, then, nobody on Caroline's U13 team is *older* than thirteen. Some may be twelve. Soccer usually divides age groups in one-year intervals (U9, U10, U11), while field hockey uses intervals of two years or more (U10, U12, U14, U19).

2. This league is fictitious.

3. Many high-level soccer programs forbid their players from participating on school teams. This is includes US Youth Soccer's long-standing Olympic Developmental Program (ODP) and US Soccer's pending Girls' Development Academy.

4. Elizabeth has since told her parents. They were not pleased.

5. The NCAA is divided into three divisions. Division I schools play at the highest level of intercollegiate athletics. The bulk of athletics-based scholarships are associated with this level. There are subdivisions of Division I based on the size (or existence) of a school's football program. Division II schools have more modest and less prestigious intercollegiate programs with fewer and more modest athletic scholarships. Division III schools, generally smaller liberal arts colleges, do not award athletics-based scholarships, so usually spend far less on intercollegiate athletics. These divisions are often referred to as DI, DII, and DIII. The discussion in this book will focus mostly on DI and DIII schools. For more details, see http://www.ncaa.org.

6. For an outstanding analysis of these historical trends, see Edward Royce, *Classical Social Theory and Modern Society* (Lanham, MD: Rowman & Littlefield, 2015).

7. A nonexhaustive list might include: Howard Nixon II, *The Athletic Trap* (Baltimore: Johns Hopkins University Press, 2014); Ronald Smith, *Pay for Play: A History of Big-Time College Athletic Reform* (Urbana: University of Illinois Press, 2011); James Duderstadt, *Intercollegiate Athletics and the American University* (Ann Arbor: University of Michigan Press, 2003); Andrew Zimbalist, *Unpaid Professionals* (Princeton, NJ: Princeton University Press, 1999); Gilbert Gaul, *Billion-Dollar Ball* (New York: Viking, 2015); Charles Clotfelter, *Big-Time Sports in American Universities* (New York: Cambridge University Press, 2011); Taylor Branch, "The Shame of College Sports," *The Atlantic* (October 2011).

8. For instance: Welch Suggs, *A Place on the Team* (Princeton, NJ: Princeton University Press, 2005); Susan Ware, *Title IX: A Brief History with Documents* (New York: Waveland Press, 2015); Brian Porto, *A New Season: Using Title IX to Reform College Sports* (Westport, CT: Praeger, 2003); Linda Jean Carpenter and R. Vivian Acosta, *Title IX* (Champaign, IL: Human Kinetics, 2005). Female athletes are also given attention in the Mellon Foundation's College and Beyond study, which has resulted in several important books (see chapter 2, note 44).

9. By no means am I belittling "journalistic" explorations about youth sports. Most of these books are excellent, but they are not tethered to social scientific theories or research methodologies, thus impairing our confidence in generalizing from specific examples to larger social trends. Some outstanding journalistic accounts include Mark Hyman, *The Most Expensive Game in Town* (Boston: Beacon Press, 2012); Mark Hyman, *Until It Hurts* (Boston: Beacon Press, 2009); Tom Farrey, *Game On!* (New York: ESPN Books, 2008); Bob Bigelow, *Just Let the Kids Play* (Deerfield Beach, FL: HCI Books, 2010).

10. Michael Sokolove, *Warrior Girls* (New York: Simon and Schuster, 2008); Joan Ryan, *Little Girls in Pretty Boxes* (New York: Warner Books, 1995).

11. Hilary Friedman, *Playing to Win* (Berkeley: University of California Press, 2013); Noel Dyck, *Fields of Play* (Toronto: University of Toronto Press, 2012); Michael Messner, *Taking the Field* (Minneapolis: University of Minnesota Press, 2002); Michael Messner, *It's All for the Kids* (Berkeley: University of California Press, 2009); Sherri Grasmuck, *Protecting Home: Class, Race, and Masculinity in Boys' Baseball* (New Brunswick, NJ: Rutgers University Press, 2005).

12. For example, Dyck talks about Canadian youth soccer players "going south" to get scholarships at US colleges since there is no corresponding intercollegiate athletics system in Canadian higher education. But this is treated as one of many factors influencing how participants think about youth sports.

13. Women may be able to make a living, though, by coaching or teaching sports. However, even this is becoming more problematic (see chapter 5).

14. There is scant reliable data on women's professional soccer players throughout the world. However, according to FIFA, women comprise only about 12 percent of "registered" nonyouth soccer players.

15. Reflecting this, graduation rates for female intercollegiate athletes are consistently higher than rates for male athletes.

16. Christopher was mistaken. Abby Wambach attended the University of Florida.

17. See note 7 above for some excellent reviews of Title IX's history.

18. The NCAA strategy was to offer national championship tournaments in many of the same sports that already had AIAW championships. In marketing this alternative, the far wealthier NCAA promised to cover all costs for schools participating in its tournaments. It was an offer schools couldn't and didn't refuse, and the AIAW dissolved in 1982.

19. There is a very clear relationship between these trends and who occupies the White House. This reflects whom the president appoints to run the Department of Education, which is charged with monitoring Title IX compliance. The department can engage in stringent oversight or lax oversight.

20. Author's analysis of NCAA and NCES data. The percentage of male athletes is slightly lower at DI schools (54 percent) and slightly higher at DII and DIII schools (59 percent).

21. According to the NCAA, between 1980 and 2015 the average size of a football team increased from 95 to 112 (DI), 81 to 112 (DII), and 69 to 103 (DIII). Schools in the "Football Bowl Subdivision," once known as Division IA, offer 85 full scholarships that cannot be divided among players. The "Football Championship Subdivision" schools, formerly known as Division IAA, can offer up to 63 full scholarships that are rarely divided. Division II football schools are allowed a maximum of 36 full scholarship equivalencies that are almost always divided up among a large number of players. There are no scholarships for DIII football players, but all team participants count toward an institution's Title IX compliance. The so-called Javits Amendment to Title IX acknowledged that equipment costs were higher in some sports (like football) and should not be compared to

women's sports requiring less expensive equipment, but this qualification does not generally extend to participants, although some legislators tried to exclude football from the original Title IX legislation.

22. This is decidedly *not* a sophisticated quantitative analysis, but a careful assessment of aggregate trends. So while I think changes in college sports opportunities were driving high school sports opportunities, I don't think that these particular data prove it definitively. I am more convinced of this trend based on interviews with people who were highly involved with youth sports during this period.

23. This new tournament is being run in conjunction with Corrigan Sports and will be discussed further in chapter 3.

24. For example, during the 2016 Memorial Day Weekend, there were four simultaneous elite tournaments for girls' soccer (five for boys). On another weekend, there were two concurrent girls' tournaments about ninety miles apart.

25. The patriarchal influences on these perceptions will be addressed in chapter 5.

26. In contrast, the much smaller world of male field hockey is concentrated on the West Coast, where it draws on players of Oceanic descent, where the game is played by males and females without any patriarchal cultural stigma.

27. The University of Southern California recently added a women's lacrosse program. Roughly two-thirds of its players hail from northeast and mid-Atlantic states.

28. Author's analysis of data from the Sports and Fitness Industry Association (SFIA), the NCAA, and the NFHS.

29. Much of this information is from Pasquale Anthony Leonardo and Adam Zagoria, *ULTIMATE—The First Four Decades* (San Francisco: Joe Seidler, 2005). This is truly considered the historical bible of ultimate and was referenced by almost every player, coach, and sport official I interviewed.

30. See http://www.usaultimate.org/spirit.

31. See Jay Coakley, *Sports in Society* (New York: McGraw-Hill, 2014).

32. The data on sports participation rates are mixed and matched from a variety of sources. One is the SFIA, which represents commercial interests within the sports industry. Even though it is a "special interest" group, the SFIA has a keen need to accurately understand the youth sports marketplace. The Pew Research Center conducts regular surveys on a variety of issues. The Center's survey covering the period of September 15–October 13, 2015, asked a number of questions on youth sports participation. D'Youville College's Center for Research on Physical Activity, Sport, and Health (CRPASH), under the guidance of Don Sabo, has also generated a wealth of data on youth sports participation, generally drawing on the longitudinal Monitoring the Future (MTF) data set on US adolescent behavior. I greatly appreciate Don's sharing with me recent unpublished reports about this subject. Slightly older but still pertinent data can be found in Don Sabo and Phil Veliz, *Go Out and Play: Youth Sports in America* (New York: Women's Sports Foundation, 2009); Don Sabo and Phil Veliz, *Progress without Equity* (New York: Women's Sports Foundation, 2011). The Aspen Institute's Project Play is a great clearinghouse for data on youth sports participation: http://www.aspenprojectplay.org.

33. This refers to "small-sided" soccer games with fewer participants, thereby allowing the young players to get more "touches" and have more fun. Competitive travel soccer usually starts with eight players per side on a smaller field. Somewhere between ages ten and twelve, players begin competing on a regulation field with eleven per side.

34. Indicated by memberships in US Figure Skating (USFS). All skaters competing in USFS events must be USFS members.

35. For interesting discussions on youth ice hockey, see Bill King, "Are the Kids Alright," *Sports Business Journal* (August 10, 2015); Esme Murphy, "The High Cost of Competitive Pre-H.S. Sports," *WCCO/CBS Minnesota* (February 16, 2015; retrieved at http://minnesota.cbslocal.com).

36. The pipelines for boys' football and basketball still run through high schools, at least to some extent, which is why those sports tend to have much more diverse intercollegiate footprints (social class and race) than female sports. Thus, there is more chance for upward mobility in these male sports, although this chance is still highly exaggerated.

37. Many thanks to Villanova student Bridget Black, who conducted this research for her senior thesis on patriarchy within international women's soccer.

38. Deducing family income from hometowns is a problematic methodology since many towns and cities are extremely heterogeneous. A slightly better approach would be to use a person's zip code. This was employed in economist Seth Stephen-Davidowitz's analysis of National Basketball Association players [Seth Stephen Davidowitz, "In the NBA, Zip Code Matters," *New York Times*, November 2, 2013]. But there can also be heterogeneity within zip codes. The gold standard for research like this would require using the actual street addresses of where players grew up and checking them against neighborhood-level census data. Unfortunately, these addresses are very difficult to obtain, and we are left with less precise measurements. So while these measurements provide a fairly accurate picture of how social class influences sports pipelines, they are far from perfect.

39. Villanova student Stephanie Uibel conducted much of this research, which was partially funded by a Vreeland-Gallagher Undergraduate Research Award in the university's Department of Sociology and Criminology.

40. The 21 percent figure is a median of medians. The same qualifications expressed in note 38 are at play here. I am hesitant to mention the schools involved until I am able to obtain more precise address data for the recruited or scholarship athletes. Teams were chosen from among the top twenty women's soccer and field hockey teams as ranked by the NCAA after the fall 2015 season. Median family incomes of students at state schools (in the aggregate) are publicly available, although usually by request. Only full-time residential students were considered. Aggregate family income of students at private schools was obtained from a variety of direct sources (e.g., school officials) and indirect sources (e.g., published documents with reliable sources). I am currently gathering more precise data on player addresses that will allow for a more sophisticated analysis.

41. For the record, those "states" are California; Delaware; Washington, DC; Maine; Michigan; Ohio; and Virginia.

42. See Gilbert Gaul, *Billion Dollar Ball.*

43. The number of male intercollegiate ice hockey players has increased only slightly during this time.

44. The states with larger girls' high school programs are Minnesota, Wisconsin, Maine, and Massachusetts.

45. The data are remarkably consistent on this regardless of the sources, which include Roper, Gallup, *USA Today*, and CBS News.

46. See Howard Nixon II, *Sport in a Changing World* (New York: Routledge, 2016).

47. There are mild penalties involved if a valid NLI is violated by either party. See http://www.nationalletter.org.

48. The NCAA recently began "permitting" future DIII athletes to actively participate in these high school events, even though they were still not committed to a school (or vice versa) and were likely signing blank pieces of paper or doing their homework while the cameras clicked. Previously, this was not explicitly permitted by the NCAA, although many high schools did it anyway since there really weren't any repercussions.

49. We will meet many of these parents in chapter 4.

CHAPTER 2: HIGHER EDUCATION AND THE YOUTH SPORTS TO COLLEGE PIPELINE

1. Thorstein Veblen, *The Higher Learning in America* (New Brunswick, NJ: Transaction, 1993); C. Wright Mills, *The Sociological Imagination* (New York: Oxford University Press, 1959). For another angle on corporatized higher education, see Debra Swoboda, Kevin Delaney, and Rick Eckstein, "A Theoretical Exploration of White Collar Organizing: Graduate Student Employees and the Future of Unions in Academia," *Humanity and Society* 11, no. 2 (April 1987): 165–74.

2. Henry Giroux, *The University in Chains* (New York: Paradigm, 2007); Henry Giroux, "Public Intellectuals vs. the Neo-Liberal University" (at truthout.org, October 29, 2013). "Neoliberalism" and "corporatization" are sometimes used interchangeably. Both refer to a genuflection before free-market principles while acknowledging the benefits of human agency.

3. Eric Gould, *The University in a Corporate Culture* (New Haven, CT: Yale University Press, 2003).

4. Veblen, *The Higher Learning in America*, 98.

5. Benjamin Ginsberg, *The Fall of the Faculty* (New York: Oxford University Press, 2011).

6. Peter Seybold, "The Struggle Against Corporate Takeover of the University," *Socialism and Democracy* 22, no. 1 (March 2008): 1–11; Richard Sennett and Jonathan Cobb, *The Hidden Injuries of Class* (New York: W. W. Norton, 1993).

7. Jennifer Washburn, *University Inc.: The Corporate Corruption of American Higher Education* (New York: Basic, 2005); Larry Gerber, *The Rise and Fall of Faculty Governance* (Baltimore, MD: Johns Hopkins University Press, 2014); Marvin Lazerson, *Higher Education and the American Dream* (Budapest: Central European Press, 2010); Stanley Aronowitz, *The Knowledge Factory* (Boston: Beacon Press, 2000); David Noble, *Digital Diploma Mills* (New York: Monthly Review Press, 2003).

8. Veblen, *The Higher Learning in America*, 99–101.

9. Gaye Tuchman, *Wannabe U: Inside the Corporate University* (Chicago: University of Chicago Press, 2009); Gaye Tuchman, "The Future of Wannabe University," *The Chronicle of Higher Education* (October 17, 2009).

10. Kevin Delaney and Rick Eckstein, *Public Dollars, Private Stadiums* (New Brunswick, NJ: Rutgers University Press, 2003); Eva Marikova Leeds, Michael Leeds, and Irina Pistolet, "A Stadium by Any Other Name," *Journal of Sports Economics* 8, no. 6 (December 2007): 581–95.

11. Veblen, *The Higher Learning in America*, 89–101.

12. Derek Bok, *Universities in the Marketplace* (Princeton, NJ: Princeton University Press, 2003); Derek Bok, *Higher Education in America* (Princeton, NJ: Princeton University Press, 2013).

13. Murray Sperber, *Beer and Circuses* (New York: Henry Holt, 2000).

14. Henry Giroux and Susan Searls Giroux, "Universities Gone Wild" (at http://truthout.org, January 5, 2012).

15. This was distilled from data found at the National Center for Education Statistics, the National Council for Public Policy and Higher Education, the Delta Cost Project, the US Department of Education, the Center for College Affordability and Productivity, the American Association of University Professors, and Benjamin Ginsberg, *The Fall of the Faculty*.

16. Knight Commission on Intercollegiate Athletics, *Restoring the Balance* (Miami: Knight Foundation, 2012); Steven Hurlburt and Rita Kirshstein, "Spending: Where Does the Money Go," *Delta Cost Project* (Washington, DC, April 2012).

17. http://www.ncaa.org/about/resources/media-center/news/growth-division-i-athletics-expenses-outpaces-revenue-increases.

18. Elka Peterson-Horner and Rick Eckstein, "Challenging the Flutie Factor: Intercollegiate Sports, Undergraduate Enrollments, and the Neoliberal University," *Humanity and Society* 39, no. 1 (January 2015): 64–85.

19. Howard Nixon II, *The Athletic Trap* (Baltimore, MD: Johns Hopkins University Press, 2014).

20. The so-called Power Five conferences have far larger intercollegiate programs than the "mid-major" conferences within DI. The Power Five conferences are the Atlantic Coast Conference (ACC), Southeastern Conference (SEC), Pacific Twelve (PAC-12), Big 12, and Big 10. Recently these five conferences have increased their influence within the NCAA.

21. There are a number of excellent historical accounts of the NCAA. A nonexhaustive list might include Nixon II, *The Athletic Trap*; Welch Suggs, *A Place*

on the Team (Princeton, NJ: Princeton University Press, 2005); Rodney Smith, "A Brief History of the NCAA's Role in Regulating Intercollegiate Athletics," *Marquette Sports Law Review* 11, no. 1 (April 2000): 9–22; Ronald Smith, *Pay for Play: A History of Big-Time College Athletic Reform* (Urbana: University of Illinois Press, 2011); James Duderstadt, *Intercollegiate Athletics and the American University* (Ann Arbor: University of Michigan Press, 2003); Andrew Zimbalist, *Unpaid Professionals* (Princeton, NJ: Princeton University Press, 2001); Gilbert Gaul, *Billion-Dollar Ball* (New York: Viking, 2015); Charles Clotfelter, *Big-Time Sports in American Universities* (New York: Cambridge University Press, 2011); Taylor Branch, "The Shame of College Sports," *The Atlantic* (October 2011).

22. Walter Byers seems to have come full circle from the days when he insisted wholeheartedly that college athletes in revenue-producing sports were not entitled to compensation as employees. See Walter Byers, *Unsportsmanlike Conduct: Exploiting College Athletes* (Ann Arbor: University of Michigan Press, 1995). His successors as NCAA president did not seem to be convinced by his conversion.

23. Rick Eckstein, *Nuclear Power and Social Power* (Philadelphia: Temple University Press, 1997).

24. There is a fairly strong consensus that equity for women's athletics has not directly *caused* the decline in certain men's sports such as wrestling and gymnastics. Rather, the incessant growth of football squads has been the main driver of the expansion of women's opportunities. If football teams had fewer members (on scholarship or not), there could have been increases in women's sports while maintaining men's sports such as wrestling. Most of the sources cited in note 21 address this issue.

25. This was established in a landmark US Supreme Court Case, *NCAA v. Board of Regents of the University of Oklahoma* (1984).

26. Rodney Fort and Jason Winfree, *15 Sports Myths and Why They're Wrong* (Palo Alto, CA: Stanford University Press, 2013).

27. This new playoff format supplants what was called the Bowl Championship Series, whereby a complex algorithm of teams and conferences playing in designated bowl games would determine a national champion in college football. Regardless of the system, the NCAA does not garner any revenues directly from these contests.

28. Mark Alesia, "How the NCAA Makes and Spends Money," *Indianapolis Star* (March 27, 2014), A1.

29. Intense research has been unable to determine the origins of this term.

30. Dale Breme and Randy Kesselring, "The Advertising Effect of University Athletic Success," *Quarterly Review of Economics and Finance* 33, no. 4 (Winter 1993): 409–21; Brad Humphreys and Michael Mondello, "Intercollegiate Athletic Success and Donations at NCAA Division I Institutions," *Journal of Sport Management* 21, no. 2 (April 2007): 265–80; Brad Humphreys, "The Relationship between Big-Time College Football and State Appropriations to Higher Education," *International Journal of Sport Finance* 1, no. 2 (May 2006): 199–228; Franklin Mixon

Jr. and Rand Ressler, "An Empirical Note on the Impact of College Athletics on Tuition Revenue," *Applied Economics Letters* 2, no. 10 (October 1995): 383–87; Robert Frank, "Challenging the Myth: A Review of the Links among College Athletic Success, Student Quality, and Donations," *Knight Commission on Intercollegiate Athletics* (May 2004); Irvin Tucker, "Big Time Pigskin Success: Is There an Advertising Effect?" *Journal of Sports Economics* 6, no. 2 (May 2005): 222–29.

31. For instance, over the past decade Northeastern University and Hofstra University eliminated their DI football programs with seemingly no ill effect. Spelman College in Georgia eliminated all intercollegiate athletics, also with no apparent negative impact. Conversely, the University of Alabama at Birmingham's attempt to eliminate its football program generated enormous opposition, and the school abandoned its plan.

32. Much of the material in this section was originally published in Peterson-Horner and Eckstein, "Challenging the Flutie Factor."

33. In addition to many of the citations in note 30, see also Brian Fisher, "Athletics Success and Institutional Rankings," *New Directions for Higher Education* 148 (Winter 2009): 45–53; Devin Pope and Jarin Pope, "The Impact of College Sports Success on the Quantity and Quality of Student Applications," *Southern Economic Journal* 75, no. 3 (January 2009): 750–80; Chad McEvoy, "The Relationship between Dramatic Changes in Team Performance and Undergraduate Admissions Applications," *The Smart Journal* 2, no. 1 (Fall 2005):17–24; Brian Goff, "Effects of University Athletics on the University," *Journal of Sport Management* 14, no. 2 (April 2000): 85–104; J. Douglas Toma and Michael Cross, "Intercollegiate Athletics and Student College Choice," *Research in Higher Education* 39, no. 6 (December 1998): 633–61; Franklin Mixon and Yu Hsing, "The Determination of Out-of-State Enrollment in Higher Education," *Economics of Education Review* 13, no. 4 (December 1994): 329–35; George Chressanthis and Paul Grimes, "Intercollegiate Success and First-Year Enrollment Demands," *Sociology of Sports Journal* 10, no. 3 (Fall 1993): 286–300; Robert McCormick and Maurice Tinsley, "Athletics vs. Academics: Evidence from SAT Scores," *Journal of Political Economy* 95, no. 5 (October 1987): 1103–16.

34. See McCormick and Tinsley, "Athletics vs. Academics: Evidence from SAT Scores."

35. See Peterson-Horner and Eckstein, "Challenging the Flutie Factor."

36. http://www.artsci.com/studentpoll/archivedissues/4_4.pdf; see also Doug Chung, "The Dynamic Advertising Effect of College Athletics," *Marketing Science* 32, no. 5 (December 2013): 679–98.

37. Data are from the US Department of Education's Office of Secondary Education, which provides an accessible database with revenue and expense data from all US colleges and universities subject to Title IX regulations. See ope.ed.gov/athletics.

38. Kate Zernike, "Few Wins but Much Chaos at Rutgers After Move to the Big Ten," *New York Times* (December 8, 2015), A1.

39. Largely in response to unionization attempts by revenue-generating athletes in football and men's basketball, the NCAA allows schools to supplement scholarships with extra money to cover things like traveling home over school breaks. Schools and conferences determine these levels. The so-called Power Five conferences pushed hardest for this "full cost of attendance" supplement.

40. The NCAA was very forthcoming with limited equivalency data at the conference and school level, but asked that the groups and institutions not be identified.

41. For example, at the University of Connecticut, just over 20 percent of undergraduates are from out of state. However, 83 percent of the varsity athletes on five women's teams (soccer, field hockey, basketball, ice hockey, and lacrosse) are from outside Connecticut. None of the twenty-one ice hockey players are in-state residents.

42. See the NCAA's Women's Sports Inventory at http://www.ncaa.org. Elsewhere, 14 percent of women's varsity tennis players are from outside the United States, as are 10 percent of women's varsity golfers. Just over 3 percent of varsity field hockey players are non-US citizens, but it is the fastest-growing geographic demographic within the sport, based on an examination of rosters in 2004 and 2012.

43. As mentioned in chapter 1, only DI and DII scholarship athletes sign binding letters of intent that officially commit them to a specific college, and only if they are receiving athletic-based financial aid. Nonscholarship athletes and DIII athletes may sign "ceremonial" letters of intent, but these are not legally binding, although people often act as though they are.

44. The College and Beyond study was reported in William Bowen and Derek Bok, *The Shape of the River* (Princeton, NJ: Princeton University Press, 1998); James Schullman and William Bowen, *The Meaning of Life* (Princeton, NJ: Princeton University Press, 2002); William Bowen and Sarah Levin, *Reclaiming the Game* (Princeton, NJ: Princeton University Press, 2005).

45. In addition to the references in note 44, see Thomas Espenshade, Chang Chung, and Joan Walling, "Admissions Preferences for Minority Students, Athletes, and Legacies at Elite Universities," *Social Science Quarterly* 85, no. 5 (December 2004): 1422–46.

46. SATs and other standardized tests are a poor predictor of college academic success, and many universities no longer require them. Regardless of their substantive shortcomings, these test scores do allow for worthwhile comparisons in schools that use them as a criterion for admissions.

47. For an excellent historical account of early decision programs, see James Fallows, "The Early-Decision Racket," *The Atlantic* (September 2001). For a scholarly assessment of early decision's bias toward the wealthy and white, see Julie Park and Kevin Eagan, "Who Goes Early? A Multi-Level Analysis of Enrolling via Early Action and Early Decisions Admissions," *Teachers College Record* 113, no. 11 (December 2011): 2345–73.

48. Some admissions officers (and other university officials) I spoke with denied that this happened, insisting that potential varsity athletes went through the exact

same admissions and acceptance process as all other students. The coaches I spoke with found such assertions amusing but not surprising.

49. This was also mentioned to me "off the record" by several DIII coaches and athletic directors.

50. Sam Weyrauch, "Banded Together," *Bowdoin Orient* (March 28, 2014): 1; Sam Weyrauch, "A Path to Campus," *Bowdoin Orient* (April 4, 2014): 1; Sam Weyrauch, "After the Acceptance," *Bowdoin Orient* (April 11, 2014): 1; Bill Pennington, "One Division III Conference Finds That Playing the Slots System Pays Off," *New York Times* (December 25, 2005); Noah Levick, James Karsten, and Kyle Olehink, "Athlete Recruitment: A Complicated and Confidential Process," *Bates Student* (April 1, 2015): 1.

51. See note 21 above.

52. These are periods of time when college programs must have absolutely no contact with active or potential recruits.

53. Nathaniel Popper, "Committing to Play for a College, then Starting 9th Grade," *New York Times* (January 27, 2014): A1; Farrey, *Game On!*; Hyman, *The Most Expensive Game in Town*.

54. Ibid.

CHAPTER 3: THE COMMERCIALIZED YOUTH SPORTS TO COLLEGE PIPELINE

1. Many thanks to Carol Rossignol at PSA for help with these numbers.

2. Former British corporation Reebok is now a subsidiary of Adidas and is headquartered in the United States.

3. Female ice hockey, like female lacrosse, does not permit checking.

4. Technically, Reebok/Adidas only bought CCM's "brand" since the company had already folded its operations.

5. This more low-key soccer league was part of AYSO.

6. As mentioned earlier, this tournament is being replaced by one cosponsored by the National Field Hockey Coaches Association and Corrigan Sports.

7. The $50,000 figure was practically a matter of consensus among the many skating coaches and families I spoke with.

8. This does not include the hundreds of teams unaffiliated with US Youth Soccer.

9. Diane Mastrull, "New Play, Big Payout," *Philadelphia Inquirer* (July 28, 2014).

10. See https://www.espnwwos.com/events/field-hockey/disneys-field-hockey-showcase. It is possible this URL will be inactive at the time of publication.

11. This name may be interesting but has no significance. It just happens to be the road where the complex is located.

12. Soccer does not seem to be on Spooky Nook's radar yet, but that shows some signs of changing.

13. Apparently the staggering growth of girls' lacrosse camps has led to a "bounty" system where high school coaches receive something akin to a signing bonus if a certain number of their players register at a specific camp. Several high school and college coaches confirmed this. The same bounty system does not seem to be present in girls' soccer or field hockey, at least not overtly.

14. See http://www.skatepsa.com/psa/PS_Magazine.html.

15. Not coincidentally, NCYS increased its emphasis on background checks after the Penn State University events concerning Jerry Sandusky.

CHAPTER 4: CREATING DEMAND FOR THE YOUTH SPORTS TO COLLEGE PIPELINES

1. As a registered youth soccer coach, I receive no fewer than ten e-mails each week announcing some outstanding upcoming tournament or international tour guaranteed to get young players to the next level.

2. Sonny Vaccaro was considered a pioneer in establishing commercial relationships between universities (especially marquee coaches and teams) and sporting goods companies such as Nike and Adidas. Vaccaro has since become a vociferous critic of the commercialized system he helped create. For a readable historical overview of this, see Joe Nocera and Ben Strauss, *Indentured* (New York: Penguin, 2016).

3. This is a combination of comments from several different individuals.

4. Mike shared this story during an interview. It was also published in the EPYSA newsletter (Summer 2014).

5. Even in these sports, pay-to-play showcases independent of high school teams are becoming far more popular.

6. Anson Dorrance and Steve Swanson are head coaches, respectively, at the University of North Carolina and the University of Virginia, two very well regarded women's soccer programs.

7. See http://www.nfhca.org.

8. Patricia is now playing on a DIII college team.

CHAPTER 5: THE MASCULINIZATION OF FEMALE SPORTS

Former Villanova student Jessica Swoboda helped immensely with the ideas and data collection in this chapter.

1. See Rick Eckstein, Dana Moss, and Kevin Delaney, "Sports Sociology's Still Untapped Potential," *Sociological Forum* 25, no. 3 (September 2010).

2. Zach Schonbrun, "Idea to Lower Rim for Women's Basketball Stirs Talk," *New York Times* (October 25, 2012); Asher Price, "The WNBA Should Bring the Baskets Down and the Fandom Up," *New York Times* (June 2, 2015).

3. This was a reference to the University of New Mexico's Elizabeth Lambert's aggressive behavior toward a Brigham Young University player in 2009. The incidences, captured on video, include Lambert kicking the ball into the face of an opponent (lying on the ground) during a restart and pulling an opponent to the ground by her ponytail. This and other similar examples will be explored more later in this chapter.

4. Mary Louise Adams, *Artistic Impressions: Figure Skating, Masculinity, and the Limits of Sport* (Toronto: University of Toronto Press, 2012).

5. Barrie Thorne, *Gender Play* (Princeton, NJ: Princeton University Press, 1993).

6. See Sharon Stoller and Jennifer Beller, "Ethical Issues in Sport," in Richard Lapchick (ed.), *Rules of the Game: Ethics in College Sports* (Greenwood, CT: Praeger, 2006). Unfortunately, this longitudinal project seems to have been terminated.

7. This refers to a player placing her thumb in or near an opponent's anus (over the shorts) during a restart when players are often bunched together.

8. See https://www.womenssportsfoundation.org/advocate/foundation-positions/equity-issues/girls-boys-competing-sports-physical-activity-settings.

9. See Joel Brenner, "Overuse Injuries, Overtraining, and Burnout in Child and Adolescent Athletics," *Pediatrics* (June 2007); David Gwinn, "The Relative Incidence of Anterior Cruciate Injury in Men and Women at the United States Naval Academy," *The American Journal of Sports Medicine* (January 2000); Sally Mountcastle, "Epidemiology of Anterior Cruciate Ligament Injuries in a Young, Athletic Population," *American Orthopedic Society for Sports Medicine* (May 2007).

10. See Michael Sokolove, *Warrior Girls* (New York: Simon & Schuster, 2008); Mark Hyman, *Until It Hurts* (Boston: Beacon Press, 2009).

11. I became aware of this at the 2016 meeting of the Coalition on Intercollegiate Athletics (COIA). The movement started in a men's DI program but seems to be spreading across divisions and gender lines. Any changes to the standard season would require NCAA approval.

12. See chapter 1, note 11.

13. Many thanks to Emma Nicosia for research assistance in this section.

14. R. Vivian Acosta and Linda Jean Carpenter, "Women in Intercollegiate Sport. A Longitudinal, National Study, Thirty Seven Year Update. 1977–2014." Unpublished manuscript. Available for downloading at http://www.acostacarpenter.org.

15. See http://www.ncaa.org/sites/default/files/SWA_Brochure_11_2011_FINAL%20%281%29.pdf.

16. Currently, women comprise about 2 percent of men's college team coaches. The numbers are slightly higher in DIII than in DI.

17. It is especially difficult analyzing trends in track and field since teams are often combined across seasons and across gender, and it's not always clear who is coaching which iteration. Things are much clearer in softball, volleyball, and basketball.

18. Rosters including coaches are available on team-sponsored websites and Facebook pages (independent of the college) and in various places on the USA Ultimate website (usually related to tournament participation).

19. Christine Williams, "The Glass Escalator: Hidden Advantages for Men in the 'Female' Professions," *Social Problems* 39, no. 3 (August 1992).

20. See Acosta and Carpenter, "Women in Intercollegiate Sport."

21. Special thanks to the Alliance's former executive director, Celia Slater, for her outstanding insights on this topic.

22. http://gocoaches.org/programs-events/wca.

23. http://www.cehd.umn.edu/tuckercenter/default.html.

24. Annelies Knoppers and Anton Anthonissen, "Women's Soccer in the United States and the Netherlands," *Sociology of Sport Journal* 20 (2003): 351–70.

25. Grainey, Timothy, *Beyond Bend It Like Beckham* (Lincoln: University of Nebraska Press, 2012).

CHAPTER 6: SAVING GIRLS' YOUTH SPORTS BY CHANGING HIGHER EDUCATION

1. There is no shortage of excellent histories of higher education in the United States. An extremely limited sample might include Roger Geiger, *The History of American Higher Education: Learning and Culture from the Founding to World War II* (Princeton, NJ: Princeton University Press, 2014); Jerome Karabel, *The Chosen* (New York: Mariner Books, 2008); Helen Lefkowitz Horowitz, *Campus Life: Undergraduate Cultures from the End of the Eighteenth Century to the Present* (Chicago: University of Chicago Press, 1988); R. Veysey, *The Emergence of the American University* (Chicago: University of Chicago Press, 1965).

2. As discussed in chapter 3, the National Council of Youth Sports and its primary benefactor (the Sports and Fitness Industry Association) are also interested in increasing youth sports participation. However, this concern may be driven more by commercial interests than the intrinsic rewards of physical activity and play.

3. These reports are available at the Project Play website (http://www.aspenprojectplay.org). They include *Physical Literacy in the United States: A Model, Strategic Plan and Call for Action* and *Sport for All; Play for Life: A Playbook to Get Every Kid in the Game.*

4. A nonexhaustive list might include these previously cited works: Nixon II, *The Athletic Trap*; Clotfelter, *Big Time Sports in American Universities*; Duderstadt, *Intercollegiate Athletics and the American University*; and Smith, *Pay for Play: A History of Big-Time College Athletic Reform*. See also Brad Wolverton, "How Would You Reinvent College Sports," *The Chronicle of Higher Education* (October 15, 2012).

5. Eliminating intercollegiate athletics would likely change the structure of boys' pipelines but would probably not eliminate them altogether since there would still be professional options available to males.

6. Game played on October 31, 2015. Reported at the Northeast Conference website (http://www.northeastconference.org). Statistical data about Duquesne are available at http://www.duquesne.edu and http://ope.ed.gov/athletics.

7. I am not "picking on" Duquesne for any particular reason. It does, however, represent a genre of midsize schools that are increasingly turning to intercollegiate sports for a "branding boost." It also has a very well organized and nonrestrictive website that allows for better research. The transparency is also quite refreshing compared to many university web sites.

8. There is a slight discrepancy between the federal government's Equity in Athletics Database (EAD) and what actually happens on the ground. EAD lists sixteen teams and the school lists eighteen. This is mainly because the EAD combines many programs into an "all track combined" category rather than separating out cross-country, winter indoor track, and spring track and field. Thus, the EAD slightly undercounts the number of teams, although it accurately counts the number of actual participants. Separating out the various track and field teams also allows Duquesne to satisfy the NCAA's seventeen-team minimum requirement (see chapter 2).

9. Data collected from http://www.villanova.edu and http://ope.ed.gov/athletics.

10. See http://www.arl.org.

11. See Smith, *Pay for Play*; Duderstadt, *Intercollegiate Athletics and the American University*; Bowen and Levin, *Reclaiming the Game*; Clotfelter, *Big-Time Sports in American Universities*; Zimbalist, *Unpaid Professionals*; Gaul, *Billion-Dollar Ball.*

12. Elite basketball and football teams are notorious for screening walk-on candidates by GPA. Especially in basketball, two or three walk-ons with 3.7 GPAs (out of fifteen total players) can do wonders for the team's academic standing.

13. See chapter 2, note 31.

14. See Nixon II, *The Athletic Trap*, chapter 7.

15. See also Clotfelter, *Big-Time Sports in American Universities*, chapter 9.

16. Nixon II, *The Athletic Trap*, 155–56.

17. Such a change in compliance criteria would require legislation changing the so-called Javits Amendment (see chapter 2), or an especially cantankerous interpretation of the Javits Amendment by the US Department of Education.

18. Using actual names would not be necessary. For instance, schools could report that the twenty-six players on the women's soccer team share ten full scholarship equivalencies, with twenty of them each receiving a half scholarship amounting to X dollars per year, and average out-of-pocket payments to the school of X dollars per year.

19. Data from the NCAA SCORE studies indicate that many varsity athletes regret not having the ability to study abroad or secure internships. See http://www.ncaa.org/about/resources/research/score-study.

20. The NCAA currently has four levels of infractions, Level I being the most serious.

21. See Robert Pruter, *The Rise of American High School Sports and the Search for Control, 1880–1930* (Syracuse, NY: Syracuse University Press, 2013).

22. It is probably more likely that high schools and school districts will "brand" themselves by boasting about their school's/district's aggregate standardized test scores, or how many of its students take AP exams. But it is still branding.

23. The Interscholastic Sports Division of the Maine Principals Association has such a restriction.

24. See Alia Wong, "The Absurdity of College Admissions," *The Atlantic* (March 2016).

INDEX